In 2021, the women who came up to New Hall been chatting to each other by email, about thei. students. They decided to make these memories into this book. The contributors are listed in the Appendix.

Some of the memories may not be entirely accurate. It was fifty years ago!

The painting on the cover is by Julian Henry Mott, now the husband of Jane Mott (née Style).

This is the Freshers' Photograph of 1971 – Left half:

Row 1: S.Addison K.Bamborough F.A.Barnard P.E.Barnard V.Z.Beardshaw M.L.Beardsley M.Bell G.Blessley
Row 2: T.Cartwright N.A.Chapman D.M.Clark G.S.Clarke A.E.Cleghorn D.M.Collyer C.M.Conlin
Row 3: D.C.Glass J.M.Gooding K.N.Greenwood J.Hammond S.A.Hardy S.M.Henley A.J.Hill
Row 4: W.R.Joseph M.C.Kemp F.L.Kenter Akcan A.D.Kidd P.C.King D.J.Lewin H.A.Lupton H.V.Martin
Row 5: R.Mordeth H.F.Morton P.M.R.Mountsteven I.A.Mullens A.M.New S.M.Newton A.S.O'Brien S.M.Perris J.M.Phillips
Row 6: J.P.Sloper G.F.Smith S.J.Smyth-Tyrrell E.M.Stafford S.Stallard A.Stewart P.Stirling J.F.Style E.S.Sutton

Right half:

Row 1: M.A.Bonney A.M.Borrett R.A.Boughton S.A.Bowen N.A.Brown U.M.B.Buchan D.Burnham J.C.Butler

Row 2: W.A.Coulson J.Couzens R.T.Coward A.S.Cox S.J.Davies J.E.Dibblee C.T.Fisher H.L.Gibbon

Row 3: S.E.Hill D.M.Hills P.J.Hilton E.B.Hyams M.E.Ignatowicz D.James S.E.Jenkins

Row 4: P.J.Massy-Collier A.C.Mawle H.G.A.Mayer P.J.Micklam D.Milburn C.E.Miller S.A.Morgan

Row 5: L.E.Radford V.H.Rees C.Roberts L.M.Robertson J.R.Rogers M.Roston N.J.Rooke M.Sarkar

Row 6: P.M.Taylor R.C.Temple F.A.Weaver A.B.Webster K.E.Wernly E.Wheelock P.G.Willmer S.M.Wood S.A.Yo

Contents

Before New Hall	5
Entrance exam and Application to New Hall	23
Interview	33
First Impressions	41
Academia	48
Staff and Regulations	76
The buildings of New Hall	81
Accommodation	98
Societies	107
Political action	121
Entertainment	130
Socialising	134
Relationships	139
Cycling	146
Food	152
Clothes	163
Punting	171
Money	174
Holiday jobs	182
Social attitudes and external events	188
How it was different, back then	193
Reflections	198
Best bits and Worst bits	208
After New Hall	214
Deaths	240

Appendix

Contributors	246
New Hall entrance exam	248
Timeline	255

Before New Hall

Applying to Cambridge University involved an entrance exam, which could be taken before A levels (which meant you went to university immediately after school) or after (which gave you about half a year to do something else).

I attended a small state Grammar school for girls. Quite a long way from home (2 buses). I found out later that I had been regarded as a swot.

Deborah Glass

I was state educated, but like others, was on a scholarship place at a GPDST (Girls Public Day School Trust) school. From the age of 16, I was focused on becoming a doctor but hadn't thought of Cambridge. However, I played lots of music and my musician boyfriend was going off to read English at Cambridge - so that probably 'sowed the seed' of applying to Cambridge. Both my parents came from very poor homes and in the 1930s, my mother had left school at 13 and my father at 16 (despite coming third in the whole of Norfolk in the equivalent of GCSE exams). I was the fourth of five children and I was the first to go to university.

Rosemary Grande (née Temple)

I was yet another GPDST pupil (Brighton and Hove) but went to Bedales School to do A levels which was co-ed: which meant I arrived at Cambridge with former classmates in several of the men's colleges, making it easier to branch out socially.

Rosie Boughton

Like so many of us, I came from a GPDST school, Norwich High School, and I was one of three from that school arriving at New Hall in October 1971. The other two were Sarah Henley & Rosemary Temple –

both Medics. Rosie/Mimi and I had been at school together since we were 10, and we are still in touch.
An inspiring History teacher had suggested in my first term in the Upper Sixth, that I "had a go" at the New Hall entrance exam.

Charlotte Crawley (née Miller)

I came from the Oxford High School, with three others, I think. We were told that masses of people applied to New Hall because of the unique general paper, so I was quite relaxed, thinking I had no chance. In the end, I had to choose between New Hall and St Anne's, Oxford, and, since I'd been at school in Oxford, it made sense to me to go to Cambridge.
Oxford High School will sound 'privileged' to some reading this, but it was a bit more complicated than that. In those days it was a direct grant school, and I won a free place there in the sixth form, having come from a comprehensive school outside Oxford, not long after my mother (who had brought me, and five other children, up on her own) died.
I very much wish now that I had taken a gap year. The extra maturity which I saw in my own children, who did have gap years, would have been very useful. However, my grandfather, who looked after me, thought I should get on with things and that was a perfectly sensible attitude, since I had no money and lived in the middle of nowhere.

Ursula Wide (née Buchan)

I'd been to a private girls' school, myself. I was very naive when I arrived at New Hall and am surprised, in respect, at how little I knew about the background of my fellow medics.

Joanna Watts (née Sloper)

I went to a highly regarded Direct Grant school for girls on the outskirts of London. In my year there were three of us who went directly up to Cambridge without taking a gap year. I'm sure this background gave us an advantage over others who were the only ones from their schools to go to Cambridge, but I never socialized with any of my school friends after the first week.

Gillian Blessley

My father worked abroad, for the British Council, and so I boarded at a convent school in Sussex, which was very academic; most of the nuns had degrees from Oxford or London or Paris, but they were very disapproving that I wanted to apply to Cambridge; they usually sent a couple of girls to Oxford. I was, like many of us seem to have been, a fourth term applicant; I think that system was just opening up.

Fiona Edwards-Stuart (née Weaver)

I went to the same school as Diana Kuh (Lewin), King Edward VI Camp Hill School for Girls in Kings Heath, a direct grant Grammar school and part of the King Edward's Foundation which consists of 5 schools in Birmingham. My father worked at Cadbury's based not far away in Bournville, as did the parents of many of my fellow schoolmates.

I studied History, Biology and Geography at A-Level, which was an unusual cross over between traditional Arts and Science, but one which certainly stood me in good stead for the kind of lateral thinking that I deduce New Hall was looking for in its student selection. I was good academically and in music and sport, but also a bit of a rebel. Diana and I played doubles in the school 1st tennis team and, if I recall correctly, did tolerably well in the inter-schools competitions.

In spite of a headmistress who consistently emphasised education for girls and encouraged us to aspire to attend university, our school had never routinely offered the Oxbridge entrance exams. When we were in the sixth form, a new Geography teacher joined the staff (Miss Moffat?), who had recently graduated from New Hall. She was very keen that a group of us should apply for Cambridge. I don't recall Oxford featuring at all! So, with a few lunchtime sessions looking at past entrance papers we were thrown into the exam. Diana and I were selected for interview. The two top scholars in the school were rejected, which did not go down well with our headmistress who greeted the news with a stony face. Perhaps she had just had a bad day. Looking back, I think this is what New Hall stood for, and possibly still does today i.e. not those who are innately bright and top of the class, but those for whom a Cambridge education could make a difference and for girls who could potentially make a difference in the world.

Diana Murray (née Collyer)

Burton on Trent, the town I grew up in, used to have a three-tier secondary school system - secondary modern, 'technical', and grammar schools. The year I started secondary school the technical school was converted to a brand-new grammar school, which I attended. Because I was academically able, I was 'promoted' from the third year to the fourth year to join the last year of the technical school intake, who ostracised me. So I concentrated on academic work. It was the school that suggested I apply to Oxford or Cambridge. I chose Cambridge because I could do natural sciences, rather than having to choose between botany or zoology. And it was the school that chose New Hall, which now seems inspired, as they had no experience of having students apply to Oxbridge. I did the entrance exam before A levels, and was asked for the usual two Es. I remember that on the day I told my school I was constantly congratulated all day. The only time I've been congratulated as much since was when I announced my first pregnancy. I felt at the time that getting into Cambridge was much more of an achievement.

Alison Litherland (née Hill)

I was at a state grammar school in a small town, where the expectation was that girls who wanted a career would become teachers or nurses. A keen new headmistress met me to encourage Oxbridge application but was slightly phased when I explained that I wanted to study medicine. My competence was in arts subjects and, as with so many girls' schools then, physics and chemistry education had been weak. The head recovered herself and declared that I could do science A levels, if I would still apply to Oxbridge. So, like many others who've written in, I had no hope of success and no feeling of pressure when I sat the entrance exams. I was in a room on my own for 3 happy hours looking over our playing fields across the town to the sea and had a lovely time exploring the questions on the paper (like others I went for "How do you know you are not now dreaming?" and "Freedom of Speech: is it desirable, is it possible?"). I was stunned to be offered a place at New Hall. Medics needed 3 science A levels to gain 1st MB exam exemption so New Hall required 3 A level grade Es for us. Even this seemed far from certain, but I gained permission to study further chemistry for myself in Sussex University Library, where I could find books with the information I needed. Physics was made achievable because I and the applied maths pupils in my year worked ourselves through the excellent A level textbook. My father was a lawyer but could help with electricity because he had worked in radar in the war! Mercifully I got 2 As and a B, which was a miracle but certainly wouldn't get me in to medicine in today's different world so I am endlessly grateful to New Hall for their 1971 approach to admissions.

Philippa Evans (née Taylor)

I attended a state girls' grammar school in Leeds, there was no tradition that I was aware of for applying to Oxbridge. I was the only person in my year who applied to/was offered a place at Cambridge, I seem to remember that one girl went to read Russian at Oxford.

I don't know whether it was intention or coincidence that the route for our annual summer family journey to stay with my grandfather in Kent, from my early teens, sometimes included a lunch stop in Cambridge as opposed to Huntingdon or a picnic in a field. I fell in love with the city of Cambridge to the extent that when a maths teacher casually asked if I'd considered applying I jumped at the idea. I also had the offer of a place at Somerville Oxford but was determined that Cambridge was the place to be.

I don't think I ever considered having a gap year. I'm not actually aware of any of my friends who did. As far as I know there was no tradition in my school of spending an extra sixth form term to take Oxbridge entrance exams - it was now or never! Anyway, as the youngest by far of four siblings, I spent most of my early life trying to catch up and, in those days, would not have welcomed the idea of a gap year "slowing my progress". How I wish I had known better; I would have been so much better prepared to make the most of university life if I had been able to spend the year experiencing more variety of life.

Dorothy Cade (née Clark)

I loved the sixth form and was probably happier then than at university. My friend and I were a foursome with our boyfriends, spending much time together at weekends and in holidays, listening to rock music, talking about literature, playing bad bridge, and sometimes smoking dope. The four of us had rented a very run down and cheap cottage in Wales for a week before coming up, where we did all these things. I felt that maybe I was more frivolous than I perceived others to be when I got to New Hall. At the same time, I was too shy to go and mix with people I didn't know in the dining hall (and it seemed expensive) so I didn't really get to know people in the College and missed many opportunities.

Pam Hilton

I was excited to being going to New Hall. Pupils at my school (GPDST) did not often get into Oxbridge and in 1971 there were 3 of us and so we were congratulated and a bit of a fuss was made, e.g. I was invited to dinner with the Chair of the governors. I didn't have a gap year because my mother actively discouraged it. She sent me to Cambridge by train and I arrived to find I had a corner room on the ground floor, the walls of which I covered in psychedelic posters and a painting of peacocks.

Alison Wray (née O'Brien)

I was at a small boarding school for girls and applied to New Hall in my upper sixth year. I had a nice letter back saying to try again next year.

As I had jumped a year previously, I did spend one more term at school with a bit of extra maths and was successful. My school was very excited as I was their first pupil to get to Cambridge.

Jane Mott (née Style)

I went to Durham Girls Grammar, which became Durham Weirside Secondary during my 6th form.
We had come to Durham from South Africa in 1964, and after initial culture shock it was a liberating 60's counter-culture experience. Then, halfway through my A levels, my parents returned to South Africa to do research. Not a liberating experience, but it helped me to see apartheid even more starkly than before.

Helen Mayer

I came from a grammar school on Tyneside and had little idea of what to expect when I was researching universities. I was the first in my family to attend university, and my school had little experience of Oxbridge applications, so advice was minimal, but I think the staff were sufficiently attracted by the prospect of a girl getting into either that they were extremely supportive. I was not confident enough to apply before A levels so was the only person from my year left in school for that final term - perhaps having few distractions was helpful! I applied to New Hall on the assumption that as a very young college it would not have the same traditions of taking candidates from specific schools as the more established colleges. I've no memory of the entrance exam and can't even guess which questions I would have answered; oddly I have a much stronger memory of the more traditional Oxford paper.

Denise Phillipson (née Milburn)

This may explain how I came to be at New Hall at all. I had been working as a secretary in the City of London where, in the sixties, women were still seen and not heard, and preferably not even seen. I had a good job and was reasonably well paid - I was the only one of the five friends sharing a flat who broke the £20 per week barrier - but I couldn't see any chance of progressing so decided to travel. A former flat mate had gone the previous year to South Africa so I saved hard for six months (no cigarettes or weekends out of London) and got a basic berth on the Edinburgh Castle, sailing from Southampton to Cape Town. There I was able to share a flat with a very bright Afrikaans girl and immediately plunged into a series of temporary jobs until I found a fascinating one with an organisation which tracked the dependents of political prisoners when they had been forcibly returned from the squatter camps to their homeland. The trouble was that to do the really interesting field work one was meant to have a degree, while I just collated the information back at the office. My boss must have got tired of hearing me whinge so said why not get a degree and I realised he was actually serious, but I shelved the idea for a while because I got the opportunity to drive from Cape Town to Rhodesia via Lesotho, Swaziland and Mozambique, looking after three small children and a large dog. Eventually making my own way down to Johannesburg the idea of a degree surfaced again and, having managed to obtain an UCCA form, I applied to six universities. I received an immediate rejection from four, but St Hilda's in Oxford asked me to sit the entrance exam, which I did in Buenos Aires, my travels having by then got me to another continent. I heard nothing from New Hall until a telegram arrived in San Francisco (yes, I'd moved on again) asking me to write 3,000 words on any subject I liked. Wow, what a request. How to decide what they wanted? Anyway, I did it sitting in the library of Hawaii University (yes, I know) and eventually received a letter from New Hall when I was in Hong Kong asking me to notify them when I was back in England and able to come for an interview. I can't believe now that I didn't get on the first plane back, but the fact is I travelled on to Thailand, Nepal and India before I came to my senses. In the middle of May I had an interview with Esther Goody and fortunately had not accepted the offer from St Hilda's. That is what I did before New Hall!

Sarah Wilson (née Stallard)

In hindsight, it's too much of a shock to the system to go straight from school to university – I'm all in favour of "gap" years or being a mature student.

Lou Radford

After school, I had 6 months working at IBM as a computer programmer, staying with an uncle and aunt, before starting at New Hall, and I know that I grew up a lot during that time. It made me think of university as being different from work, as opposed to being a continuation of school.

Jo Edkins (née Dibblee)

A gap year never occurred to me – nor was ever suggested. I was very keen to get to New Hall and start the Cambridge experience. Like Lou and Wendy, I agree that a gap year can be extremely valuable in so many ways. I was certainly very green and immature at 18 and I too took a long time to 'grow up'. I feel that I probably didn't make the most of opportunities that were offered while I was at Cambridge, and for me, this was certainly due to lack of maturity.

Anne Muir (née Borrett)

After the entrance exam I had 9 months in California as a student with American Field Service. I lived with a family and went to High School with their children. I'm still in touch with them. It was a fantastic experience. It taught me an awful lot but it was also tough. I suspect that while some of us were sensible human beings by that age, there were others, including me, for whom it just took an awfully long time to grow up.

Wendy Joseph

What interesting conversations about gap years. I had never heard of having a gap year until I was being interviewed by Rosemary Murray. She asked whether I'd like a year off before starting university and I didn't know what on earth she meant! I said 'no' and explained that I didn't want to be dependent on my parents any longer than necessary. Now, of course, I can see the value in 'growing up' terms. I was young for my year, and it would undoubtedly have been a good thing ... but all I could think of, there and then, was that if I didn't go straight to university from school, I would have to carry on working in the factory where I worked in the holidays!

I suspect that in wanting to attract more state school pupils the academic staff just didn't realize how little some of us knew about going to university (in my case, nothing); or, indeed, the narrowness of our experience - and probably, in my case, imagination!

Maureen Bell

No-one called them 'gap years' in our day, of course. It was just the two terms left if you did entry after A levels.

I didn't get a place at New Hall in my first attempt. At the interview Esther Goody asked if I would try again if I didn't get in; I remember desperately trying to work out what was the 'right' answer. Esther told me years later that another candidate had said she wouldn't, so I didn't get in until the next year - she wanted both of us.

But it meant that I had the chance to work in Rome for 7 months. It was fabulous. Rome is the perfect city to explore on foot and to suit changing moods - archaeology, art, architecture, markets, people, everything. I grew up a lot; discovered I really missed studying so was keen to do so when I came to Cambridge that autumn; and I survived the pressures of the Italian men who flocked round British girls so felt no need to go mad on men when I arrived.

It also led to my lifelong love of Italy - I studied Italian/British migration for my PhD back in Cambridge a few years after graduation and have continued a 40+ year longitudinal study on 'my' village and Bedford.

Siân Crisp (née Jenkins)

I had two terms to wait, having done the exam as a seventh term one, but I was "only" 18 when I did it, as in Primary School I'd "jumped" a year...... you could do that then. No Foreign Parts for me, but a menial job (Sterile Supplies of all things) in a Preston hospital, which meant employment amongst the 'Salt of the Earth'.

I count this as one of my most serendipitous and informative experiences, working with these (far from) ordinary people, and finding out what made them tick. I hope that doesn't come across as patronising because it's not meant to be! So much to learn about Beryl and Ethel, Jack and Marjorie, and I was "only" sheltered by a grammar school..... so, what ignorance of working people must be prevalent in those enclosed by a private school!

What this did not fit me for was, of course, the Men question. A lot of us appear to have found this difficult. There were so many boys at Cambridge, and they obviously found us women novelties too! I think if many of us considered our grim experiences, we would be subscribing to MeToo! Absolutely ghastly behaviour. Gauche. Two terms' gap could no way anticipate that.

Sue Whitham (née Addison)

I applied to New Hall after my A levels and then had nine months to fill. I wanted to leave home but wasn't brave or imaginative enough for an adventure into the unknown. I responded to an ad in The Lady magazine and became a mother's help on a farm in Northamptonshire. I would be away from home but in a safe environment. It was only for eight weeks, during which time I was to get used to the house, the children and their routines so the parents could go skiing for a fortnight at the end of February.

It was a complete eye-opener for me. My home was a council house, my parents had separated, and my mother was hard up. My employers lived in a large house and were very comfortably off. They belonged to an affluent farming community. The girls, aged 3 and 5, not only had their own bedrooms but a playroom downstairs. They weren't told off if they left half a plateful of food and they were encouraged to talk with the adults at mealtimes.

The couple had an active social life, with frequent parties and get-togethers for drinks. I was treated pretty much as part of the family. The mother liked chatting when we were busy together and I heard some detailed and quite racy gossip about their friends. It was a new and fascinating world, but quite superficial, I remember thinking, in my youthful, lofty way. The only adult books in the house were those I'd brought with me and those I was buying from a second-hand bookshop in a nearby town.

Back home in early March, I'd had the offer of a temporary office job nearby when I realised I couldn't bear the prospect of six months at home (I wasn't getting on with my mother) and reached for The Lady again. I applied to be an au pair girl for an Anglo-French family in Le Havre and two weeks later I found myself waiting at the ferry terminal after a sleepless night crossing from Southampton. I had written a letter of application to the mother, giving a neighbour's 'phone number (we didn't have a telephone) and had spoken to her once, briefly. Waiting for her to pick me up, I was scared. I'd never been abroad before and knew that my grade A in A level French wouldn't help much if anyone actually spoke to me at normal speed. For me, this was a HUGE adventure.

The world I was entering could scarcely have been more different from the conservative farming life I'd glimpsed, or my own experience. They were left wing graduates: she a trained social worker but working as an English teacher, and he a geneticist currently doing his military service, with a day 'release' each week to continue his research. Their friends were mostly other socialist professionals, and conversations usually became intense discussions, although I couldn't always follow their meaning.

I always spoke in French with them and in English to their two young daughters. After about three months I began dreaming in French and eventually spoke fluently. For a month in the summer, we, with various brother and sisters, all stayed in his parents' large house in the

Auvergne. The family relationships were complex, the politics diverse and the frequent arguments noisy and exhilarating to witness. I loved being the fly on the wall!

Unlike Sue (Witham) I'd had plenty of experience with 'the salt of the earth' and had concluded that a little salt goes a long way. Within those two families I discovered new worlds and different attitudes to living. Observing how they brought up their children and discussing different ideas about, and approaches to, childcare, probably made the deepest impression on me, as I'd spent my earlier teens struggling against my parents' authoritarian upbringings and mindsets. Although they don't know it, my own children have benefited significantly from what I saw and learned.

My three quarters of a gap year was not a managed developmental opportunity like my nephew's marine conservation experience in Fiji, a dozen years ago. It was a time filler. But looking back through fifty years. I can see that it was one of the most intense learning experiences of my life. To be immersed, albeit temporarily, in lifestyles so different from anything I'd known, stretched me intellectually and emotionally. It couldn't reverse the lack of self-confidence and social skills of the previous eighteen years, but it did switch on the light.

Sue Attridge (née Wood)

My route to New Hall was rather back to front in comparison with most of you applying straight from a UK school. My early life was somewhat nomadic, due to my father's academic career, initially travelling between Scotland (where I was born) and West Africa Gold Coast (now Ghana) before the family immigrated to New Zealand where I had most of my schooling. However, my final sixth-form year in 1966 was back in the UK, split between 2 terms at a school in London and an autumn term at the Cambridge tech before returning to start university in New Zealand. It was a bit like a gap year break as I was travelling and studying but without any pressure to sit exams. There is no way I would have been ready to apply to Cambridge at that point, as I was young for my year and the academic standard of the upper sixth in London was at least a year, if not more, above the standard in New Zealand in those days. However, I loved the experience, and the dream of applying to Cambridge in future was kindled. After studying for 4 years at an antipodean university and gaining a first-class honours degree in English I finally fulfilled the requirements for applying to Cambridge, who graciously traded in my four-year degree for the first year of an undergraduate tripos. My father advised applying to New Hall as he rightly felt I would fit in more easily to a more modern and open-minded college. I'd had an introduction to Old English and Old Norse as part of my English degree and was keen to pursue my interests, so the Anglo-Saxon and Old Norse Tripos was the perfect choice. I was lucky to get a government scholarship to cover the New Hall fees for the two years, but I worked to earn my own airfare and pay for a holiday en route. The two terms between completing my NZ degree in Dec 1970 and flying to the UK in September 1971 was like another mini-gap year, when I was earning money, becoming more independent and planning for an exciting experience that would change my life. I made the trip with my closest friend who was going to study at the Courtauld Institute of Art in London: two young ladies let loose on the world via stops in Fiji and Mexico City with a wonderful sense of freedom. I gradually felt more at home in the northern hemisphere and had a wonderful Scottish aunt who travelled with me in the Easter holidays to Sweden, Norway and the Orkneys in search of rune stones, Viking boats and other archaeological treasures. While I was never planning to return to New Zealand immediately after graduating, I didn't think then that it would be another 9 years before I flew back for a holiday with a husband and two young children.

Aileen Regan (née Kidd)

I applied and was interviewed before A levels and was disappointed to be turned down. But it turned out very much for the best. I was lucky enough to have a fantastic 8 months in Northern Newfoundland, working for the International Grenfell Association in their hospital at St Anthony. I worked as anaesthetic assistant and had a lot of responsibility for the drugs and equipment. Best of all, I got to watch all the operations! A great start for a medical student. But, with hindsight, I wondered why I didn't question my suitability for the medical profession. I was gauche, immature, and had not the slightest idea how to utter a word of comfort to the poor frightened patients who were awaiting their anaesthetic...

I loved the period in Newfoundland (I was actually paid $75 a month, with nothing to spend it on, and food and accommodation thrown in, so was able to repay my father for the air fare and have some savings for the first 2 terms.). It certainly made me accustomed to life away from home and made me more self-sufficient. It took me many more years to grow up, and to learn to communicate with patients!

Sarah Watson (née Henley)

I attended a direct grant school for girls and applied to New Hall after taking my A levels.

I spent a few months as a technician at an agricultural station doing field work and laboratory testing. It was challenging but gave me a good introduction to the workplace and a summer job to return to.

Hilary Martin

I do think it is a shame that society makes people feel that certain careers are more valuable than others. It reminds me of my gap year working as a nursing auxiliary in our local cottage hospital where I was taken under the wing of a delightful auxiliary who I thought at the time must be about 80 years old but in retrospect was certainly younger than I am now. She and I were paid the princely sum of £8 a week for the job and she taught me so much more than the basics of the job. She absolutely loved it and took such pride in doing everything thoroughly. She must have struggled with me as my first job was cleaning the telephone with disinfectant. I simply couldn't see the point, but she gently persuaded me of the importance of the task. She would be in her element in these COVID times and on reflection I now understand that she trained in the pre antibiotic era where basic hygiene was the only tool to prevent transmission of infection.

She never did manage to teach me the perfect "hospital corners" on the ward beds, another job that I thought was pointless but gradually she made me see that doing the job well and cheerfully to the best of your ability was so satisfying whatever that job is.

The highlight of her week was the visit of a Consultant Physician from our nearby district general hospital to deal with complicated patients. Everything had to be immaculate and extra cleaning was required. He arrived with great ceremony at the hospital to be greeted by an entourage of Matron and some nurses and came to the casualty department where she and I had laid a tray with a starched tray cloth and his lunch after which he had a post prandial nap on the casualty bed. I did have a fleeting thought that this is what a career in medicine could be like for me, but it was not to be! He was actually very pleasant and always thanked us graciously. For my mentor that was a source of great pride.

Jan Sherman (née Phillips)

I had a place at UCL the previous year, but at only 17 and a half, decided to wait a year and applied to Cambridge. I don't remember the exam but do remember that New Hall was the first interview and still during term. With the modern architecture and real students, it made an infinitely better impression than empty cold Newnham by candlelight in a power cut.

I spent the next 9 months as an au pair in France, learned German and travelled a bit in Italy and Yugoslavia. All good experience for self-reliance, budgeting on a shoestring and generally growing up - and I still speak French.

Jane Dottridge (née Rooke)

My mother, my aunt, my grandfather, my grandmother and even my father, who had come over from New Zealand to do his PhD, had all studied at Cambridge University though all at different colleges and we had visited often so it seemed a logical place to go. I had also decided I wanted to study Engineering and the course at Cambridge was one where you studied all aspects of engineering for two years and only specialised in your third year which suited me as I wasn't entirely sure what branch of engineering I wanted to go into. I think I chose Engineering because people told me I couldn't do it because I was a girl, and I was determined to prove them wrong and because I guess I was competing with my older brother who was already studying engineering. I had nine months off between school and university because I applied to Oxford and Cambridge for entry after I had done my A-levels. I spent those 9 months working as an apprentice with GEC-Marconi Instruments in St Albans where they moved me around different parts of the factory including testing components, assembly and workshop practice using a lathe and milling machine for the first time. It was fun and also incredibly boring at times, but I have a clear memory of arriving at Cambridge in October 1971 and being very glad that I was at last somewhere I could actually use my mind again as I felt I hadn't done that much during the previous nine months.

Helen Morton

After A levels at a state secondary school, I trained as a nurse at University College Hospital, London, loving it and becoming an SRN. However, as my life changed and I had seven very young children to bring up (four steps) I wasn't able to be a 'proper nurse' with night duties etc., so, since we had by then moved to Cambridge, I thought a degree would lead me to teaching, which would obviously fit in better in terms of hours and holidays.

Alison New

I had a family death just before the entrance exam - I had had a great summer touring east and west coasts of the USA with my uncle, Gwyn. We planned that I would go to Radcliffe (that is - the women's college paired with then all-male Harvard), giving up any ideas of medicine as that wasn't an undergraduate degree in the States, as Gwyn lived in

Cambridge Massachusetts. His death in a car crash - I was waiting for him at Heathrow at the time - turned everything over. No sooner had I got to Cambridge UK (the Radcliffe suggested I would be better off in the UK, a very kindly refusal on their part) than I gave up my medical sciences place as I felt Natural Sciences were so much more exciting. Hm, subconscious capitalisation I note crept in there. I know Esther Welbourn was less than pleased, but if it was my dissection place that went to Marguerite Kemp, then then it was a double blessing.

Sally Morgan

Entrance exam and Application to New Hall

At Cambridge University, students applied to individual colleges, rather than the university as a whole.
See Appendix for the New Hall entrance exam paper 1970.

You may remember that New Hall had a very different entry exam from Newnham and Girton (the only 3 women's colleges then) – I recall answering a question about a planning application for a caravan site on a beautiful cliff top. A perfect topic for Social Anthropologists – and I think there were 12 of us who started in Arch/Anth that year, an enormous proportion of the intake. There were several engineers too, and a fair proportion of state educated women (I was one of them).

Siân Crisp (née Jenkins)

I came from a grammar school and would have found entrance exams for Oxford and other Cambridge colleges - with their emphasis on Classics - very hard. I think the New Hall exam was designed to find good brains with potential.
Seeing the exam paper took me straight back to the little schoolroom where I was taken - all alone - to sit it. I could almost smell the chalk. I'm pretty sure I had a go at 'Food' and 'How do you know you aren't now dreaming' - less sure which other I chose but I suspect it would have been a poetry one. But what a great exam paper ... no wonder it produced us!

Wendy Joseph

Unlike you, Wendy, I was ensconced in a small 'dining' area in the Home Economics Dept and given coffee and biscuits by the Home Ec. teacher! VIP treatment. Not a stick of chalk in sight!

Anne Muir (née Borrett)

I was in a room on my own for 3 happy hours looking over our playing fields across the town to the sea and had a lovely time exploring the questions on the paper (like others I went for "How do you know you are not now dreaming?" and "Freedom of Speech: is it desirable, is it possible?").

Philippa Evans (née Taylor)

I see that someone has found a copy of the entrance exam we took. I was relieved to find that the one question I remember doing, 'How do you know you aren't dreaming?', was actually on it and I hadn't mis-remembered. But I didn't remember any of the other questions at all, and indeed I'm amazed to think that I might have been able to answer any of them. But someone mentioned that they enjoyed doing the exam. I did as well - I remember having a hugely enjoyable morning. It was the first time ever that I had been asked to use my intelligence, reasoning and imagination, instead of just regurgitating stuff I'd been made to learn by heart. And I remember I took it in the deputy head's office - he gave it up for the morning, as I think it was the first time anyone from the school had even applied to Oxbridge, let alone got in.

Alison Litherland (née Hill)

New Hall was the only Oxbridge college I tried for, during my first term in the sixth form. My real intention had been to go to one of the new universities and I only applied because my boyfriend did. It was fascinating to see the entrance exam again and to realise it was as off the wall as I remembered. The two I recall doing were whether free speech was possible or desirable, and how I knew I wasn't dreaming at present. I've no idea what the third question was. Whilst I was sitting in the room doing the exam, the school secretary brought us coffee in cups with the school crest on, which I had never seen before. I remember offering this as evidence that I was unlikely to be dreaming, as it was such a mundane but odd discovery that the school had its own china, never normally used by pupils.

Pam Hilton

The paper does indeed bring back memories - but, strangely, I can only remember two of the questions I answered. I was shut in a little room off the staff room and a teacher would pop in to check I was still there from time to time. What I DO remember vividly is allowing one hour per answer and reaching the last hour unable to find a third question I fancied. I stared at the paper, re-read it endlessly, stared at the wall in front of me (no windows) for a whole half hour before thinking I just HAD to pick anything and get on with it . . . and did something (the one about poetic language?) in a rush. I'd never struggled with an exam paper before, so that frozen half-hour wasted was a frightening (and therefore memorable) experience!

Maureen Bell

I'm pretty sure I did the question on the escalator – having done Physics and Maths A levels, even though I was applying to do Economics. I'm puzzled though, because I was sure there was a question about decimalisation and I can't find it. Perhaps I twisted one of the questions and used it as an example.

Wendy Spray (née Coulson)

I have only the dimmest recollection of sitting the exam paper. I can't remember which questions I answered scribbling away all alone in a shabby classroom at my school. Looking at it now, the paper we apparently sat is both intelligent and quirky, and the fact that New Hall recruited its undergraduates using this unusual method was one of the things that made me put it above Girton (even though a beloved aunt had gone there) and Newnham (which I knew nothing of) in my list of choices.

The other attractors were the architecture – the idea of going to a modern college was appealing. I liked the look of the place from the photos in the brochure. More venally, I had a hunch that as neither Girton or Newnham had Fellows in Archaeology and Anthropology and New Hall had the anthropologist Esther Goody on the Fellowship it would be likely to have more undergraduate places (it did!)

Virginia Beardshaw

The entrance paper: I remember writing for an hour all about water. I think as potential scientists we had to do 3 one hour answers: one scientific, one general and one arts.

Rosemary Grande (née Temple)

I remember the entrance paper so well as it was unlike anything I had ever seen before - my comprehensive school in South Yorkshire prepared us for Joint Matriculation Board A Levels and that was it. I only sat the paper because someone else in the school had intended to apply to New Hall and was persuaded by the Headmaster to try Oxford instead and I got substituted somehow. I sat the paper on my own in the Deputy Head's office with people peering through the door at intervals. Section C had questions that more or less related to A level knowledge so two could be attempted, but I could not understand the majority of the questions in Section A and almost resorted to assessing the caravan site (q 12). I was saved by 2 things. First, I had just read a dystopian science fiction novel by Harry Harrison called 'Make Room Make Room' and second, a student on teaching practice at my school had given a General Studies talk on Malthus. Question 4 'Food' could consequently be approached from the 'running out of it' angle. Thinking about my answer to this, 50 years on, what was dystopian science fiction in 1970 seems now not so unlikely. In the book the planet's population has exploded. The 35 million inhabitants of New York City run their TVs off pedal power, riot for water, fight for soya/lentil 'steaks' and sweat beneath a sweltering sun. An award-winning film 'Soylent Green' based on the book and starring Charlton Heston was released in 1973. I saw this film with my then boyfriend from St Catharine's.

Angela Bailey (née Webster)

The unique New Hall entrance paper most definitely benefited me. Although I am not sure exactly which questions I answered, I could probably hazard a guess it was my gateway to Cambridge.

My Direct Grant school in Devon was at the time not very strong on Sciences. We did not cover any organic Chemistry and did not complete the Physics A level course. I only managed to pass the exam using a small "crammer" which my brother gave me. He encouraged me to apply to New Hall because he thought I would have a better chance of a non-subject oriented exam. Also having been at Clare 5 years ahead of me told me that the nicest girls he met were from New Hall.

Our headmistress was a London graduate and loyal to her Alma Mater so did not encourage applications to Oxbridge.

Jan Sherman (née Phillips)

I remember the three questions I answered: the Bertrand Russell quotation; the fake versus the genuine art work; and poetic language being figurative. I was fortunate in that the grammar school I attended had some young and challenging teachers who expected us to discuss ideas way beyond our set texts and curricula. Indeed, whether a fake can be better than a genuine work of art was a question that had taken up a whole double English lesson. Although I chose not to tackle them, the topics of 'Food' and 'Chance' were a surprise and struck me then, as they still do now, as indicators of an interesting and challenging approach to thinking and learning.

Sue Attridge (née Wood)

I too was attracted by the general knowledge character of the exam. I did the question on free speech (q11), the one about art forgeries (q16), and the one about the man riding up an escalator (q27b). I expect my answers for the first two were complete drivel! I was also accepted at Newnham, but preferred New Hall, which seemed more forward thinking. My school discouraged students from applying to both Oxford & Cambridge, on the grounds that "the other place" wouldn't appreciate being put second.

Gillian Blessley

My father persuaded me to apply to New Hall – I had wanted to join my sister at trendy Sussex - so I took my New Hall entrance paper in a lonely lecture hall in South Africa, just me and the invigilator. I seem to remember quoting R.D. Laing in a piece about the family. Fortunately, I didn't answer a question about whether I'd rather be a sheep or a goat, as I had understood this literally!

Flying back to England, I vividly remember the thrill of crossing the Sahara, and then the northern edge of the continent. At that moment I swore to never go back to South Africa – and I didn't until the Mandela era – so I barely saw my parents during the further 10 years that they postponed their return.

Helen Mayer

I took the entrance paper in 1970, in my fourth term of Sixth Form. I don't remember answering the history questions, although I suppose I must have done, but I do have a memory of answering the one about dreaming and reality - goodness knows why! All I know now is that I still couldn't answer most of them.

I was astonished to get an offer: two 'Es' at 'A' Level to take up my place. This gave me the freedom to read widely, especially English and German literature, in my final two terms.

Ursula Wide (née Buchan)

The exam paper looks terrifying. I don't remember doing it, and certainly not which questions I did!

I applied two years running, and was disappointed to be turned down, after interview, in my pre A level year (I did subsequently ask Esther Welbourn, our director of studies for medicine, what had happened to my potential in the intervening year - I don't think she gave a very clear answer!) but I was very glad in the end as I had a great gap 'year' (2 terms), which helped a lot in teaching me independence before I arrived.

Sarah Watson (née Henley)

I was delighted to get into New Hall and like several others relished the broad exam paper though I have very limited memory of what questions I answered (I think I did the one on space travel and its impact on wisdom).

Karen Greenwood

I remember well the New Hall entrance exam paper, which confirmed my impression of our college as so much more interesting than Newnham and Girton, whose traditional style paper I also took. It was just fun to think about the pros and cons of assorted items as currency, and how fast a battery would move if all its energy were converted from chemical to kinetic (sorry - I haven't read the copy of the paper that someone has sent round, these were from my memory, which is increasingly fallible).

Sally Morgan

The exam paper does seem impressive in hindsight. Was New Hall engaged in some incredibly prescient widening access experiment which the rest of Cambridge has taken 50 years to catch up on? I only remember answering one question - on Anarchism - which, as I was very keen on George Orwell at the time, I passionately defended! Afterwards I wondered if I should have been a bit more even-handed.

Ros Coward

My entrance exam was bizarre. At the request of my school English teacher, I sat the entrance exam a year early, before doing A-levels. She thought it would suit me, and as she seemed to be the only teacher at my school who respected that I did actually have a brain in my head and was not just a naughty girl whose mantra seemed to be "Yes, I know, but WHY?", I thought I might as well. I think "Food" was the main question I answered, and I wrote my thoughts about the clashing needs of spiritual and carnal satisfaction! And then a bit on fake v genuine works of art - yay, a chance to spout off about the 'haves' and the 'have-nots'! Total freedom of expression, no pressure – I loved it!

What an absolutely inspired and inspiring Entrance Exam - we all seem to agree on that! I got an interview and was offered a place if I achieved 2 x Grade E at A level. I was summoned to the Headmistress and anticipated congratulations – but no! I was told not to tell any of my friends at school as it would intimidate them in their A level efforts. It was like a "telling off" (again!) and made me even more desperate to leave school!

I felt under terrible pressure by having to get 2 E Grades – what if I couldn't even achieve that? So much for the confidence of youth – ha!

Lou Radford

I had to sit the paper in a tiny visitor's parlour behind the chapel, in my convent school, in a room completely cut off from everything and everyone I knew. I quite liked exams, but as I glanced through this initially my heart rose, I thought the entrance paper was so exhilarating and so totally different from the endless mock A levels and the boring Oxford papers. I also chose the essay on Food, using Man is what he eats as an analytic to assess the impact of colonialism and imperialism on national culture… how pretentious was that? but I absolutely loved it, wrote pages and pages in free flow enthusiasm. And then the dreaming one too, where I remember describing in very precise detail my physical surroundings without now being able to remember why. I can't recall a third choice. The history teacher, who was a wonderful old nun, came in at the end and picked up my reams of writing with a sad sigh.

Fiona Edwards-Stuart (née Weaver)

I went to a mixed modern grammar school which did not, as I recall, promote Oxford and Cambridge entrance and staying on for an extra term to do the entrance exam. However my father and brother went to Cambridge and I was encouraged by my parents to apply to New Hall and I was enthused by the idea of a modern college with only a general entrance exam. My memories of the exam are that I managed to use the questions to write about the discovery of DNA (having recently read the

Double Helix), and evolution (the Origin of the Species) and Animal Behaviour.

Liz Stafford

I vividly remember the Nuffield entrance exam used by New Hall and can even recall several of the questions from it 50 years later! One was about taking a torch battery and converting its electrical energy into mechanical energy and estimating how fast it would travel. Another was estimating the cost of heating the hot water for a bath and since I had never paid an electricity bill in my life it was an interesting exercise. I had to work out the volume of water needed, the amount of energy needed to raise it from mains temperature to hot water and guess the cost of electricity. I calculated the cost at around £1 but concluded that I had overestimated the cost of electricity because that seemed rather expensive!

Helen Morton

My memories of New Hall really started with meeting a New Hall graduate when I was on holiday in Morocco in the late 60's. I told her that I had been thinking about applying to do a degree in Social Anthropology as a mature student and she recommended that I apply to New Hall. Without that recommendation, I would never have even considered applying to Cambridge.

Ros Morpeth

I can remember being intrigued by a college that wanted to be different and choose on the basis of answers to a range of random (or so it felt) questions and hardly test our subject knowledge. I was chuffed when I was able to turn down a place at Girton and choose this interesting place instead – and anyway it was a shorter cycle ride from town! I hadn't wanted to apply to Cambridge, having grown up in Oxford as I wanted to get away from the elitism. However, I was persuaded by a combination of having already found a boyfriend at Peterhouse and my brother who said Cambridge is the only place you can do Economics! I knew little about it having done Physics and Maths A levels, but I wanted to do something with more of a human side and felt Economics would satisfy that. I think it probably did.

Wendy Spray (née Coulson)

New Hall as such was not a significant factor in making Cambridge so special, but I knew it was because of that peculiar entrance exam that we were there at all. So, enabling, rather than anything more. And, in comparison with Girton, architecturally and socially dull, or Newnham, architecturally and socially conventional, we were in by far the best available option.

Fiona Edwards-Stuart (née Weaver)

Interview

When I went for interview (for History) I was asked why I'd answered the questions intended for philosophers. I think I just said that they looked the most interesting. I still like the idea that they were looking for potential rather than results. Bafflingly, I have a vague memory of Rosemary Murray asking me about bookbinding at interview. I said that my grandmother had been an apprentice bookbinder but I knew nothing more about it. It still seems like a strange subject to pick on.

As far as I recall eight of us were accepted for History and eight for English but by the time we arrived at college four of the historians, including me, had swapped to English. Why was this? In my case I think I was influenced by a charismatic teacher at my boyfriend's school (he was a recent Cambridge English graduate and my boyfriend was going up to Queens' to read English) and the last straw was the History reading list which suggested reading 'Jane Austin' (sic) as background. I don't know now why a typo confusing a car and an author seemed so annoying to me at the time.

Pam Hilton

My interview started off with one of the English fellows asking me all about Elizabethan ballads, which surprised me as I was applying for medicine. Rosemary Murray then asked me about community work I had done (which I hadn't said I did) so I thought she maybe had the wrong application form in front of her. Neither asked me much about medicine or the various interests I had written about on the application form. It seemed to me that they wanted to see if you could 'think on your feet'.

I went to a recital at Kettle's Yard on the night before my interview (Brahms's E minor cello sonata), followed by a party at Magdalene College. I must have been living life more dangerously in those days. Certainly my parents didn't seem to be bothered.

I hadn't really wanted to come to Cambridge until that evening.

Rosemary Grande (née Temple)

Oddly, I remember the interview at Girton more clearly than the one at New Hall, partly because there was no power and the cavernous Girtonian Hall looked wonderfully Gothic and romantic by candlelight. I remember a lot of Classics candidates there, who seemed a bit on the snooty side. Archaeology and Anthropology didn't rate with them I felt (doubtless defensiveness on my part). I sat another entrance paper there, this time in Geography, one of my best school subjects, and had some very formal interviews.

The New Hall interviews were more relaxed. The other candidates seemed friendly but I felt shy. I remember being surprised to be interviewed by Rosemary Murray, being too naïve to realise that we were actually of some significance to her.

I didn't get in to Girton, but before I got their rejection letter, New Hall wrote to offer me a place, so that was that. I felt so lucky.

And I was.

I've always been proud to have gone to Cambridge, and pleased to have studied anthropology. It was great to study a non-school subject – it felt liberating.

Virginia Beardshaw

My only recollection of the interview is meeting Maryla, who was a fun friend throughout my time at New Hall.

Hilary Martin

I did not expect to even be called for interview and I did spend much of the first year with what the young now call "Imposter Syndrome", waiting for someone to tell me they had made a mistake and I shouldn't be there.

My memory of the interviews with Dame Rosemary and Esther Welbourn seem to consist of technical discussions about sailing. I did wonder whether they were just looking for someone for the sailing team. I participated fully in the sailing throughout my time, probably to the detriment of academic work.

I felt that the people I met at interview, including the ones showing us the ropes, were friendly and relaxed in sharp contrast to those at the Oxford interviews. There was also a power cut during my stay in Oxford and all the heating was off so I had to trek down to Marks and Spencer's to buy thick socks and a jumper. It seems so trivial but that really made my decision to accept the New Hall offer rather than Oxford when to my amazement they arrived.

Jan Sherman (née Phillips)

The recollections of people's entrance exams and interviews have been fascinating and reminded me forcibly how lucky I was just to be requested to write 3,000 words on any subject I liked, I imagine because I was applying late from overseas. There is absolutely no way I would have been able to write for an hour on three different topics from any of the papers I have seen recently, but perhaps that justifies my decision, when I was 17, to bypass university and get out into the world to earn some money.

What I wrote about, describing an experience while working in South Africa, was apparently sufficient to warrant an interview, but I was relaxed enough about it to continue my world travels for several more months before returning to England, when I was invited to come to New Hall for a day in May 1971. I do remember arriving rather hot and out of breath after hurrying up Castle Hill, having taken a bus from the station. I was interviewed by Esther Goody, and my first experience of the kindness of Mr Ellis [*head porter*] was when he directed me to her room, which I think was on the lower level of Fountain Court. I remember absolutely nothing of the interview, but I do remember being so nervous at the thought of being interviewed by Rosemary Murray in the afternoon that I couldn't face having any lunch so walked round the garden and then settled down in the Library. It was there that Mr Ellis tracked me down with a note from Miss Murray that she was extremely sorry, but a summons for a meeting on urgent university business meant that she did not have time to see me and would arrange a suitable time the following week.

A couple of days later I received a letter from Miss Murray saying that she felt it was unkind to put me to the expense of travelling to Cambridge again. At that point my attention froze as I thought it meant my dream was shattered, until I read "so I look forward to welcoming you to New Hall in October". Phew!

Sarah Wilson (née Stallard)

I have a clear recall of the interview with Janet Moore and Joan Stevenson-Hinde to read Natural Sciences. The interview felt as though they were looking for something I knew very little about, which did not take them long, as they focussed in on genetics. I feel I spent most of the interview saying, how interesting, and offering to go home and read more about that.

Karen Greenwood

I remember when I came up for interview that I shared a room with a girl from a well-known girls' school who was full of confidence (unlike me), and full of plans for the drama societies she was going to join when she came up. This totally bemused me as I had no idea what to expect of the university. When I arrived in October to take up my place, I was strangely reassured to see that she was not there.

Alison Litherland (née Hill)

When I was invited to interview, my history teacher tried to persuade me to wear a skirt and to put my (long) hair up in a bun, both of which I refused to do. I got myself from deepest Sussex to New Hall, and back again the same day (because I was not allowed away for the night), and I remember very little about the interviews with Helen Clover and Miss Murray, or anything of the other girls there, who all seemed very poised and confident, and rather snooty, but I was very taken with the buildings, which I had not seen before. And then I walked back through the town, along Kings Parade to the station on a complete high.
When I was summoned to the Headmistress a few days later, she had already opened the letter from New Hall addressed to me, and read out

the 2E offer, but insisted that I tell none of my peers and above all that this was no excuse not to continue with my studies and to do as well as possible for the good of the school. I did not begrudge this at the time, at all, and I was simply, secretly, thrilled, without quite knowing why…. I did get good grades though; one of the advantages of a boarding school is that there are fairly few distractions. And East Sussex County Council, as well as being generous and very prompt with a full grant, gave me an extra £30pa as a book bonus!

Fiona Edwards-Stuart (née Weaver)

The interview at New Hall was with Janet Moore and I really enjoyed it. She was a wonderful person, kind and generous. The interview included being handed a skull and being asked about it. It was like a dog but not a dog, teeth too small and backwards pointing... A seal, of course.

Deborah Glass

The interview, where I waited outside the interview room listening to the dauntingly confident candidate ahead of me, convinced me I wouldn't get in. I remember being astonished when the offer letter arrived. My mother came up with me on the train and I cried when she left. I thought she wasn't going to cope without me!

Ros Coward

In November 1970, New Hall summoned me for a day of interviews and college tours. I can't remember anything about the interviews, but I very clearly recall being "shepherded" around college to the interviews by a 1st year English student called Mary Allen, who went on to become Secretary General of the Arts Council. Mary was a keen thespian and enthused at length about Footlights and Cambridge life generally, as between interviews she poured me cups of black Lapsang Souchong tea with tiny twigs floating in it. I'd never even heard of Lapsang tea, but I fervently wanted to become a Cambridge student like Mary. Amazingly, a letter arrived in early December from NH offering me a place to read History on 2Es. That letter boosted my confidence hugely and that same day I passed my Driving Test on the first attempt, despite my instructor telling me I wouldn't pass.

Charlotte Crawley (née Miller)

My mother, my aunt, my grandfather, my grandmother and even my father, who had come over from New Zealand to do his PhD, had all studied at Cambridge University though all at different colleges and we had visited often so it seemed a logical place to go. I had also decided I wanted to study Engineering and the course at Cambridge was one where you studied all aspects of engineering for two years and only specialised in your third year, which suited me as I wasn't entirely sure what branch of engineering I wanted to go into. I think I chose Engineering because people told me I couldn't do it because I was a girl and I was determined to prove them wrong and because I guess I was competing with my older brother who was already studying engineering.

I don't remember very much about the interview other than finding out that Rosemary Murray knew my aunt who studied chemistry at Cambridge in the 1940s. It's a very small world!

Helen Morton

I was interviewed at New Hall by Rosemary Murray who agreed to give me a place after discovering I was intending to do the washing, cleaning etc. myself. She was amazing! The college also let me have extra time when I developed an ectopic pregnancy in my third year.

Alison New

Never put anything on your CV to pad it out unless you are prepared to talk about it! I remember travelling on the slow train from Worcester, looking out at the wonderful English countryside with its remnant mediaeval landscapes, wondering what it would all be like, what I would be asked and keeping my expectations low so as not to be disappointed. Like many, I was the first in my family to attend university, and if that university could be Cambridge, I knew my family would burst with pride. Could I do it? Everything was going well until I was called in to talk to Rosemary Murray. Her benign appearance and manner hid an eagle eye and sharp intelligence. She looked down my CV and picked on the one thing I had used as padding – membership of the National Trust, which in fact was only family membership. "What was the last property you visited?". My mind went blank – I said my favourite house was Cothele, a Tudor manor house in Cornwall. I thought, if she asks me any detailed questions about this I am sunk, but she said "what do you think the Tudor residents of the house would have made of the radio?" I love theoretical nonsense questions like this.

Diana Murray (née Collyer)

Travelling to New Hall for an interview, I was very nervous and didn't know what to expect. Friends had told me to prepare myself for a formal interview with at least four academics on a panel and this made me even more apprehensive. I turned up at the porter's lodge and said that I had come for an interview with Dr Goody. I was directed to her office and I can remember standing outside trying to steel myself for a gruelling interview. I knocked on the door and a friendly American voice invited me to come in. There was Esther Goody sitting in an armchair, surrounded by papers. She was dressed in jeans, a tee shirt and a suede waistcoat. I immediately felt overdressed in my rather formal interview outfit. Esther and I talked for over two hours about anthropology and she mentioned that she felt it was a difficult subject for students straight from school because they hadn't had much time to experience life. During those two hours I realised that I had opened up and revealed more about myself than I ever would have allowed myself to do in a 'proper' interview. I couldn't believe my luck when I was offered a place for part 1 Archaeology and Anthropology to start that autumn.

Ros Morpeth

I was interviewed at LMH (Lady Margaret Hall) in Oxford first and hated everything about the experience: the candlelit interview ("I'd like to pick up on something you wrote in your essay but can't see to read it" has stayed with me for 50 years), the bitter cold of the college and the fog enveloping the town, the students in gowns. It felt completely alien. I was supposed to stay a second night there as it was too far to go home, but another candidate, equally horrified at the conditions, invited me to stay in London with her family before travelling with her to Cambridge the following day.

I can't say I fell in love with New Hall as a building but I felt much more comfortable there. Even the interview felt more welcoming, although I was both delighted and distracted by a squirrel darting around outside the room in Fountains Court! Still I wasn't at all certain it was the place for me, but I had some time between interviews and went into town to look around. I walked past the entrance to Christ's and looked through the gateway, and seeing those beautiful buildings was the moment I knew I wanted to be in Cambridge and would be bitterly disappointed if I didn't succeed. It was wonderful then to be offered a place - and even more satisfying to reject the offer from Oxford!

Denise Phillipson (née Milburn)

My interview was very exciting because I had to go by train from my boarding school and stay overnight at New Hall. At some point during the day two other girls and I met three male interviewees who invited us out for the evening. I don't think my head mistress would have approved of our activities had she known! The next day I made my way to Oxford for an interview at St Anne's College, which was very nice but I had fallen in love with Cambridge and New Hall, and there was no question about which to choose when both offered me a place.

Jane Mott (née Style)

First Impressions

Self-confident I was not; nor ever became so during my time at Cambridge. My abiding memory of my first day at New Hall was of watching from my window, which looked over the car park, as others arrived, accompanied by their proud mothers and fathers.

Ursula Wide (née Buchan)

I too felt pretty overwhelmed by what I perceived as the confidence of others. Like Ursula I'd had a free place to a single sex Direct Grant school but had grown up on a council estate. I imagined everyone came from 'posh backgrounds' so was insecure around female friendships at New Hall, connecting with others who in retrospect I realise were similarly feeling their way. Some of those friendships remain important today. But I also think that being surrounded by so many men (boys, really) shaped how we experienced New Hall social life. We were so outnumbered, and they were so eager, it was almost easier to have male friends. I certainly spent a lot of time down the hill in the men's colleges!

Ros Coward

I was from a state school, and felt socially awkward, as though there were rules that I didn't know. I also remember being intimidated by everyone else who, it seemed, did underwater flute playing or were published poets or astonishingly beautiful.

Deborah Glass

Arriving at New Hall in October 1971 for my first term was an eye-opener. Coming from a state school in a Midlands market town I was bemused and often baffled by so many new experiences: porters who called me 'Miss'; terrifying sherry parties; a fellow student who, apparently magically, already knew which Oxford college her 13-year-old brother would be going to; wearing a gown; riding a bike for the first time (one-handed after I fell off and fractured my arm); being locked out of the building on the dot of midnight.

Maureen Bell

Socially, I felt an outsider at Cambridge University. This was compounded by the shock of dealing with my father's premature death in my first year. I came from a state grammar school, and was the first (alongside my sister) in the family to be able to attend University, because of state grants that our generation were so lucky to be awarded. I had no understanding of all the social conventions, traditions and hierarchies on display at Cambridge University. That was also disconcerting and led to a lifetime research interest in social inequalities. I had never been to a cocktail party until my supervisor in economic history, Dr Von Tunzelmann, invited me to one. There I met new friends that have lasted a lifetime; and from there I migrated to the disco basement of St John's College where we danced on many an evening to rock and roll music, including Alright Now by Free and Jumpin' Jack Flash by the Stones. So much fun!

Diana Kuh (née Lewin)

I'm fascinated by how many of us felt a little out of place. I was on a scholarship at a direct grant school, which was fairly academic. As far as I recollect my 18-year-old self, I was very serious about academic work, but not about life. I had never been a 'big fish' at school – probably ranked about fifth or sixth in my year, with my closest friend (who turned down a place at New Hall to go to Sussex with her boyfriend) always way ahead of me in terms of results. So, it was no surprise to find a place full of people who seemed far cleverer and more knowledgeable about almost everything.

Pam Hilton

I was pleased to find New Hall "classless", compared with the town colleges. I was the sole Music student, so had to make my way alone.

But there were loads of musical opportunities in Cambridge; and loads of strange musicians! Hmm! Very strange!

As it had been obviously so hard to gain entrance (only 6 lady musicians in my year, the others being at Girton and Newnham), this meant the place came with a certain fitted "confidence", and a kind of "assurance of competence", as if you had "beaten" a lot of aspiring persons at interview and having sat for the other two colleges, I can tell you the waiting room was alarmingly full!

Sue Whitham (née Addison)

Like many others, when I arrived, I felt quite nervous and wondered whether I really was good enough to be there. I expect I appeared quite confident, just as others did to me, but it is only now that I am seeing how many of us came from state schools and modest backgrounds. Good for New Hall – not only encouraging women's education but also social inclusion. I was, however, overwhelmed by the preponderance of men from privileged backgrounds who were really most unappealing and did tend to keep in their own peer groups. The Rugby players and the Boat clubs were perhaps the worst, and I never shall understand how the colleges put up with their drunken brawling in some of the most beautiful rooms in their colleges and the damage that they caused.

Diana Murray (née Collyer)

I came from a state grammar school as did many others – they were good schools and at least where I came from (Guildford) better than the local independent schools. Coming to New Hall was certainly the first time I met people from public school and with markedly different backgrounds to myself. However, I do think everyone had to put on a show of confidence arriving at university and most probably didn't feel it underneath. In the end I met people I got on well with and made lifelong friends.

Pauline Whitney (née Micklam)

My first impressions were - The social life! I had been at a girls grammar school and hadn't really had that much to do with men other than my brothers. The whole idea of all the clubs and societies and activities was pretty exciting. And because I was studying engineering there were 250 students in my year of whom only five were women and 245 were men so it was an interesting experience and very different to life beforehand. The other engineer at New Hall was Susan Young, known by all as Scottie, and we spent a lot of study and social time together.

Helen Morton

In reply to the question 'were you a grammar school girl who found it hard to fit in?', I am heartily grateful that no one at the time suggested that as a 'grammar school girl' I might not fit in. If they had I would have run a mile - I hadn't fitted in at my small-town grammar school and I'd had enough of not fitting in.

I arrived at New Hall full of optimism for a new start, totally lacking in social skills and with a huge desire to make up for lost time. I remember feeling hugely embarrassed at my response to the nurse after our arrival - when she asked 'and do you have a boyfriend' my response was 'not yet', implying that rectifying this was first on my to-do list.

I found the other students friendly, but apart from two close New Hall friends I didn't do most of my socialising in college. I found friends through societies, parties, and friends of friends. And as most students were men, I had many platonic male friends. I did notice many people from a very different background to mine, but didn't feel I needed to fit in with them. I remember noticing a certain type of (not New Hall) student who were expensively educated, over confident, and not very bright. I avoided them.

Alison Litherland (née Hill)

I loved the ambiance of Cambridge and think I spent at least most of my first term (and much of the next three years) wandering around believing that I was in a dream.

It was a different world. Judging by the responses here there must have been so many of us thinking that, coming from a state school, we were different from most around us!

Dorothy Cade (née Clark)

Experiencing Cambridge as an overseas graduate from New Zealand but on a British Passport, and reading for an undergraduate degree (Anglo-Saxon and Old Norse), meant that I didn't fit neatly into any clear group but I had the advantage of being able to move within a number of circles.

Having overseas graduate status meant I had the luxury of a split-level room to myself, a free dinner once a week in hall with sherry (of course) beforehand, membership of the Grad Pad where I remember seeing Stephen Hawkins once at a nearby table, and the right to stay in college during the vacations as long as I wanted.

Aileen Regan (née Kidd)

My father was working in Nigeria at this time, so on the first day, I had to get myself and my few possessions to Cambridge on my own somehow, I can remember splashing out on a taxi from the station and reflecting that I would not know a single person in Cambridge. I had a single room on H staircase, next to the infirmary, very small and dowdy but it was mine and I loved it; a single electric ring to build a life from. The rooms were allocated almost alphabetically, so mine was the second last before Eve Wernly (RIP) opposite. She and Annie Stuart, who had the first room on the landing, were both reading Japanese, which seemed so exotic. Emily Smith, who had the room next to Annie, was reading classics, which also seemed quite rarefied. There was sherry for the historians with Miss Clover that first evening, about which I was a bit anxious but it was a very friendly evening, where I met Ursula Buchan for the first time, with whom I am still friends. Supper in Hall that first evening was completely grim, but after that, once lectures started, everything got busier and better. There was just so much on offer, societies to join, countless causes to espouse, AmDram

(Amateur Dramatics) to enjoy, the town and the Backs and the Sidgewick site to explore. I too remember the incredibly stimulating Steiner and Pevsner lectures, and the Barenboim concert, and the picture loan library at Kettle's yard, without realising that there were so many other peers from New Hall doing the same things, although Ursula and I usually went together.

Fiona Edwards-Stuart (née Weaver)

One of my earliest strong memories of Cambridge is of cycling down Castle Hill to a party at the beginning of term in my long skirt with the wind blowing my hair all over the place, and suddenly feeling overcome by joy and exhilaration - nobody in the world knew where I was or what I was doing! Real freedom! Yes, I was apprehensive and nervous, but also excited - it was the beginning of my adult journey, away from a close family with 4 younger siblings, and I resolved to make the most of it that I possibly could.

Lorna Robertson

Sitting around Louise Ramsay's (Gibbon as was) kitchen table, my son Tom asked 'What was Mum like at Cambridge?'
Louise took her time. After a long pause she said, 'She worked very hard'.
Unglamorous, but probably true.
I'd come from a Quaker boarding school in Yorkshire with a firm nonconformist work ethic and a definite feminist slant. I was a dual national UK/US. My family were in Greece when I started at New Hall. My kind of mixed international background was more unusual in 1971 than it is now, but Cambridge was welcoming.
Rosemary Murray's talk on our first evening chimed with the nonconformism in a way that would make me forever uneasy. She suggested that we should aim for a 9 to 5 working day, like our peers in the world of work. Her strictures haunted me throughout my time in Cambridge, and beyond. I never seemed to achieve it, although by a great stroke of good fortune I had first year supervisions with Ros Morpeth. Classed as

a 'mature student' at the advanced age of 24. Ros, who went on to be CEO of the National Extension College, was formidably well organised. I followed in her wake. Under her expert leadership I never missed an essay.

Virginia Beardshaw

I found negotiating the 1st year pretty hard. Yes, there were lovely people to talk to and I can remember staying up late solving the world's problems, but it was hard getting used to being away from home. It was difficult being woken by the cleaners wheeling something down the corridor every morning, and trying to cook cauliflower cheese on one ring - and there were essays to write.

Wendy Spray (née Coulson)

Just snippets. A sense of setting off on a spaceship adventure with lots of other friendly earthlings, mutual excitement crowding out any anxieties that followed. A thrill at my first view of the building (I hadn't been for an interview). Walking down corridors that somehow whispered to me that I'd arrived, there was no going back. Feeling like a clumsy stranger at sherry introductions with Rosemary Murray.

Helen Mayer

Academia

In Cambridge, the university covered lectures and exams. The college covered individual learning. For each subject, there was a college Director of Studies, who arranged supervisors to set work and hold individual or small supervisions to discuss it.

I've fished out my copy of the 1974 prospectus - which lots of you perhaps never saw, since aimed at applicants. I was on a working group set up by Kate Pretty and Kate Belsey to do what is now called 'widening participation' and we produced a prospectus as part of that. I had to organize the photographs - at short notice - and so grabbed friends and indeed anyone around to pose for them.
This photo shows Kate Belsey (a real supervisor) pretending to supervise a couple of people. The chap was my then boyfriend, but I'm sorry I can't remember the name of the other 'supervisee'.

Maureen Bell

I read French and German. It was really exciting to discover a world of literature beyond Racine and Corneille and to be able to go to as many lectures as I wanted in any subject. It's a pity that I never, ever learned how to write essays. The night before I was due to hand one in would find me looking at pages of notes and multiple versions of my first paragraph, wondering how on earth I was to make a sensible argument out of it all in time.

Emma Wheelock

I only went to the occasional lecture by lecturers I really rated, including George Steiner, who wasn't lecturing on my subjects, but spoke, as I remember, about life, the universe and everything, in a most dramatic and charismatic way. I used to do most of my work in my room or at the university library, where I would turn up in time for cheese scones in the cafe at 11am. When I left, I asked the cook there for her recipe and I still have it. It started, three pounds of flour....
My supervisor for Spanish was Lorna Close, whom I adored. She gave me so much freedom to study what I wanted, never criticised, but questioned, and got me to question everything. I once told her I couldn't come to supervision because I had to make myself a skirt and she totally got the importance of that. Another time, she warned me, as I arrived at the door of her room that there was a very large black spider under her desk, so I chose to skip that session too! There were always piles of sherry bottles outside the door of her and Dorothy Colemans' offices. I remember my interview with her there, where I told her I had taught myself Spanish under the covers at night, because my school didn't teach Spanish. She encouraged me to learn Portuguese, too, which I never did, but I did take up Russian in my second year and then studied it as part of my degree. I am amazed that I was allowed that freedom!
The first essay she set me in my first week was to write in Spanish on "solitude". I remember sitting crying in my room, looking at books and poems on solitude and feeling intensely lonely. It sounds sad, but actually, I was learning to notice and question my own experience,

describe it and compare it to similar experiences in writers and thinkers I admired. I studied Modern Languages, which meant basically foreign literature read in the original language. There was nothing practical about the course. Everything I read was not only of academic interest but spoke to the burning concerns I had at the time. What is love, whom do I love and who loves me? What is solitude? Is there a God? What happens when you make a decision based on intellect, or emotion, or instinct? How do you reconcile these things? What is sex for? and friendship? Can anyone help anyone else and if so, how? (I spent some time working for the student equivalent of the Samaritans and ended up getting stalked, which put me off). What is my purpose in life?
I did not really come up with answers to any of these questions, although I am much better at making decisions nowadays. I hope I am still asking questions and learning about them through life and the literature and art that I enjoy.
Talking about the freedom we had to change subjects, mix and match: someone mentioned being allowed to do a literature paper as part of a medical degree. I was allowed to do the tragedy paper from the English tripos.

Penny Stirling

I relished the independence of college life and the relative informality of New Hall suited me. I studied Modern and Medieval Languages and the only supervisions in college I can remember were with Dr Coleman, who was my Director of Studies and whose enthusiasm for her subject was as infectious as her knowledge of it was daunting. She was the exception among my supervisors in that she made a good show of seeming interested in what I had to say. The others were probably more honest: I struggled with the dissection of texts and having to wade through interminable articles on the books I was studying, and the conclusions I drew were probably not up to much. I readily took up a linguistics option that opened my mind to different ways of thinking about language and literature and was partly taught in seminars which I found far less intimidating than supervisions and more relevant than the lectures, and a Tragedy paper from the English tripos which offered scope for broader reading. It was several years after I left Cambridge that I went back to reading literature for pleasure again. I was shocked at how little importance was given to the spoken languages. Am I right that the only oral test we had happened before the beginning of the first term?

Mary Anne Bonney

As I was reading Anglo-Saxon and Old Norse, I had tutorials in several other colleges and only fully appreciated later how fortunate I was to be taught by such colourful academics like Ray Page, who was the modern embodiment of an ancient Viking and recited Old Norse poetry in a truly inspiring manner. He also had the original Anglo-Saxon Chronicle on a shelf in his room and would casually reach for it to illustrate a particular passage. I doubt that would be possible these days.

Aileen Regan (née Kidd)

After the first year, all my supervisions were outside the college. I was accepted to do a Part 2 in Social and Political Studies, with a Part 1 in Archaeology and Anthropology: however, in the event I switched to Anglo-Saxon, Norse and Celtic for my Part 2, attracted by the subject (I had been on several digs) and by the prospect of a small, intimate school, instead of the hurly-burly of SPS. In practice, it didn't really end up that way - I rather envy those of you with supervisors who seem to have taken a real interest in you as a student and as a person, though I enjoyed the subject.

The really significant outcome, for me, was that a group of us ASNC students developed a project to reconstruct part of an Anglo-Saxon village at West Stow, near Bury St Edmunds, using the traditional tools used then – experimental archaeology. This took up a lot of my two years of ASNC studies, outside of term time, and was a significant distraction in my final year since half the group were from the year above and had already graduated. The project was academically sound – we even gave a paper at an Oxford symposium – but was entirely unsupported by Cambridge: in fact, was rather frowned on as a diversion from proper study.

I learned a lot of new things at West Stow. How to interpret drawings; how to split wood, adze, and thatch; how to seek and obtain necessary permissions and sponsorship; and how to navigate living with a fairly random group of other people, in a remote cottage with no mains services, in all seasons. The houses we built then, and in the year or two after graduation, are still there as the centrepiece of West Stow Country Park, and have been added to since by subsequent student groups. But it took me a long time to be proud of this.

Rosie Boughton

I'm still not sure that English, in the way we studied it was really a discipline, but I loved the opportunity, as part of the reforms brought in for our year, to do two dissertations in the final year. It was a huge amount of work and Miss Hammond told me afterwards that the faculty were reconsidering it as almost everyone who took this option did very well in the dissertations but less well in the exams than would have been expected.

To add to the recollections of bizarre teaching, we had joint supervisions on practical criticism at the Advisory Centre for Education. One day I recall arriving a little late and running up the stairs, hearing the supervisor talk to someone in the hall below. He then arrived in the classroom and spoke throughout in a squeaky voice which he claimed was the result of an unspecified illness, though when I'd heard him talking downstairs his voice was perfectly normal. On the other hand, Kiernan Ryan, still a post graduate student then, was an excellent supervisor who really challenged me to think; I was so pleased to see later that he became New Hall's Director of Studies for English.

Pam Hilton

I have always beaten myself up about not making the most of my 'English at New Hall' experience. I didn't sink, but I certainly didn't swim! The lack of academic support was shocking, as was the lack of guidance about what was actually on offer, and what was expected of us. In fairness to New Hall and to our tutors, we were afforded the complete freedom of expression and range of study which had attracted us to the college in the first place, but to be plunged into that environment directly from school was daunting to say the least. I rather envied the scientists, because in sciences there was a "body of knowledge" to be absorbed, something that had a good beginning, a meaty middle, and that actually led to some tangible achievement! I do have one outstanding memory of the English experience though – does anyone else remember going to a much-touted lecture on Ibsen by George Steiner at Sedgwick? I queued for ages and managed to get a place inside the lecture theatre, but to my horror, Steiner quoted Ibsen in what was presumably Norwegian, with references to other quotations in Latin and probably Greek, and I left the theatre in disgust, as I thought it was elitist and unworthy of my time! I was referred to in a local review as someone who had walked out. I don't think I was mentioned by name, but I was mortified, while remaining fairly irritated with the erudite man himself!

Lou Radford

I confess that over the years (and particularly because of teaching at various other universities) I've looked back and thought how shockingly little academic support we had. The supervision system meant weekly essays (good! I enjoyed the intensive reading and late-night scramble to write it up) which weren't ever given a mark (not so good! so how did I know how I was doing?) In fact it wasn't until Prelims that we had any marks at all. What was presumably intended as freedom from competition and a fostering of individual interests etc., at the time felt more like isolation and uncertainty.

Individual supervisions took some getting used to. Miss Hammond was indeed patient with my inability to connect with George Herbert's poems. She didn't even flinch when, in a Practical Criticism practice session, I denounced as insipid and sentimental an 'unseen' poem by

Wordsworth. In my first year, after a really hard but exciting week wrestling with Piers Plowman, my postgraduate supervisor suggested that next week I should tackle Chaucer. When, naively, I asked which of the Canterbury Tales I should read, she replied, terrifyingly, 'All of them, of course!' So I did; though I confess to skipping 'Melibee', an omission never yet remedied. While the New Hall supervisors showed an interest in what I had to say and established something of a personal relationship, for the rest of the three years we were sent to many people at other colleges, sometimes for only 3 weeks before moving on to a new person. Only a few seemed much interested in the undergraduate/s in front of them (usually one, but sometimes two, when we went in pairs). One supervisor at a men's college, to whom I was sent for a few weeks on the Victorian novel, insisted on my reading my essay aloud while he lounged, apparently semiconscious, by the blazing fire. He hardly ever interrupted me to comment or question. By the time I had completed my weekly monologue, and he had shaken himself and then bustled about making tea and toasting crumpets (yes, really!), there was remarkably little of the hour left for any discussion of the novels in question. Either my essays were too mind-numbingly tedious for him to engage with, or he just didn't like teaching. Or, conceivably, both.

A school friend at another university had seminars - which sounded like wonderful inventions to me, in that they were a chance to discuss and argue things out in a group. Individual supervisions were a mixed blessing. Kate Belsey (being then relatively young and new) spotted that seminars could be helpful, but the few she organized were not very productive.

When it came to the dissertation Miss Hammond, hearing my intended topic, suggested I go and see another unknown person at another college and because I had no idea what the whole dissertation thing entailed, I didn't go - and just wrote it by myself with no guidance during the long vac. It wasn't a distinguished piece of work! It was only years later that I realized how little explanation we were offered at any stage about what was expected. Lectures were take-it-or-leave-it affairs and by second year Raymond Williams's were the only ones that could get me into a lecture theatre by 9.00 a.m.! Cambridge certainly encouraged independence in learning, which is desirable. But the Cambridge way was, looking back, one which left you to sink or swim on your own - and consequently for some people it was, I think, damaging. I just accepted what it was like and didn't worry about it over-much.

Maureen Bell

Like Maureen, I reflected afterwards on the lack of general academic support and the notion that we should get on with things and presumably ask if we needed help. It did seem that the quality and personality of our supervisors was a key factor. I have a memory of going to Fitzwilliam for a supervision with David Starkey (Tudor and Stuart history). I can't remember whether he was still doing his doctorate or was a post-doctoral Fellow at the time. He was however much the same in attitude and demeanour as he appears now! In one exchange he described me as a 'minor intellectual'. He was being quite condescending, but I privately felt quite flattered! Another supervisor really fired my interest in social and economic history, and I also gained a great deal from my sessions with Quentin Skinner at Christs on the Political Thought module. Another Supervisor – a doctoral student – gave me such long reading lists each week I felt swamped. He was brilliant, but not very helpful. I always came away feeling told off and as if I'd been given a Dunce's hat. These mixed experiences and the lack of attention to the process of learning certainly made me keen to help my own students to learn effectively and to 'jump through the hoops'. By then study skills were promoted on most courses anyway.

Anne Muir (née Borrett)

I read Modern History, which I enjoyed hugely. I did not know it, but it has proved to be a very useful study for any kind of journalist since it essentially consisted of acquiring a lot of information and then distilling it into something logical and readable. I liked my fellow historians at New Hall very much, as well as my supervisors, although most of them were outside college. One of my history supervisors was Miss Kathleen Wood-Legh. She lived in a house the other side of Lammas Land, which was rather a pleasant bike-ride away, near Fen Causeway. The house was rather dark, the reason being that Miss Wood-Legh had been blind from childhood. She was by then in her early seventies. I don't remember anything I learned from her, except not to use the word 'adaption' but rather 'adaptation' (a strange random memory) but she made a profound impact on me, nevertheless. She would ask me to read my essay to her, and then we would discuss it. She would repeat whole sentences back to me, verbatim, which was both embarrassing because of their banality, and deeply impressive. From her I learned the important life lesson that I should never use any kind of disadvantage as an excuse for not trying my best.

I was the victim of an awful muddle in my first year. I liked my first Supervisor of Studies at New Hall very much, but she failed to tell me that I had to study a medieval paper for Part I. Nor did she organise a supervisor for me. I bear her no ill will, but it was quite unfortunate, and would have dished my chances if I had wanted to go on in academia. I was too timid, or passive, to make a fuss, as I would undoubtedly have done nowadays. As it happened, that muddle did me no harm at all in the long run.

My second Supervisor of Studies, Zara Steiner, was one of the most remarkable women I've ever met, and a wonderful teacher. The only problem was that she would never put supervision times in her diary, since she said it undermined her memory. As a result, on more than one occasion she was double-booked. I wanted to go to the USA to study after Cambridge, and she was very helpful as far as seeking out funding that I could apply for. In the end, I did not go, but I was grateful to her for taking me seriously.

Ursula Wide (née Buchan)

So, what was the point of New Hall? I think we all enjoyed it? Perhaps not sufficient cause in itself, but we were exceptionally well educated, at a time when not every girl had that opportunity. From an academic point of view, I thought New Hall did us historians proud. We seemed to have complete freedom of choice about what papers we chose, and the choice was very wide. All my supervisors were outside college. David Starkey at Fitzwilliam was an excellent if startlingly harsh supervisor, and once I recovered from the initial shock of his confrontational ethos, he certainly sharpened up my critical thinking, and made me reduce my word count. Otto Smail at Christ's managed to totally immerse the tiny group of us who were studying the third Crusade into the daily life of Outremer, introducing us to alternative contemporary sources, Islamic, Armenian and Jewish as well as Latin. We came out of any seminar with him, blinking with surprise at being back in present time. Unfortunately, I cannot remember the names of all my supervisors, but they were all very good, stimulating, patient, guiding rather than dictating. In my last year, for history of political thought, I had a young research fellow called Richard Tuck, who is now the Professor of Government at Harvard, and he was just completely brilliant. He gave supervision in his home, a lovely house on Parkers Piece. What a total luxury to have had those one-on-one quality teaching hours. All my supervisors were male, most of the lecturers were male, but I was never ever patronised or made to feel in any way that I did not deserve to be there. There were so few girls really, when we went up, and it was so easy to make friends with everyone. I think most of our male contemporaries were initially much more frightened of us than we of them, or so they always said. Perhaps we were just there at a lucky time. I still have many of the male friends that I made from different colleges and walks of life, as well as my New Hall group of friends, a few girls from Newnham, and from Clare and Kings' the following year.

Fiona Edwards-Stuart (née Weaver)

Unlike several of my fellow New Hall first year historians, (I remember Ann Borrett, Ursula Buchan, Di Hills & Fiona Weaver), I found Part I History incredibly dull – a far cry from the sparky history teaching I'd had for A level. Our Director of Studies set me, and maybe all of us, our first essay – it was entitled, "Pope Boniface VIII was an anachronism – discuss". Who the hell was Boniface VIII and why did he matter so much? It all seemed so remote to me. The next essay was on the origins of Gothic architecture, and its spread from France across Europe. This was much more my bag, but I still felt generally disappointed with history at Cambridge.

My other supervisor was an even older scholar, Dr Kay Wood-Legh, who had in 1965 published two thick volumes on British medieval chantry chapels. Blinded by childhood measles, Dr. W-L lived in a cul-de-sac beyond Newnham, in a house festooned with heavy Nottingham lace curtains. Of necessity, essays had to be read out to her and as the November afternoon light faded, eventually I always had to ask her if I could turn on the lights? She was a dear old thing, with a great love of Gilbert & Sullivan, but I'm afraid she contributed to my growing disillusion with History.

Towards the end of my first term, I felt sure I would not be able to pursue history for two years and so decided I'd like to switch to Architecture. I went for an interview, and astonishingly, I received a positive response. But fortunately, my father persuaded me that I did not possess any of the requisite skills to be a successful architect and that most probably none of my buildings would stand up. Dad, now 94, was absolutely right, physics and maths were not my strong suit! But the outcome of this exercise was that I did make arrangements to do a Part II in History of Art and Architecture, come Autumn '73. Thereafter I did a fairly minimal amount of History and scraped through the Part I exams with a third.

At last, from October 1973, I could immerse myself in subjects I adored – History of Architecture and Art. I exchanged the huge and drafty Seeley Library, for the much cosier Scroope Terrace at the far end of Trumpington Street, beyond the Fitzwilliam Museum. There were only just over 20 students in each year of Art History – so the whole experience was completely different to reading History. We had some brilliant young supervisors, plus very distinguished and established Art and Architecture Historians, with lecturers dropping in to Scroope

Terrace from other universities and museums. Our Director of Studies at New Hall was Dr Virginia Spate, who spoke softly with a slight Australian accent. She was very different to Prof. Michael Jaffe, who conducted mildly terrifying study sessions in the Fitzwilliam, in front of appointed paintings. Jaffe loved putting us on the spot with searching questions about paint pigments, obscure Greek mythology etc. – but these sessions were invaluable lessons in how to look at and understand works of art. Connoisseurship.

Charlotte Crawley (née Miller)

Arch and Anth students at New Hall were largely well taught by graduate students from across the colleges. In my third year I had Caroline Humphrey (now a Dame and a Fellow of King's), whose research was amongst the horse herders of Mongolia. The romance of this contrasted with the Downing site, home of the Faculty of Archaeology and Anthropology and much else scientific. They were very gloomy Edwardian and early 20th century buildings set in tarmac, unrelieved by greenery, often with a chill Cambridge wind zipping through them. Hating coats, as I still do, I was very probably never warmly enough dressed.

I can't remember any amenities for students in the Faculty except a bare sort of room where we could eat food we brought in with us. No Faculty meetings or get togethers. Students of today would be underwhelmed.

We didn't realise it at the time, but the Faculty was at an inflexion point. Meyer Fortes, who had been William Wyse Professor of Social Anthropology since 1950 was winding down, and would be succeeded by Jack Goody, Esther's husband, in 1973. This created an awkward situation for her, and if my memory serves me rightly, I believe she was asked to resign as a Reader in the Faculty – something many of us were indignant about. She implored us not to make a fuss. Would this happen today? Did it happen then? It seems archaic in the extreme if it did, like a bad dream.

Thinking about it now, I remember the Department as having a colonial flavour, which was about to be dissipated by the Francophile Jack Goody who had returned from a spell in Paris getting to grips with Claude Levi-Strauss and structuralism. His wide interests brought a fresh perspective that was badly needed. A change from ethnographic studies from across the vanishing Empire.

There were a lot of us in the year group because we were doing three subjects at the start. Because they were new to everyone, attendance at lectures was quite good, although I don't really remember getting to know anyone from other colleges. A pity.

For Part 1 we did Archaeology as well as Social and Physical Anthropology. This seemed to mean Neolithic hand axes, of which there were hundreds in the Faculty Museum. One hand axe seemed, and was, very like another. I found them dull. Ditto Physical Anthropology, which at that time was the study of skulls and bones of early hominids, of which there were precious few in the early 1970s. Little did I imagine how the subject would expand and develop with new discoveries and techniques to colour in the map of human evolution. Nowadays I find this fascinating and read whatever I can on it.

One of the rooms off Fountain Court was Esther Goody's, our Director of Studies. A wonderfully kind and understanding woman, I remember her sorting me out so sympathetically when I got panicky over second year exams.

I have vivid memories of walking all the way through John's on the way to the first day of Finals in the School of Pythagoras on a radiantly beautiful May morning, full of nerves and heightened senses. Crossing the Bridge of Sighs, beauty all around me, I remember everything being drenched in sunshine. The late spring flowers of Cambridge were a dream of delight. I knew how lucky I'd been to spend three years there. Social Anthropology was fab. I was taken with how other societies worked and what they put an emphasis on in their organisation. Reading about Australian aboriginal societies has stuck with me and has maintained its fascination. And I always tell people that it was helpful for my subsequent career working in the NHS.

Virginia Beardshaw

The Archaeology and Anthropology department was very old fashioned and out of date with current research and practice. I wasn't really aware of it at the time although the lectures on World Civilisations by Professor Grahame Clark had clearly not been updated for a while along with the glass slides used for illustration. I really enjoyed physical anthropology but never got my head around social anthropology which seemed at best patronising to what would now perhaps be called first nation peoples, as did the strange collection of dusty anthropological objects in the museum (but I did love the totem pole). I did Archaeology part II and really enjoyed a lot of the teaching and studying. We had a course of lectures by J K St Joseph on aerial photography. He had such a boring style of delivery, but the content was interesting – well to me anyway. By the last lecture in a weekly series of eight, I was the only one left in the audience. He carried on as if nothing had happened, not acknowledging my presence. I think he would have given the lecture to an empty room. When he died, my colleague and I were invited by his widow to take his papers for the archive of RCAHMS (the Royal Commission on the Ancient and Historical Monuments of Scotland) where I worked for my entire career. We also later rescued the archaeological papers and artefacts accumulated by another of my tutors, Brian Hope-Taylor, when he died. Brian was an excellent teacher, but notoriously bad at writing up his excavations and, following a mental breakdown, left the department. When I entered the archaeology profession after graduating, I realised how poor the archaeology department at Cambridge was compared with other universities, for example Edinburgh, or Newcastle and my degree was not highly valued by my contemporaries in the profession. Some of the dysfunctionalities were set out by another member of the department, Professor John Coles, who published his memoires shortly before he died last year. It was rather salutary reading and a scenario that I recognised. I am glad to say that it is much bigger and better today and better respected.

Diana Murray (née Collyer)

We had an enormous number of books and articles to read each week for essays in all three subjects – but you could always get all the reading materials from College, Department, University libraries – unlike the LSE where I spent a future year. And we were so privileged to be taught by the people who wrote the books – to be able to ask them the questions raised.

The Part 1 practical exams where the Medics (who took Arch/Anth Part 1 as an easy option before the rules were changed to make them study medical final Parts) were chucking around the skulls and stone tools we were supposed to be identifying in turn until the whole thing descended into farce; Prelims in the Grad Pad on a Bank Holiday Monday with all the families loudly picnicking and playing by the Mill Pond outside; and then Finals in the thick walled cavernous silence of the School of Pythagoras.

I would like to say that New Hall's Academic support on the Arch/Anth Part I and Social Anthropology Part II was very good. We had some good, if demanding, supervisors who read the essays they set and expected us to have read the extensive book lists and made helpful comments. Lectures were often good too. I came back to do a PhD a few years later and was shocked by the lack of any real guidance or input at all.

Siân Crisp (née Jenkins)

Adding to your defence of Social Anthropology I think it was difficult putting the three disciplines together for Part 1, but I found some of the Soc Anth lectures fascinating, particularly Jack Goody and Edmund Leach (A Runaway World). One thing I never understood, however, was why the department was so dismissive of Jane Goodall, bearing in mind she had come to Cambridge as a mature student for her degrees - perhaps because she studied chimpanzees rather than obscure human tribes in Bechuanaland or New Guinea! I remember quoting her in an essay and being very much put in my place, but it didn't stop me following her work later when I needed light relief from sheep and cows in my post New Hall life on our Exmoor hill farm.

Sarah Wilson (née Stallard)

Esther was my director of studies and my supervisor for some parts of the course. She was a brilliant teacher, her feedback was always thoughtful, encouraging but critical as well and made me want to strive to do better.

My first supervision was memorable. I had supervisions in the first year with Virginia Beardshaw who became a good friend. Our supervisor was a graduate student and was I guessed a bit younger than me. To put us at our ease he asked us what had made us decide to study anthropology. I said that I had picked up a book by Margaret Mead called Coming of Age in Samoa, by chance and I was fascinated because it challenged so many of my assumptions about family and culture and I went on to read more about anthropology and more books by Margaret Mead. I can remember him saying that he wished he had a poster in his office with the words "Thou shalt not read Margaret Mead". I guess she was considered too populist to be taken seriously as an academic.

My time as an undergraduate was amazing, it was life changing and eye opening especially when I got involved with setting up the Women's Paper in SPS which I was able to take as a student for part 2. Most importantly, I met so many wonderful people and some of those have become lifelong friends. I know that I am very lucky to have had this experience and it shaped the rest of my life.

Ros Morpeth

I studied Medicine. What with Medicine being somewhat all-embracing and having a boyfriend in Pembroke I didn't spend much time at New Hall itself. One of the best times was the long vac term which I remember as a halcyon time spent in the sunshine (working) in New

Hall grounds; most of the other students were not there so we had it to ourselves.

Joanna Watts (née Sloper)

Yes, we worked hard as Medics - 5 long days, finishing with a 5pm lecture and, on 3 evenings, a 6pm supervision and then Saturday mornings. I don't remember minding; I suppose I knew nothing different! I agree, Rosemary and Jan, we were so lucky to have Jean Thomas as both a tutor and supervisor. I had nothing of Rosemary's fashion sense, so remember nothing of what she wore or the decor in her flat, but do remember her delightful smile, personality and teaching. And the sherry! Then there was Esther Welbourn, who mothered us all, and round to Fitzwilliam for physiology with Dick Hardy. The pharmacology long vac term involved a lot of punting, I remember.

Sarah Watson (née Henley)

As a Medic in my first 2 years, my memory is that it was hard work and that we had lectures and practicals 6 hours each weekday and 4 hours on Saturday, with supervisions and essays to fit in after those hours. There was a huge amount of knowledge we needed to acquire, and lectures were the only way to gain up to date input. We had to get a good 2:1 in each subject to be counted as having passed the 2nd MB preclinical medical exams.

Having done the optional long vac term in pharmacology, I was free to do my longed-for arts subject in my 3rd year. What a wonderful opportunity! Having not even O level scripture, I was allowed to do part II theology and to choose 4 pretty much unrelated papers - I so wanted to make the most of this chance. Trying to grasp the ways people from Old Testament times to the modern day thought about belief and life, in a department with an open questioning approach, was so exciting for me. I stayed up all night reading Dietrich Bonhoeffer's writings and trying to get my head around ideas like covenant. One supervisor did ask in exasperation "Why do medics only think in straight lines?" but in general all were very tolerant of this escaped medic ploughing clumsily around in their field.

Philippa Evans (née Taylor)

As Philippa has said, Medicine was very hard work. We had little free time between lectures, practicals, supervisions and writing essays, so didn't have much time to wander the backs and enjoy the beauty of Cambridge. I remember flying down to 9am lectures, going past Kings Chapel and never giving it a moment's thought as to its beauty. Generally, I had inspirational supervisors. I also felt that I was extremely lucky to have a fantastic and hardworking supervision partner. She was always so constant in her approach to study, and her steady hard work provided a yardstick against which to measure my own performance. Not sure how we managed to fit in socialising.
It was the same with all the natural scientists. We were so lucky to have the amazing Jean Thomas as one of our supervisors (biochemistry). She was phenomenally clever, extremely glamorous, and her beautifully elegant rooms seemed to coordinate with her outfits, usually shades of black, purple and white. Her mane of shiny, long black hair added a further level of sophistication such as I had never witnessed before. Inspirational. She was so very different from all my school teachers.

Rosemary Grande (née Temple)

I do remember the glamorous Jean Thomas who was a fantastic teacher and managed to teach me some Biochemistry despite my total lack of knowledge of organic Chemistry.
The Saturday morning lectures in the First year were on Embryology given by Dr Bull I think who managed to teach full time despite being very deaf. However, at times it was quite hard to hear what he was saying particularly at the beginning of the lecture because he started talking whilst rolling down the automatic blinds so that he could start the slides. The blinds made thunderous clanking noise which completely blocked out his voice. I do seem to remember that a few of us got together and sent a representative of the group armed with

carbon paper to sign us all in, as was required and take notes to be distributed later so we didn't all have to get there for 9 o'clock every Saturday.

The Long Vac term in the Summer was a highlight with picnics and punting and some Pharmacology supervisions outside on the grass in New Hall

Jan Sherman (née Phillips)

I read Natural Sciences and echo the contributions about how hard we worked. 3 lectures a week (including Saturday mornings) for each of 3 subjects, together with half day labs on Monday, Wednesday and Friday as well as 3 supervisions and 3 essays a week. Terms were short and very intense. Janet Moore was an amazing Director of Studies throughout my 3 years: always supportive and very aware of us as young women away from home building new lives. Jean Thomas was my tutor though I hardly saw her. Joan Stevenson Hinde took on more of a role when I took Psychology in the second and third years. It was amazing to be part of lectures with over 500 students (particularly physiology with the medics) and also to have supervisions in pairs, individually and in small groups both within college and in other colleges.

Karen Greenwood

I studied Natural Sciences and particularly enjoyed the practicals where I met many of the people I am still in contact with today. In the summer holidays I travelled to Syria and when I returned, I was diagnosed with Hepatitis A. Although it was only mild, and I recovered quickly, later in the Autumn term I struggled with low moods and was told by the doctor that this was an after effect due to vitamin deficiency (B as I recall). I mentioned all this to Janet Moore, my Director of Studies, and was surprised to receive a parcel of smoked salmon in my pigeonhole, sent by her to feed me up. (Being a bit gloomy at the time, at first I thought someone had sent me a rotten fish.)

In my third year I specialised in Experimental Psychology and although the curriculum was very dominated by rat behaviour, I enjoyed the Brain Physiology lectures by Sue Iverson. As a young woman who was interested in feminism, I was particularly impressed that she was teaching us whilst heavily pregnant and had lined up her husband to complete the course of lectures if the baby was early.

Liz Stafford

The Natural Sciences courses and supervisions were well organised but outside of the college, apart from Jacqueline Mitton. She was the astronomy correspondent for the New Scientist's and taught us to write accessible technical English, but not a lot of physics. The broad base of the natural science degree gave us a really good grounding in science plus maths, and allowed students to change subject easily, so after the first year, I reorientated from physics to geology. The emphasis on working things out and creative thought, plus writing skills honed on several essays per week, gives Cambridge graduates a great start. When I did an MSc at Birmingham the following year, there was much more to learn and less to invent.

Jane Dottridge (née Rooke)

Those of us doing Natural Sciences were very fortunate to have Janet Moore as our tutor. She was a wonderful, energetic, warm woman with a great zest for life and much empathy with students. She was very encouraging and hospitable and would invite us to dinner at her lovely house in Swavesey. Academically, I struggled and being shy and unconfident, I found some of my supervisions a strain. One male supervisor had a confrontational style and enjoyed robust conversation and I felt hopelessly inadequate and couldn't wait for the hour to end.

Alison Wray (née O'Brien)

I had often visited Cambridge from home, when we had overseas visitors usually, so felt very comfortable going there to live. Despite only living 50 miles away in North London, I virtually never left

Cambridge during full term: for Natural Sciences, we had lectures and practicals 6 days of the week, 3 or 4 subjects each with work to be submitted at weekly supervisions, and there simply wasn't time. The 8-week terms were very intense. I would sleep for hours to catch up once I did go home.

Sally Morgan

I studied Natural Sciences, which meant choosing three options in each of the first two years. One of the options I chose was physiology, which was studied with the medics. I found it utterly confusing and after a few weeks was able to change to geology - I appreciated how easy it was to switch subjects.

I remember having a real block about writing essays and would write and cross out and re-order repeatedly - oh for the cut and paste of current times. Our director of studies, Janet Moore, who others have very rightly praised, was very patient with me, and allowed me to submit lists of bullet points instead.

For us natural scientists, there were also field trips and long vac terms. A geology field trip in Arran was particularly memorable and fascinating. I remember the joy of chipping off pieces of rock with my geological hammer, and the exhaustion of always being the last one to arrive at a rest point on long hikes. The long vac terms included day field trips, which I remember as being days of torrential rain. But it was delightful to spend those quiet four weeks in Cambridge.

Alison Litherland (née Hill)

I did Natural Sciences. Academically I felt no link to New Hall. My director of studies was Dr John Leake at St John's and no supervisor was at New Hall.

The first year was very challenging. The number of lectures, practicals and supervisions was impressive and the material seemed very difficult. Miraculously I achieved a 3rd. Years 2 and 3 went much better, and I managed a 2-2 and then a 2-1, which set me up to do research.

Hilary Martin

I did physiology with the medics but had to rush across Downing Street from biology to make the lecture in time. I remember always ending up at the back by a group of boys who smelled bad. In desperation one week I left early (I think with Karen) and we sat elsewhere. Sadly, the same bad smell. It turned out that it wasn't personal hygiene exactly, the medics came straight from dissection and brought a cadaver laden formaldehyde smell with them.

Anatomy lectures were at 2pm, lots of slides and a darkened room, I used to catch up on my sleep, unlike now I don't think I snored.

We went to a lecture on sleep, the first by the (now) Prof Sir Colin Blakemore who was clearly destined for greatness, my supervisor (a less beautiful individual) muttered darkly that he "probably wore coloured underpants and ate yoghurt on his muesli in the morning". The lecture was entertaining as well as informative but no mention of yoghurt.

I, and others did have problems with some of the experimental work, pithed frogs, decerebrate rabbits and the worst for me were the dead rats with still moving foetuses. I protested about this to Janet Moore who was sympathetic, but we were doing medic's unit.

We did work hard, lectures and practicals every weekday, lectures on Saturday morning, then 3 tutorials a week and essays.

Deborah Glass

I was lacking in experience and don't think I ever moved away from a "them and me" attitude to academic staff and a way of learning. I guess many of the Maths lectures which I dutifully attended went straight over my head. I certainly do wish that someone had sat me down at the beginning and suggested that collaboration and discussion was the way to go. After the first term in the sixth form I was the only girl in my year at school studying Further Maths, and again as the only member of our college year to complete the three years in the Maths tripos, my learning was much too isolated for my own good.

Dorothy Cade (née Clark)

I read Maths and Computer Science. Computer Science tripos was just a single year. I don't know if anyone else in New Hall had done it before. I was the only girl on the course (from any college) in my year. Our supervisions were all organised by the Computer Science department as the colleges didn't have the expertise. My New Hall Director of Studies was a Mathematician and wasn't sure what her duties towards me were re Computer Science. I told her – just give me a big meal at some point. So she did!

Jo Edkins (née Dibblee)

My course was Maths with Physics in the first year moving to just Physics for the second and third years, chosen because they were my favourite subjects at school. Having previously found Maths quite easy I certainly hit my ceiling at Cambridge. My memory is of a huge lecture hall where we had to watch as the lecturer wrote lots of symbols and numbers on the board with chalk, ending up QED. If you got lost part way through there was no way to ask a question or catch up really. Some of them gave out those purple handouts; others just expected you to make notes and also use the text books of course. Supervisions were at St John's College and were helpful, but I think I was lucky to get my third at the end of the year. This was partly due to a lot of time socialising with one or two particular young men and also joining various clubs and societies and generally trying to make the most of Cambridge.

I enjoyed Physics far more and there were different modules to choose from so although much of the quantum mechanics was way beyond me, things like astronomy and cosmology were fascinating. In the third year, we were amongst the first to use the new Cavendish Labs out to the west of Cambridge. I think the lecturers were genuine enthusiasts and wanted to pass that on. I ended up with a 2:2 which was a relief, and decided I never wanted to do an exam again! The work had been hard and intense with the 8-week terms but also exciting to be there, in Cambridge, with some of the best physicists in the world.

Jane Mott (née Style)

I think engineers at New Hall had a different experience to most other students because there was no Engineering Fellow at New Hall in those days and so all my tutorials and my tutorial partners were outside the college - in my first year at St John's and in my second and third year at Sidney Sussex with Donald Green. I think that made me feel less affiliation to the college and more to the Engineering Department and most of my socialising was with other engineers rather than the other students at New Hall. I had glandular fever in my 2nd year and was sent home so I missed 3 weeks of lectures but I was fortunate that my friends had taken notes of all the lectures and I just about managed to catch up and pass my exams, though I fear that complex numbers will always remain a mystery to me!

Helen Morton

For Economics, if I remember rightly, it was two essays a week, and I had no idea how to write an essay or take notes from heavy Economic History books. At the end of the first term I had tonsilitis and a raging temperature, and the nurse injected me with antibiotics and looked after me until my brother could come and take me home. I wasn't at all sure I wanted to return, but I did. Happily, I was sent to Miss Hammond in the summer vac. She took me in hand, and after that I managed better. We were very lucky to have such care taken of us.

I chose to do a dissertation in my third year comparing the push and pull factors of migration in Africa.

Other memories include being awestruck by the way in which Prof Brian Reddaway would give such amazing explanations of what would happen to the economy on a macro-level if this or that was done. Of desperately trying to revise. Of working on the Sedgwick site sustained by delicious cheese scones from the University Library. Cambridge became easier and more enjoyable once I'd settled in, though it was hard work for the weeks we were there.

Wendy Spray (née Coulson)

A few remarks about the Music course: There appeared to be no structure to the study. I was surprised things did not move onwards and upwards from A-level. Where were the Set Works? Goodness, one might pass through the place never having heard the "St Matthew Passion"!

Many men in my year appeared to spend their time organising concerts and so on, but doing little actual work, and getting away with it. We 6 girls (myself from New Hall, 2 from Girton, 3 from Newnham) had a better work ethic, but lectures were very ill-attended, and inevitably lecturers focused on their specialism. There were no lectures in the Summer term and we never saw the Professor.

There were classes called something like Orchestration, or Keyboard Skills, run by those eminent choral directors (men, of course) who were household names, but who could not communicate those skills at all. We learnt little. I recollect a particularly shocking "class" at Caius, in which nothing was learnt beyond smutty "jokes". Only went to that once!

It was indeed, fend for oneself. The excellent Dr Brown at Fitzwilliam dealt with practical aspects which had "answers", such as transcription, harmony and counterpoint, tablature. These were tasks which could be completed.

The other aspect of music, viz. What to Study? was terrifying. There is quite a lot of music to choose from! What do you know, at 18/19? You can't just open your mind and let the truth slop in, without guidance. In my 2nd year the enlightened Dr le Huray at St Catherine's was my supervisor, and he got me reading parts of Kant's Critiques.... now there was an expansion of mind! But other than that, supervisors were content to let me choose my interests. Yes, and fiddle with kettles. Or, in the case of a bloke at Sidney, talk about his divorce!

I think that this wishy-washy laissez-faire attitude was wrong. But, again, what do you know at 18/19? Having only seen one university, you assumed this was the norm. It was a given that one could write an essay, but no advice was offered upon how to structure a dissertation. Fend for yourself. Apart from Dr Berry at Girton, the Gregorian Chant doyenne, the place was all run by men! Lecturers, supervisors, conductors.... some very weird musicians, as I have already said. Prejudice. Condescension. One eminent examiner is reputed to have said "no female will get a First on my watch". A veritable Poison Garden! I hope it is not like that now.

Sue Whitham (née Addison)

I was another struggling student on the fringes who had almost no academic support, although at the time I did not realise what was lacking. I switched subjects in my first week and was the only architect at New Hall until one year later, when Helen Mayer joined in the year below. My Director of Studies was an art historian. She meant well but had nothing meaningful to contribute to my education.

The Architecture School was small and functioned a bit like a college of its own. There were five women in my year, two from Newnham, two from Girton, and me. Sexism was rife among some of the faculty – including a Structural Mechanics lecturer who opened his first lecture (oblivious to the women present), with an off-colour joke with a punch line of "Nut Screws Washer and Bolts"! I found it difficult to be competing so closely with men who seemed to be a lot more confident than I was. Supervisions were with a group of young men from assorted colleges, and were dry and academic, mostly theory of architecture. I don't recall any essays being assigned; we would just meet & discuss. I found my supervisor a bit dull, and after a while drifted away. In my second & third years I didn't even know who my supervisor was. Was somebody getting paid for supervisions that I never went to? I have no idea.

Many, but not all, people worked in the design studio, where teachers would pass through and comment on their work. At the end of each project, there was a "crit" (critique) where each student presented their design to the assembled class and faculty. All architecture schools that I know of function this way. It is an effective system, but often soul crushing, especially for students like myself who lacked confidence in their design work. I have yet to meet anyone, anywhere, who actually enjoyed crits.

There was no grading of students' portfolios until the end of the year, when there were also exams. As a result it was easy to avoid crits altogether. I didn't like working in the studio with people looking over my shoulder (and still don't), so worked by myself at home. I did fine with anything that I could learn from a lecture or a book, but nobody taught me anything about design until late in my third year. Consequently, I didn't really understand what it was that I needed to do to improve my work. Every term (or year, whichever it was) I would go to the required meetings with my Director of Studies & Tutor, who would both scold me gently for not working hard enough but not provide any constructive advice; and I would nod my head, promise to do better, and go away. And nothing changed.

The neglect from New Hall was compounded by what was going on in the Architecture School. The professor, Sir Leslie Martin, died unexpectedly in my first year. A new professor was appointed after a year's search but was killed in a car crash six months later. I later found out that during this time there were heated battles among the faculty, so there was little energy left for the students. Finally, late in my third year, I was given a new Director of Studies who actually taught in the Architecture School and assigned supervisions with someone who helped me polish my portfolio. This helped enormously. I scraped a 2:2 but was frustrated I could not do better. In hindsight much of my problem was that I was too isolated and had fallen through a lot of cracks, rather than it being all my fault as I believed. In New Halls' defence I will say that this sink-or-swim approach was fairly common at the time; and that the university bent over backwards so that people rarely failed outright. But it was not a happy experience for me.

Gillian Blessley

I managed OK with part 1 English but changing to law in my last year was a real shock. I got glandular fever as well, and began to feel I couldn't do anything. I remember the kindness and support I had from

Ken Polack who was supervising me (down at King's because we didn't have law at New Hall) and the relief when it was over. I think it was the intensity of those short terms that I remember most, where everything seemed a triumph or a tragedy with not much in between. I look back on it as a wonderful experience even if not always joyous one.

Wendy Joseph

Staff and Regulations

*The college had Directors of Studies and Supervisors (see Academia).
The Tutors were available to help us in our personal lives.
The domestic staff included porters, who manned the Porters' Lodge, and bedders or cleaners, who cleaned our rooms.*

I particularly enjoyed recalling Catherine Belsey's approach to personal tutorials: "He's not worth crying over. Let's have a gin and tonic."

Ros Coward

There was a university rule, seemingly absurd now, that undergraduates had to spend a certain number of nights within the university precincts in order to take their degree. If you wanted to stay out in the evening after the doors were locked – I think it was at 10pm – you could sign out a key in advance, but the key had to be returned by something like 7am the next morning. I did that only once, before going to a party. Later, I decided to spend the night with my boyfriend. I was terrified of the consequences if I didn't return the key on time, so over the protests and disbelief of my boyfriend, got up at about 6:30am and cycled back to college through deserted streets to return the key! After that, no more keys for me!

Gillian Blessley

I got married in my second year, and so had to go and report this to Miss Murray, the only time I saw her after interview. There was some minor administrative problem about what name I was to use for my exams, but I mentioned, I think, in passing that I was due to have a baby in early October. This was seemingly much more complicated, not for the obvious reasons but because the Maternity hospital was not within the University bounds, and some way of remedying this would have to be found. She suggested a nursing home which might be eligible, so I agreed to investigate. She asked for my address, with whom I would be living (2 other New Hall girls, my husband having already been posted abroad) and no further interest was ever taken or expressed. I did ask if I would be able to apply for a place in the graduate crèche (no, not for undergraduates) and whether I could apply to the proctors for a car permit (no, because that was restricted to certain officers in specific societies) That was it. In fact, the baby was early and I was back in Warkworth Terrace in time for full term and my first supervision; but no-one from New Hall ever checked up or followed through. I thought nothing of it at the time, my mother came for a couple of weeks, lots of people were quite happy to babysit on an occasional basis, including and most especially Caroline Higginbottom, whose husband Edward was the organist at Corpus, and who conveniently lived beside the Sidgewick site. Thinking back now, I realise that although Miss Murray seemed entirely indifferent, it was probably simply that she just did not know what to do, so did nothing. That was fine.

Fiona Edwards-Stuart (née Weaver)

I was one of several mature students that year along with Sarah Wilson and Alison New and I can remember smiling when we were told that there were a few places including night clubs, that New Hall students were not allowed to visit. New Hall took *in loco parentis* very seriously. Catherine [Kate] Belsey was my very empathetic tutor.

Ros Morpeth

I didn't see much of my moral tutor. At the interview she asked me what holiday jobs I had done and when I mentioned working in a Bar, she asked whether my parents minded. That wrong footed me completely.

Deborah Glass

Oh, the gate hours! They caused problems, because in 1970, the law changed the Age of Majority from 21 to 18. So we were adults, and didn't see why we should still be treated as children. The authorities didn't see it that way.

One of the photos sent in reminded me of a story - the one of the open walkways through the college. My boyfriend came to the Porters' Lodge from my room a minute or so too late, and saw that the door was locked. So he ran along that walk way to get to the back exit. That was locked after the main gate, so he beat the porter to it.

I suspect that the porters knew all the regular boyfriends. The porters certainly knew all of us! I remember seeing a porter with the freshers' portrait looking at each student as we came in on our usual business, then looking us up on the photo, memorising our names. I was seriously impressed! I would not be capable of such a feat of memory, even then.

Jo Edkins (née Dibblee)

I particularly remember 'kicking out time', and how it changed each year we were there (as medics, we were allowed all 3 years in college). The first year was 10pm, the second 11pm, and the third, if I remember rightly, 2am. These 'magic hours' were sociable and fun, as everyone escorted their departing boyfriends to the door (they were never allowed to prowl the corridors unaccompanied!). Outside the door, couples would be draped everywhere saying their goodbyes for the night.

It may suggest I was a bit boring, but I for one appreciated the departure deadlines in the first 2 years - it saved having to decide when 'enough was enough'!

Sarah Watson (née Henley)

I arrived in my single room on E staircase to find that the floor was beautifully warm. Consequently, I lost no time in removing the legs from my bed (probably using a spanner from my bicycle tool kit) in order to benefit from centrally heated slumber. Within a couple of weeks, I received a terse letter from the tsarina of New Hall bedders instructing me to replace said legs immediately because, (and I kid you not), the lady who cleaned my room was "finding it impossible to dust under the bed"!! I was doubly gutted: firstly, because my cosy cot was no more and, secondly, because my belief that everyone who worked or studied at Cambridge University was super intelligent had, in that moment, been shattered.

It is only very recently, nearly fifty years on, that it has finally crossed my mind that the letter in no wise indicated idiocy on the part of the writer, but was probably meant to be sardonic. So much for my own super-intelligence…!! Ha Ha!

Maryla Carter (née Ignatowicz)

Yes, I too took the legs off my bed. The College told me I couldn't do that, but the reason was different: my bedder couldn't make my bed if it was on the floor and it made the college sheets dirty. 'No problem', I said: I will use my own sheets and make my own bed! The legs stayed off! My bedder was a lovely person and we got along very well.

Gillian Blessley

In my first and only year in college, there were those wonderful ancient bedders, kind and motherly. And the porters, particularly Mr Ellis, were cheerful and patient and loyal beyond belief. Because I got married in my second year, to someone who needed security clearance, some faceless men came to College to interview me (although I was living out at the time). Mr Ellis recognised them immediately for what they were, and told them in very clear terms that he could guarantee that I was no risk but he would also not tell them where I could be found. He subsequently told me that MI5 and 6 recruited New Hall Modern Linguists on his say-so; was that true I wonder? I had once borrowed a car for something early one Sunday morning, and it would not start. Mr Ellis went down the corridor, just before 8am, knocking quietly on 4 doors which he knew would have men behind them, to get them up and out to bump start the car for me. I think those rooms were mainly 3rd years; I hope I did not disturb any of our year!

Fiona Edwards-Stuart (née Weaver)

Mention of the Head Porter, Mr Ellis: he really did have a phenomenal memory for names and took a genuine interest in everyone's welfare. He always seemed to know if anyone was having a particularly good or bad day. Although my room for two years was in Beaufort House my quickest route was through the college and across the garden and I used to stop and chat on my way through. He also seemed to get the low down on regular male visitors, I guess through a Head Porters' network, and would keep a close eye on the progress of any particular liaison if he thought it would end in tears.

Another character was Mary, one of the domestic staff, who came in each day from a fenland farm. I had an arrangement to collect milk regularly from the kitchen and woe betide me if I skipped a day - "Milk doesn't grow on trees". When she overheard someone bemoaning no letters in her pigeon hole she said "Well, those as don't write don't get".

Sarah Wilson (née Stallard)

My ground floor single room had a window onto the courtyard; it somehow became a designated through-route for after-hours young men.

Helen Mayer

I was in one of the single rooms on the ground floor in New Hall and let in young men late at night on several occasions. I had a relationship for most of the first year with a man from Churchill and got to know the path through to the college very well. I clearly remember coming home from Churchill early one morning and the porter just looking at me sadly and saying, 'oh Miss Greenwood'.

Karen Greenwood

The buildings of New Hall

These were built in 1960s. See "Timeline" in the Appendix for more about the current and previous buildings of New Hall.

The best-known building in New Hall is the famous dome, with the Hall beneath it. At breakfast, we would wait for the wonderful central serving hatch to arise from the centre of the floor with all our food. I enjoyed sitting eating breakfast, while looking at the modern art on the walls.

Jo Edkins (née Dibblee)

The dining hall was always very cold and rather stark - although quite impressive. In recent years they have improved it hugely by insulating it better, having the wonderful paintings on the walls, making the tables narrower so you can talk across them more easily and getting rid of the huge mushroom topped lights that they used to have. A really beautiful hall now.

Rosemary Grande (née Temple)

Here is the photo of the library from the 1974 prospectus - Anne (Borrett/Muir) and Sue (Wood/Attridge) will recognize yourselves in the library. I am in the library by the catalogue in a long skirt.

Maureen Bell

I'm in the library photo in the 1974 prospectus, 'working' at the central desk.

Sue Attridge (née Wood)

I enjoyed working in the library, with its high roof and plenty of windows. I would sit at a table looking out into Fountain Court, watching the large goldfish swim up and down. If I got bored with Maths, I would pick a book at random from the shelf behind me. I found the Bacchae (by Euripides) rather startling, but it was a change from Maths.

The JCR was split-level as well, with a balcony round the edge. The New Hall architect obviously liked that feature. Once, some society left leaflets to be read on the table at the top. They made excellent paper aeroplanes when thrown from the balcony.

Jo Edkins (née Dibblee)

Fountain court

The only thing I remember about my admission interview is that I thought Fountain Court was rather beautiful and I decided I would be just as happy in this college as in any of the old ones (not an option until the following year I think). Later I wondered whether the money had run out before the front gate was built. I seem to remember an unpromising double slab of brown wood and a dark corridor leading to the Porters' Lodge.

There was always an odd smell of some kind of floor polish (made of linseed oil and Jeyes fluid I decided). My first ever Valentine card was delivered in the pigeon holes by the Porters' Lodge. Disappointingly it turned out to be from an insurance company touting for custom and not a secret admirer.

Emma Wheelock

I love the building, and the modern entrance is so much better now, grander, less of an apology. I liked the smell and loved the warm floors.

Deborah Glass

I am amazed at the modern smart entrance - I seem to remember we just dumped our bicycles by the dustbins and went in an ordinary door, straight into the hallway with the Porters' Lodge.

Sarah Wilson (née Stallard)

I loved the buildings, which for me created a light, airy (but warm) space, giving us a contemporary freedom. My sense was that they allowed me to be free to live in current times in a creative way which was life-enhancing. For me it paralleled the freedom to find out about modern scientific knowledge (in my first two years as a medic) and to read/hear modern writing about ways of thinking about life/belief (in my third year doing part II Theology). This was about a world opening up and enabling me to explore and live more fully.

Philippa Evans (née Taylor)

I wish I had taken pictures inside my room but I never did. What happened to the split-level steps? I was lucky to have a split-level room to myself and it could be a challenge carrying things up and down. I am sure they would be condemned these days, but they were certainly a talking point

Aileen Regan (née Kidd)

Did anyone else have mishaps on the space saving stairs in the double height rooms? It was not a good idea to attempt to walk down them in platform-soled clogs. Balancing on the stairs was nearly as hard as balancing on a bike carrying stuff for lectures, shopping and a hockey stick.

Angela Bailey (née Webster)

I did have trouble with those stairs in the split-level rooms – and I too had impossible non-flexi-soled clogs! Those stairs were SO steep and narrow, and I used to go down backwards because I didn't like the long pane of glass at the bottom, and I got vertigo looking down! I was not a fan of those rooms…

Lou Radford

I had just spent 6 months working in Rome, when I arrived, and loved the bare brick walls which reminded me of life in Italy rather than the wallpaper and clutter of the UK. I soon covered them with posters and my home today is happily very cluttered.

Siân Crisp (née Jenkins)

I had a pleasant, if small, room to myself, on C staircase overlooking the car park, and very much liked having somewhere to cook simple meals. But I'm not sure I ever entirely got used to the internal brickwork, however skilfully it had been done. I also remember how dull the New Hall garden was in 1971 - all grass and birch trees - which succeeded in putting me off modernist gardens for life. It was not at all as it is now, thanks to the talents of the present Head Gardener, Jo Cobb, and her team. I was very involved with the design and making of the New Hall 'Transit of Venus' garden at Chelsea Flower Show in 2007, some of which came back to be erected, or planted, in the college grounds.

Ursula Wide (née Buchan)

In my first year I had the upstairs half of a shared room on the top floor. In my memory there was a tiny roof terrace outside.

Emma Wheelock

I had one of the upstairs rooms, which shared a balcony. No-one ever sat in this balcony. Huntingdon Road was very noisy, and anyway, the balcony faced north, and was damp and cold. But I used to put my milk outside on the balcony, and the cold kept it fresh.
My memory of the long top corridor at New Hall was the way that the rooms pushed into it from one side, and the bathrooms from the other. So to walk along it, you had to weave from one side to another. We used to claim that if you had drunk precisely the right amount of alcohol, then this swerving came naturally...

Jo Edkins (née Dibblee)

My room (a single one) had a red nylon carpet which I was very proud of. Sadly, it did not encourage me to get out of bed early as I would get a mild electric shock when I first touched something metal e.g. a tap. It took me a while to work out what was happening.

Joanna Watts (née Sloper)

The College Buildings! Get your woollies on! Cold white brick. Public loos were fashioned from this. What a sordid "front entrance" there was back then, along a funny little passage full of kitchen clatter and smells! It could hardly be believed. There has been a great improvement: in fact, when I visited a few years ago, I was taxed that it was the same place! The building was busy being the Architects' Statement rather than a welcoming and warm place to live in. It was not, to quote le

Corbusier, a "machine for living in". (More a Blockhaus). If it were this, it was a sadly deficient machine. What a ridiculous dining room, for example. Complete waste of space. Never homely, never welcoming or relaxing, never intimate, never warm. What a gimmick, that rising servery. But kooky, all the same. Bleak white staircases. Slippery pseudo-marble. Brrr! The curtains did little to dispel the chill. Those split-level rooms, again, full of health and safety perils. Why design stuff like this? Weird. The underfloor heating was another strange phenomenon, leading to real stuffiness. Does/did anyone find Fountain Court architecturally satisfactory? I used to think the Fellows' rooms to the south the most "normal", since they looked out onto the gardens. (They also looked rather like council "deck" housing, with their walkways!) I thought that draughty veranda useless. Perish, freeze. Well do I recall venturing along that from C staircase to get milk. I see it has been boxed in. What a surprise. When I went to Town colleges, I found they had so much of interest.... panelling, quirky rooms and staircases, etc.... a new college could not have these, of course, but it did seem unnecessarily stark and chilly. Fitz was modern too, but it had its warm purple brickwork. Am I alone in this antipathy? Or have I been reading too much Pevsner? I certainly don't get turned on by the references to Agra, Byzantium or Hagia Sophia...... goodness me, this is sub-zero Cambridge, not the sultry East!

Sue Whitham (née Addison)

I completely agree. And I'm sure I was told that the designs for the New Hall buildings were prepared by an architect for a competition for a college building in South Africa. The design was the runner up in the competition so the architect persuaded New Hall to take on the plans. It certainly always seemed to me that the buildings and layout were designed for a warm country and not for the cold, wet and windy atmosphere of Cambridge!

Helen Morton

Several people have mentioned their response to the architecture. I think I was oblivious to its aesthetic merits or otherwise but quite liked it as a place to live. I remember the library as being light and airy, the lawns as a great place to sit and revise, and the hall and the dome being utterly magnificent. I seem to remember that the urban myth was that an owl lived up there. I also remember the long corridors with a communal fridge at one end and a phone for calling home at the other. I don't think I used either very much.

Alison Litherland (née Hill)

It is interesting to read such radically different responses to/memories of the buildings. Those accounts leave me wondering what I really felt at the time ... New Hall was new, different, not beautiful but somehow befitting what felt like a step forward in life - and such a contrast to St John's where I spent a lot of time. I did think the dining hall business was unnecessary and a bit ridiculous - but then so was the ritual of dinner at the old colleges, though perhaps a bit more romantic. To this day I don't know why I was lucky enough to get one of the large single rooms - I definitely would not have coped with a split-level dog-leg staircase shared one.

I lived in South London (not far from where I was born) for 10 years or so after Cambridge and loved the South Bank - maybe partly because the architecture reminded me of New Hall.

Several people have mentioned the smell of the cleaning stuff/polish in the corridors - it is a smell I occasionally catch a whiff of and it takes me straight back to the college. I have an old friend who lives just off the Chesterton Road and the last time I visited her we went to New Hall (I can't call it by its new name) to see the art collection and the gardens - so much more beautiful now. And that smell was still there.

Nicola King (née Brown)

Does anybody else remember the college being cold? My rooms (first year in a tiny room with a balcony in Fountain Court, second year in a single split-level room in Fountain Court) all faced north so were very cold and rather cheerless despite an array of plants and posters. In my adult life I have come to realise just how much I love the brightness and warmth of sun in a room - so I don't think I ever found any of my rooms warm and welcoming. Fortunately, the first two years as a medic were so frantic (and with all the socialising too) that I never had to spend much time in them. I remember clearly loving going off to tea in rooms in college which had the late afternoon sun streaming through the window. Both my rooms in college had so little space for entertaining other people. I remember once having six people in the room in January and we had to have the balcony doors open. It was a stupid design, I felt, having balconies which looked good but were useless when you were mainly in college in the winter months.

Rosemary Grande (née Temple)

There's something worrying me about all this. It has been mentioned that New Hall was cold. My memory is quite different. My second year digs were cold (and damp), and the Maths lecture rooms were bitterly cold. Outside in winter, the Cambridge wind chilled you to the bone. But New Hall itself? My room, in year 1 and year 3, was beautifully warm, with underfloor heating. I remember the feel of warm cork against bare feet, getting up in the morning. Yes, the walls were pale grey brick, but they weren't cold. I don't remember the Hall as being cold either, although I only went there for breakfast. And there was always lots of hot water for baths.
As for the buildings - well, the grey brick walls were annoying, as they absorbed blue tack. The stairs inside the rooms took a little getting used to. The outside balcony WAS cold, but useful for keeping milk fresh. But generally, I found the quirky architecture fun.

Jo Edkins (née Dibblee)

Yes, Jo, I remember New Hall as warm, with good heating and hot water.

Philippa Evans (née Taylor)

I agree. The underfloor heating was lovely and warm and the sun shone in the big window in front of my downstairs desk. I enjoyed the scent of freshly mown grass as it wafted through in late spring.
I felt lucky to have a bedroom upstairs with a little enclosed balcony that also let in light.
We had a lovely chatty cleaning lady who emptied the little bins every day I think and provided clean sheets fortnightly so were quite spoilt compared with many students.
I really enjoyed my quirky split room

Aileen Regan (née Kidd)

I too have good memories. No recollection of being cold. Everything was quite fun to live in.

Sarah Watson (née Henley)

I think I'd better clarify my remarks on the building! What a lot of remarks have come in about the warm rooms. Yes, they were warm, and most of us put up posters and drapes on those bricks. And vastly superior to the general temperature of digs!
What I disliked for chill were the "public areas", viz the draughty walkway, and the dining room (surely an Amazonian feat to find that place warm). Warm cork floor in your room, cold cold tiles along the walkway.
Any critical views on the general architectural design? Or were we too busy to notice? Brutalist 60s concrete is a Marmite thing, isn't it? New and exciting to some, stark and impersonal to others.
 And can anyone say why it was that the channels in Fountain Court were never green, as are most places where fish live? I used to feel sorry for those fish.... no plants. A white environment, like the students' one.

Sue Whitham (née Addison)

Because I had a room in Beaufort House, in New Hall itself I really only experienced the corridors and dining hall, which I agree seemed extremely draughty. Being born and largely raised in the soft West Country what I remember most vividly is the bitter wind whipping through the city, straight from the Urals via the flat fenland. Sometimes I had to be very conscientious to bicycle to a 9 o'clock lecture.

Sarah Wilson (née Stallard)

I loved having my own single room and the quirkiness of the modern architecture. Neville House was relatively unwelcoming; I remember it as rather dark and shabby.

Joanna Watts (née Sloper)

I certainly agree about the lovely warm rooms. I don't particularly remember being cold in the dining hall, and accepted the draughty main walkway as a given – no different from crossing courts in more traditional colleges. I remember feeling that the stairs in split-level rooms were potentially hazardous, but having single rooms in both first and third years I never had to test them out in the middle of the night for example! I was very happy to be in a relatively clean modern building with modern conveniences, but I have never liked the starkness of concrete and the grey look which generally wears badly.

I was in Fountain Court in my third year and loved its quietness and convenience. There was a fairly large kitchen and I particularly remember when Alison Mawle cooked vast amounts of kedgeree there – which I'd never eaten before – for her 21st Breakfast Party. Lovely. There were also plenty of bathrooms – never a queue for a bath – but they tended to house very large spiders, probably as a result of being below ground level on outside walls! The rooms looked out over the Court with its fish. I certainly remember greenery. I do agree with Sue W. however in the general impression of stark whiteness for several months of the year at least. Like Aileen I was also acutely aware of that biting wind in Cambridge, especially on Castle Hill, in the colder months.

Anne Muir (née Borrett)

I only lived in Hall for the first year. I knew nothing about architecture but thought that New Hall was wonderfully modern/space age and the whiteness made it really stand out. I was very proud of living in it (but I suppose, now I do know a bit more about architecture, I do have a soft spot for modern brutalism). The dome, the food arriving through the floor, and even the draughty walkway seemed to me to have a certain 'wow' factor. And the underfloor heating was amazing (though I do remember how quickly the eggs we had bought to make pancakes went off in the heat).

Unlike Sue (Whitham), who lived in the upstairs part of our double room, I didn't have to negotiate those dreadful split staircases multiple times every day. In the days of wearing clogs (and in Sue's case carting a cello up and down) they were indeed a nightmare. Putting a window at the bottom of them (however much the glass was reinforced) did seem like total madness.

Maureen Bell

I enjoyed the NH buildings. The Dome with the futuristic servery, was as dramatic as the Halls of the ancient colleges down Castle Hill. I remember a big celebration in 1972 when New Hall was granted its Royal Charter. A huge buffet was spread out under the Dome, and we were invited to dig in. So we did, most greedily. I remember glazed hams with NH dolphins embedded in their aspic coatings, and other 1970s style treats.

But the college and many things in Cambridge were often freezing once we were away from the NH underfloor heating. This applied especially to the open walkway by Fountain Court (glazed in to good effect soon after we left) and the rooms off Fountain Court.

Virginia Beardshaw

I liked the uniqueness of the building which seemed very modern to me and I thought the food ascending into the dining room was quite extraordinary.

Alison Wray (née O'Brien)

There was so much to love about the buildings of New Hall. In those days (maybe not now!!) I chose the new, innovative feel of the college as opposed to the older and seemingly darker and claustrophobic atmosphere of an older college. Like many others I was very aware of the "special" and welcoming aroma of the corridors - was it the floor polish? The interesting split-level room complete with sink and cooking ring, the zig zag feel of walking the corridors, the imposing dome, the rising serving hatch and the novelty of bare pale grey brick walls all created in me a feeling of being somewhere special.

In contrast I also loved the big old wooden desk with plenty of drawers for all my work-related needs and a lovely view over the quad.

Dorothy Cade (née Clark)

My strongest memory of New Hall is the distinctive smell of the building. I thought it emanated from the bare bricks and mortar, enhanced perhaps by the heat seeping through the cork tiles. Even fifty years on it conjures up the excitement of a new beginning, a time of possibilities, living in a 'modern' building, at once part of the ancient university and apart from it. The bare bricks suited the posters, rugs, plants and other decorative flourishes their inhabitants brought to their rooms and were in keeping with the college's freedom from what I perceived to be the stuffy and irrelevant trappings of the older colleges. The only times I ever remember wearing a gown were for the graduation ceremony and, very occasionally, for dining in one of the other colleges. My first year room was the top half of a split-level, C something I think. The sloping wooden ceiling, underfloor heating and the shared balcony overlooking the Huntingdon Road which was good for keeping milk cool, were all plusses, as was the extra privacy that came with being at the top. Among the downsides were the recurrent awkwardness of waiting for a tactful moment to descend and cross my roommate's half to get to the door when she was entertaining and the inordinately loud ticking of her alarm clock which I resorted to burying in her bedclothes if she was not around. She spent more time out than I did, which had the happy side effect for me that I got to know a number of her numerous friends, who had trekked all the way up Castle Hill only to find that she was not there. They were characterful rooms but far from ideal for sharing.

Mary Anne Bonney

I liked the modern buildings but found the open walkways very draughty and I'm really pleased that they are now all enclosed in glass.

Helen Morton

I have mixed feelings about the buildings. I loved the fun element of the dining room dome and the library, and liked my room (a single one on the ground floor) with the white brick walls and warm cork floor. I remember it often being strewn with drying clothes. I covered the walls in posters.
As for the beds…. There was a wooden rim, and the mattress was below this level, which made them uncomfortable both to sit on and to share. Ros Coward's brother and his girlfriend once borrowed my room for the night when visiting her; he told me the next day he feared he would carry the imprint of the rail for life. But at least they were a really good length, unlike those between the windows in the double rooms. I recall someone telling me that the architect had begun by setting out the window pattern and then fitted the rooms in to this, which left the rather short gap for the lower room beds.

Pam Hilton

Rather like the entrance paper, the buildings of New Hall spoke volumes about the type of college it was, including the less than practical zany stairs in the double rooms, the splendid but cold dome, and the moat that leaked into the dons' rooms. I'm sure it is more comfortable now, but the open corridor across the centre, the cork tiles which needed to be endlessly and repeatedly buffed, and the stainless steel sinks, were all so different from home and so stylish! I loved the white walls, and how well posters looked against such a background.

Sally Morgan

In my first year I was in one of the split-level double rooms. And I found I enjoyed sharing, but not until after a rather shaky start. I felt intimidated by my first roommate and moved to share with a new friend I'd made on the first night.

I was in the top half of the room, and I found it both companionable and private. And I think the top half had a door to the neighbouring room where another friend lived. And I found this sense of living on top of each other really suited me and meant I was never lonely. We had friends in common so weren't generally disturbed by each other's guests. I had a boyfriend in a central college and spent time in his room when privacy was needed.

Alison Litherland (née Hill)

I was allocated a shared room. I had the bottom of the split-level as my roommate had arrived first. The rooms were not really suitable for two separate individuals to share unless you were bosom pals. With no criticism of my roommate, I felt very cramped in what was my small space with people walking through frequently and at all hours, visitors, chatter and boyfriend canoodling when I was trying to work and no privacy when I wanted to invite my friends in. I used to inhabit the library which I found cold (and no coffee) and when that was not possible, I spent time in the bathroom to get a little peace.

Diana Murray (née Collyer)

I was the upstairs roommate of Diana Murray (née Collyer). I am relieved that she was so polite about me, because I thought I must have been the roommate from hell! One particular episode stands out: my boyfriend was in King's and had discovered an unkempt corner of King's Fellows' Garden which was absolutely magical by moonlight. It was strictly off limits of course, but we used to sneak in there some nights. There was giant hogweed growing in the garden, and my boyfriend persuaded me that I had to have a stalk to decorate my room in New Hall. We stole in after Diana was in bed and tied the Hogweed up to the railings, all the while whispering & giggling, which I am sure woke Diana up. The hogweed was huge – the flower head came up above the top of the upstairs railings and looked wonderful from above. Less so from Diana's level! I am now embarrassed at my behaviour then, I still had a lot of growing up to do. After Diana moved out I luxuriated in having the entire split-level room to myself.

I think many of the shortcomings of the buildings that others have remarked on were the result of lack of funds. I suspect many budget cuts were made during design & bidding in order to preserve the core features of the design, especially the Dome, which must have been hugely expensive. The exposed brickwork is one thing that comes to mind, and I am sure the original design had a proper entrance, which was simply deferred to a later date. Hence the entrance by the dustbins which we all remember so well.

Gillian Blessley

Who didn't find the dome and the rising service hatch exciting? I also loved to escape to the library in my first (more studious) year –peaceful silence and watery views. I recall the single electric ring; the wooden pigeon-holes; the phone boxes, the much-frequented full-length mirrors in the corridors.

And an ambivalence that we seemed more progressive than – but also more excluded from - the ivory tower at the centre. And travelling between the two – a secret refuge in the simple whitewashed interior of St Peter's Church on Castle Street, the elation of cycling along the backs.

Helen Mayer

Cambridge New Architecture by Philip Booth & Nicholas Taylor, published 1970, describing New Hall, writes of "the survival of a life tenancy on part of The Grove, where entrance to the college from Storey's Way is to be provided." That would explain the odd scruffy entrance we all remember. But at some point, presumably this plan was abandoned, and the smart modern entrance is now in Buckingham Road, off Huntingdon Road.

The buildings of New Hall are listed grade II*, which is used for "particularly important buildings of more than special interest". The description is

"Women's college. 1962-6. Chamberlin, Powell and Bon. White brick, concrete, some polished some bush-hammered. Some flat roofs; hall and library with concrete vaults. Two linked courtyards, the larger with residential accommodation to three sides; the smaller with hall to east and library to west. Mostly three storeys. Hall of Greek cross plan with circular staircases in the angles, and roofed by dome of eight leaves, with indirect top-lighting introduced between. Internally it has segmental arches on four pairs of slim columns. JCR of double height. Interiors of brick and concrete. Library rectangular with barrel-vault, groined for segmental arched windows on the flanks; heavy simple 'cornice'. Galleried interior. Hall and Library are linked by double-height walkways with some offices and meeting rooms behind. Irregular fenestration to residential blocks which have split-pitched roofs, and double-height rooms to upper storey."

Jo Edkins (née Dibblee)

Accommodation

This is the room from the 1974 prospectus. We 'borrowed' a particularly attractively-decorated room - I'm sorry, I don't remember whose - and packed it with people. I am looking earnestly at someone's record collection. Note the presence of a couple of men, since we didn't want prospective candidates to think we were a nunnery.

Maureen Bell

Greetings from the occupant of the room with all the pictures, Swiss Cheese plant etc. I was Char Miller and in 1974 I lived in Room F19 (I think that was the number).

I was JCR Secretary that year, so I had one of those two-level rooms to myself, except that on the lower level was a Gestetner duplicating machine, on which the College JCR magazine was printed, plus an ancient typewriter and a filing cabinet.

This photo was taken on the upper level. I'm fairly sure I am sitting on the floor, 3rd from left leaning against the sofa. I had just embarked on Part II Art History, hence all the pictures, somehow blue-tacked onto NH brick walls! I think Anne Borrett is to my left in the photo. Like me, she read History Part I.

Charlotte Crawley (née Miller)

Maureen recruited me for the photo shoot for the 1974 Prospectus. I really enjoyed the experience. (I'm the one with the wooden bead necklace, second from the left in the picture of a 'Supervision'). I loved the underfloor heating and remember the smell of polish after the bedders had buffed it with their machine. As for pictures, I remember a picture lending library, certainly in my final year. I haven't been to the College for several years now and wonder what changes have been made to the living accommodation, given the extensions and appeals to finance upgrades/renovations.

Anne Muir (née Borrett)

College bill, belonging to Anne Muir (née Borrett)

Like Anne, I remember the smell of the corridors; it was quite distinctive.

Sue Attridge (née Wood)

I had a single room in Hall for my first 2 years then moved out to a rented house in Albert Street near Jesus bridge. I loved that too. We would stay on after term and come back early. Lengthening the time when there were no lectures, we could enjoy the town.

Deborah Glass

In the first year, I lived in a ground floor room in New Hall and developed good friendships with a number of other undergraduates, several of whom (Penny, Wendy and Alison) I shared lodgings with on Chesterton Road (in my second year) and the College house on Madingley Road (in my third year).

My memories of New Hall included: the friendly and endlessly supportive porter, Mr Ellis; the substantial buffet salad we signed up for on Sunday evening; occasional requests from young men who knocked on my door and asked to climb out of my downstairs window in the middle of the night; and the relaxing swishing sound of the floor being swept in the morning in the New Hall library as I attempted to complete the latest essay.

Diana Kuh (née Lewin)

I loved the New Hall building and feel I was very lucky to live in hall all three years. In my first year I shared with Sylvia Perris, in my second year I had a single split-level room and in my final year my room was on Fountain Court.

Hilary Martin

After the first year in New Hall I subsequently lived for two years in college accommodation on Thompson's Lane, a warren of terraced houses near Magdalene Bridge now demolished and replaced by modern apartments. Living there meant a lovely view across the river and into Magdalene's fellows' garden. It also meant perishingly cold winter nights despite extra vest, bed socks, dressing gown and multiple blankets, and large bills for heating, because of my constant use of the gas fire. Finding out that New Hall did not accept women for their PGCE year and that I was therefore expected to transfer to Hughes Hall (another all-female institution) I ventured to be different and applied to the newly woman-friendly Churchill College instead. Thus, inadvertently, I became the first woman ever to have attended both New

Hall (as an undergraduate 1971-4) and Churchill (as a postgraduate 1974-5): the only really distinguishing feature of my Cambridge career!

Maureen Bell

Having applied while I was working abroad, by the time I was interviewed by Esther Goody in May 1971 all the rooms had been allocated, but I was happy to be offered anything and for two years lived in Beaufort House. I think I realised at the time that not living in college meant I was not as sociable as I might have been and in retrospect, I wish I had made more of an effort to get involved in college activities, but I never regretted my decision to come to New Hall.

Sarah Wilson (née Stallard)

In my first year, I shared a split-level room with someone who regularly had her boyfriend to stay over with her in her single bed. We hardly ever spoke, but one day I found my very loud alarm clock missing and eventually found it wrapped up in all my jumpers in my bottom drawer. We silently drove each other mad, until one day I came back, and she'd moved out, so I had a double room to myself until the end of the year. I threw a party, inviting everyone I knew, probably about 20 people; in my memory, it is the best party I ever had.

I also remember that, when I lived in Chesterton Road, my parents couldn't phone me and I had to phone them from the phone box across the road. Once, someone came up the river in a punt as far as Chesterton Road and picked me up outside my front door. Very romantic! The gesture, not the man, I'm afraid.

Penny Stirling

I remember happy times in our shared houses in Chesterton Road, lying in bed in my attic room listening to swans flying down the river, and in Madingley Road - a lovely house. I remember ringing home from the pay phone - sadly the news was not good as my father was seriously ill.

Wendy Spray (née Coulson)

I lived in college for the first 2 years and then moved with 3 others to a little house in Albert Street off Chesterton Road which was a great experience.

Karen Greenwood

In my first year I lived in New Hall in the top half of a shared room. In my second year I moved out of New Hall and lived in a rented house with friends. This as I recall was against the rules as you were only allowed to live in registered properties. Somehow a group of us managed to get round this as we knew a graduate who could vouch for us. In my third year I lived off Mill Road which was the poor end of town. I enjoyed getting involved with local children, working on a summer play scheme.

Liz Stafford

In my second year I was lucky enough to have a single room on H staircase opposite Camilla Toulmin, who was studying Economics in the year below us. She remains a good friend. Together we have walked more that 2,000 miles of footpaths across England and Scotland, arguing and putting the world to rights together with our husbands and an assorted cast of characters gathered in along the way. An outstanding way to understand the country and how its different regions are put together, as well as seeing a range of sites (churches, standing stones, lovely villages, derelict mills, mines, factories, and canals) we'd otherwise pass by at speed in a car.

In our third year Karin Bamborough, Rosie Boughton and I colonised the upper half of 34 Warkworth Street in the Kite, by Parker's Piece. The flat was notable for having a bath in the kitchen and a freezing cold loo stuck on the back of the house. Our landlords, Ralph and Ida Wackett, could have been invented by Dickens. This pair were petrified by the hard left tenants of the flat below ours, postgraduate lawyers of a Stalinist persuasion, very anti-American and so not at all taken with me. I could easily imagine them transporting me to a gulag.

All life took place in our kitchen. Loads of visitors, lots of cooking, so many conversations. I acquired my lifelong taste for the Archers, played out on Rosie's Roberts radio, which also brought us news of the evolving Troubles in Northern Ireland and the grim proceedings as the Vietnam war ground to its miserable conclusion. We had no telly and didn't feel the lack. I still listen to the radio more than I watch TV.

Virginia Beardshaw

I only lived in for my first year in one of those split-level rooms that other people have already talked about. I was very grateful I was on the lower level of the room as the stairs were very steep! In my second year I had to live out and I found a semi basement room in a house on Midsummer Common which suited me very well as it had the merit of being much closer to the Engineering Department at the bottom of Trumpington Street and meant I didn't have to cycle up Castle Hill at the end of each day. The family were very nice and I used to do occasional babysitting for them which also meant that I had a bit of family life which was good and I decided to stay there for my third year rather than moving back into college.

Helen Morton

In my second year I lived on Chesterton Road in a big bay windowed room overlooking the Cam and Jesus Green. The landlords lived in the basement and kept a vigilant eye on us which, looking back now, seems so strange. In my third year I was at the college house in Madingley Road. So I was fortunate in my accommodation and my house mates, Di, Penny, Nicola in particular.

Alison Wray (née O'Brien)

In my second year I lived in Memorial Court in Clare College; a New Hall friend somehow discovered that Clare was open to having some second year women to help their first female students settle in. These first years, though, were far more sophisticated than us and I don't remember ever having much to do with them other than pointing out that when boiled milk had turned black, it and the saucepan should probably be disposed of. I greatly enjoyed having my own two rooms at Clare: a bedroom and a large sitting room, with a gas fire for toasting crumpets, and a view of the comings and goings to the University Library, conveniently nearby for study and home-made cakes at teatime. The walk into town through the College gardens and across the river was a delight, as was the availability of a college punt which I seem to remember pulling over the rollers for a trip to Grantchester. It was through the record library at Clare that I learnt to love early music. I also discovered the joy of college chapel services and the music that could be listened to, in lovely surroundings, several times a week. Lunchtime concerts at the Fitzwilliam were another favourite as was exploring the paintings and pots of the museum. I do not know how I failed to visit Kettle's Yard while I was at Cambridge – I was probably suspicious of having to ring the bell to get in and the aura of exclusivity that created.

Mary Anne Bonney

After the first term, I was found accommodation in a student house in Silver Street. A room to myself even if the east wind rattled through the window and it was very old fashioned. That was the term of the miners' strike and I remember working by candlelight wrapped in a blanket as the electricity was cut off.

In my second year, I went to live in Clare College. I had been singing in the chapel choir and those girls associated with the college were offered a place to help the new intake of girls to the college in 1972. I think there were 8 of us. We were given newly refurbished rooms in Memorial Court and our responsibilities were to buddy up with the new girls. It was a good system and I wished New Hall had done that for us. My college life then refocussed on Clare. I even tried to change college but was told that it was just not possible to leave New Hall, so I remained kind of suspended between the two. There was still a lot of uncertainty about the admission of women into Clare college, which I am sure was shared elsewhere in the rather reactionary university.

After a Commemoration dinner at which the choir had been singing, I recall talking to one of the dons who confessed that he was very perturbed about the intake of women. When asked why, he explained very seriously, that he did not think there would be enough intelligent women in the country to fill all the places. I was completely lost for words for a moment but was able to reassure him that I was certain there were plenty of intelligent women around who would excel with a Cambridge education. He was most certainly a product of single sex education followed by academic appointment and consequently a complete disconnect with the world outside the ivory tower. I found a lot of people like this at Cambridge both then and when I have subsequently been back on official business.

Diana Murray (née Collyer)

I did love living in the centre of town in my third year in Neville House - by then, I was studying History of Art so it was brilliant for seeing friends.

Rosemary Grande (née Temple)

Although I wasn't initially attracted by the New Hall building, I did enjoy living there. In first year, I arrived before my roommate so had the upstairs section of a double room. It was spacious enough and I loved the fact that the rooms felt cosy; this advantage was lost when they turned off the heating I think on May 1st each year - just at the time when revision for exams was starting and there was little choice but to sit there reading and freeze! There was something very special about the atmosphere in the corridors early evening - people wandering around in and out of each other's rooms as they were cooking, and The Archers playing through many doors. In my final year I had a very pleasant room in Fountains Court. It was quiet and peaceful, the cooking and laundry facilities must have been among the best in the university given the small number of people using them, and the view onto the court with the water was very restful.

Denise Phillipson (née Milburn)

In my third term of the first year I moved out into digs with 5 other students, all men. We found an accommodating MA who was willing to say they were living with us, so that took care of the residency requirements. We decided the house would be a commune, which meant setting up a central study room and eating together, but not much else. I was the only person who ever cleaned the kitchen! Two of the men were a bit thuggish and had a falling out with one of the others. At the end of Michaelmas Term they kicked the rest of us out; I never understood why. So much for Peace and Love!

Gillian Blessley

Societies

There were many university and college societies for all kinds of interests. They were run by students.

I have a very vivid impression of horizons opening up when I arrived at Cambridge. There was a societies fair, and you could join anything and try anything.

Penny Stirling

Honestly, I have absolutely no recollection of there being a fresher's fair, that was something I must have missed, as I always wondered if there was anything "going on" and it took me ages to discover groups!

Lou Radford

During the first few days many of us went to the Societies Fair. Numerous clubs and societies had stalls in a vast hall somewhere in the centre of Cambridge and I decided to join several to try out and perhaps drop some of them later. The Union Society was a must for me, with interesting debates to watch, though I did not participate, and I also learned to play snooker, after a fashion, there. I joined the canoe club - you could borrow a canoe to paddle up and down the Cam.

Jane Mott (née Style)

I joined the Union Society at the fresher's fair - it took all of the grant which New Hall made to each of us to boost our out-of-college Cambridge experience as New Hall was felt by some to be so far outside the town centre. It was worth it, and I loved taking the little passageway down beside the Round Church for debates and occasionally films. The ADC theatre was also our end of town, and Kettles Yard even closer. I remember concerts there and sitting so close to the performers that I could hear one lady cellist chomping her teeth in time to her playing. Disconcerting - literally.

I can't remember why I chose to go to a recruiting session for Linkline - a kind of student-orientated Samaritans, but I was impressed by Chad Varah who was setting it up, and somehow, I was selected - perhaps precisely because I did not say much to the 'desperate suicide risk' in the role-play. I think Linkline was still too new to be helpful to many students, but it taught me something. We manned a telephone overnight in a room loaned by Kings, but in the morning had to wash and prepare for 9am lectures in the public toilets!

Sally Morgan

I joined CUEG, the underwater exploration group, tempted at the freshers' fair by something different. On Friday evenings we trained in scuba diving at the Parkers Piece swimming pool. I made friends from other colleges - all men. We made our own wetsuits from kits, gluing together the thick rubber edges, and covering the seams with tape. We had a couple of great diving holidays, in Devon and Scotland.
In the second and third years I was roped onto the committee of the medical society. One perk was having dinner out with the speakers - in long dress or skirt! We met some interesting people, including Raymond Baxter, who presented Tomorrow's World.

Sarah Watson (née Henley)

I quickly joined the sailing club, called the "cruising club". I was an enthusiastic dinghy sailor and had made myself a wetsuit, so was immediately recruited into the university team. I had great fun in the team throughout the three years and I must have had a sailing half-blue each year.

Hilary Martin

I joined the Canoeing Club (not sure of its exact name) and remember having several sedate, though not very adventurous excursions up and down the Cam from Thompson's Yard where the Boathouse was then located.

In my second year I co-founded an International Folk Dance Society with a friend, as we'd met a delightful person whose passion was European, particularly Hungarian folk dancing. She was Swiss and had settled here when she married a Cambridge academic, and willingly agreed to teach us. It was a very small group and we performed round the town, including on Midsummer Common after finals. I don't think we were very good, but we thoroughly enjoyed ourselves.

I also joined the Catholic Chaplaincy group in my first year. We met in various people's rooms, and I remember Prof. Anscombe coming along on several occasions as she was a devout RC. My abiding memory of her was of her sitting on the floor, listening to our conversations and occasionally shouting out 'Rubbish!' I don't recall her being very encouraging of our naïve philosophical explorations!

Anne Muir (née Borrett)

To some extent my focus became university rather than college. I did run the New Hall art collection loan scheme for one year. This allowed college members to borrow pieces from the collection to have in their rooms. I had a Lowry in mine. But my record keeping, and the college's, was so casual I'm surprised they ever got any back! I also took on the role of college rep on the English Joint Academic Committee. It sounds dull but it was a time of revolution in the English Faculty so was actually quite exciting. The wonderful Raymond Williams was on the committee, so was Stephen Heath who inspired me to join the great English Faculty semiotics and structuralism battle - on his side!

I'm struck by how we all had such different experiences of Cambridge – some music, some sport, some subject- based. It's almost as if we were at different universities.

Ros Coward

I joined the Tiddlywinks club. Because. It was frivolous and fun, and we once went to Oxford to play against their team - for a 'quarter blue' (which didn't exist except in the minds of the Tiddlywinks club). Then there was a memorable occasion at the end of a sit-in when we played against the proctors. The rules were complex, there was plenty of wine, and a good time was had by all.

I also joined something called the scouts and guides club, not because I was interested in guiding but because they went horse riding once a week. So I learned to ride by charging around the Cambridgeshire countryside on a collection of bad-tempered ponies owned by a vet in a village near Cambridge.

Alison Litherland (née Hill)

New Hall 2nd X1 Hockey team

I think I was the only person in New Hall in our year to play hockey for the university.

Angela Bailey (née Webster)

I swam for the university swimming team in my second and third years and joined a really fun mixed group of friends which became the focus of my social life. I was women's captain in 3rd year and it was hard work putting together a team as there wasn't much competition for places amongst the women. The college gave me a travel grant to go on a swimming tour during the long vac of 1973 which was a memorable camping trip to the south of France (with some swimming matches involved!).

Pauline Whitney (née Micklam)

I didn't even attempt to enrol for any of the sporting activities that I had done at school, but instead joined the Clare ladies boat. I must have been founding member, being part of the first intake of women in the college. We had excellent training from one of the Clare men's boat and became quite a creditable crew. I still have the (half pint) tankard that we won at the Norwich regatta. In my final year, I lived in a house in Chesterton Road, overlooking Jesus Green, right opposite the bridge over the river, where the ice cream van would ply its trade all through the summer weeks when I was trying to revise for finals. The only time we could get onto the river to practice was 6.00am, so I duly dragged myself out of bed and cycled across to the boathouse at least a couple of times a week. I have never been fitter!

Diana Murray (née Collyer)

I played lacrosse for the university in those first two years, and learned to play squash. In my third year, I rowed with Emily Smith in the first ever New Hall eight (a boat lent by Fitzwilliam.)

Charlotte Crawley (née Miller)

We played squash late at night. Once my partner went to play squash at the Pembroke courts which were well out of town, only to find someone practising bagpipes. Presumably he'd been banned from elsewhere. The only time I remember going out of Cambridge in termtime was when I visited the National Trust property, Ickworth House. It was far too difficult cramming everything into the very short term., especially as a medic.

Joanna Watts (née Sloper)

We also played late night squash on the Clare courts and also table tennis both of which I regularly lost.

Jan Sherman (née Phillips)

I wasn't sporty. Running about in sweaty aertex shirts was not for me! Walking, cycling, and punting kept me fit. There was a table tennis room in the college, which we made use of quite often. Going to watch the Bumps in the summer was fun.

Jane Mott (née Style)

Singing was a constant for me in all three years. I was too timid to audition for CUMS, fearing that my weak sight reading would disqualify me. So instead, I sang in college choirs. In the days before mixed colleges the men's college choirs were avid for women singers. So no auditions there and they were delighted to have you.
 I can remember singing in the Emmanuel choir for a couple of terms, and then Pembroke but the most memorable was singing Monteverdi's 'Orfeo' in the summer of 1972 at Jesus.
The music was challenging, quite unlike anything I'd sung before. I think now it was an ambitious choice for a college choir, but that the music scholar who directed it was reflecting the first inklings of the early music revival that was taking off across Europe in the early 70s, which he wanted to be part of. While he struggled getting us to sing the notes, and to find people who could play authentic instruments, there wasn't a lot of time to rehearse what was intended to be a fully staged production held out of doors in the Jesus cloister.
First sight of the costumes was less than encouraging: mine, as a 'nymph', was made from flesh coloured crimplene with an unbecoming bunchy elasticated waist. I don't know who made them or who it was that choreographed our dances, but both were clumsy.

Rehearsals were chaotic. The low point was when the stage gave way with a crack as we nymphs galumphed around doing a less than sprightly dance during the dress rehearsal. So much for health and safety in those distant days.

The stage collapse and heavy summer downpours meant a hasty change of venue. We abandoned the cloisters and crammed into the chapel. I was even more confused than before, about where we were meant to be and when. To call the production 'under rehearsed' is a wholly inadequate description. I begged my friends not to come and see it, and when they loyally did, I was mortified.

But there was an upside. It was an introduction to early music like none other and I've loved Monteverdi ever since. I've been a keen amateur singer ever since.

Virginia Beardshaw

An embarrassing moment for me was when, as a soprano in CUMS, I arrived a little late for a rehearsal of what I think was Verdi's Requiem. I had to slightly shuffle along my row to get to my place, which I did as discreetly as possible, and started singing, with my head up and my score level with everyone else's – but alas for me, my score was upside down. This minor detail was immediately noticed by David Wilcox (conductor) and he stopped the rehearsal (imagine!) and asked me to leave immediately, and not to come back! Long story short, a fellow choir member said I would just have to apologise and grovel, which I duly did, and I was allowed back into the hallowed throng at the next rehearsal – another mortifying experience! I loved singing with CUMS. My other musical foray was a folk group called "Lou's Boys" - I sang, the boys played the accordion and the fiddles. I loved it and for a short time we had a sort of fixture at a pub on Monday nights, it was great fun and we seemed to be quite popular, until one night the landlord, without telling us, put in a stage platform about 2 inches high, with a little spotlight in the rafters, shining on me – I completely froze, joined the audience and never sang with them again, – they changed to "The

Boys" and the "Lou" was dropped! Never mind – it was fun for a while, and it didn't spoil my love of singing, I just stuck with choirs after that!

Lou Radford

Someone (I don't remember who) talked me into joining them in a college choir singing Faure's Requiem. I didn't even know I was an alto at that point, and I learned the art of listening to my fellow singers. One of the many unexpected joys of a university education

Alison Mawle

I loved singing with the Queens college choir- Mag Soc (St Margaret's Society). I had never sung before and have often sung in more recent times - so that inspired my love of singing - and was also such a relaxing thing to do- away from academic pressures. It was so friendly too.

Rosemary Grande (née Temple)

On Sunday evenings I helped out at FEAST, an arts organisation that showcased contemporary writing and music by students. I remember its prime movers, Stephen Poliakoff and Ben Mason from Kings and a cohort of us from New Hall. Griff Rhys Jones, Jane Rogers and Sarah Dunant were amongst the contributors. FEAST operated an early Open Mic system. Programmes were variable, with some very good things. They took place in King's cellars. Afterwards we'd populate the King's bar.

Virginia Beardshaw

I took advantage of the shortage of female singers in the men's colleges and sang with Queens' choir a couple of times – most memorably a performance of Vaughan Williams' Five Mystical Songs by George Herbert in the Senate House, with the wonderful Richard Jackson as guest soloist. My only acting experiences were odd – Richard Axton put on a performance of Piers Plowman using the original language, so I think we were unintelligible to most of the audience – though if they couldn't make head or tail of what we were saying at least they could admire the beautiful (and echoing) cloister in which we acted. With some Churchill students I was involved in a play put on for local primary schools – I was a troll and after the first performance the three trolls were asked to tone it down as we had scared the children too much.

Pam Hilton

Probably like many others, I fell in love several times at Cambridge. However, my earliest and longest lasting love-affair was with early music. It was such a privilege as a woman in Cambridge to be able to sing in choirs at the men's colleges and in our first term I chose to sing the divinely beautiful Monteverdi's Vespers at Jesus College. It remains one of the most affecting musical experiences I've had. Such exquisite music. Subsequently I've sung many glorious works and now indulge my passion for renaissance music by singing each week in a wonderful small church choir at morning or evensong services. I'm not a believer myself but just adore the masses and motets we sing by Palestrina, Victoria, Byrd, Tallis and the like.

Lorna Robertson

I spent most of my spare time singing! I joined CUMS (Cambridge University Music Society) which was course a very large chorus and was directed in my first 2 years by David Wilcox and then by Philip Ledger. It was great for singing large-scale works and performing in Kings Chapel and the Corn Exchange. I also joined a small chamber choir, called I think the Purcell Singers or Purcell Society, which I remember as being very challenging and good for my sight reading - very different to CUMS. And lastly I joined the Corpus Christi chapel choir as the college only had male students and so needed to import women for the soprano line. The arrangement was that you sang evensong in the chapel on a Sunday and then you were given a free dinner in college afterwards which I thought was great. We had an annual Choir Dinner with a four course meal and wine from the college cellars which was very enjoyable. I did join a motorbike club in my first year and went out on rides on the back of the motorbikes which was fun.

Helen Morton

I found that of all the things I excelled at when I was at school, there were few that I could continue comfortably. Singing was one and I joined a 'rock' band in my first term with boys from Churchill and Magdalene. It only lasted one term, but we played at the 'sit-in' at the Senate House – I never really understood what the 'sit-in' was all about, but we tried to entertain the crowd. We did various gigs including one at Oxford university. I am pretty sure we were dreadful but it was fun. We were called Tramp, no idea why.

I also sang in Clare Chapel choir – coming from a church music background with a father and grandfather who were organists and choirmasters, I was on firmer ground there. I had not realised until I looked it up just now, that the chapel choir was only founded in 1972, so I must have been one of the founding members, with Peter Dennison as the first Director of music. (Just missed John Rutter who took over in 1975). We not only sang in Chapel but gave other concerts, joined CUMS as a semichorus on more than one occasion, and went on tour to Coventry Cathedral to fill in when their choir was on holiday. We tried to perform Lucia di Lammermoor – somewhere in London, but we were badly under-rehearsed and I don't think it was a good performance. Otherwise it was pretty good and I came across a whole new repertoire of music which I still love, though most choirs I now sing with, find the pieces hard to master.

Early on, possibly from the Freshers Fair, I joined the ADC theatre as stage crew. It was a great group of people and I learnt a lot about backstage work. I mainly did props, costumes, scene shifting, but I did stage manage a couple of productions including "The Boyfriend". There were some superb productions and actors including Sarah Dunant, Griff Rhys Jones, and Douglas Adams. We went on tour with The Footlights to the Edinburgh Festival and to the Round House

Theatre in London. I met my first boyfriend there and although we went our separate ways after he left Cambridge after my first year, we are still friends today. He was one of the founders of the Shaft of Darkness Club – which met each term for a black tie dinner - with awards for those who had messed up backstage – hence shaft of darkness when there should have been light. On one occasion when visiting the bank to get out some cash (no ATMs in those days) when my bank balance had slipped into a small overdraft situation, I was called in to see the bank manager, who wanted to know why I was subscribing to a Satanic organisation. I was able to set his mind at rest, but those were the days when bank managers cared about you and your finances. The SOD club is still going and celebrated its 50 years in March 2019 with a dinner in Selwyn College.

Diana Murray (née Collyer)

Studies aside, I found university life quite difficult at first. I was used to living at home with six brothers and sisters and was too shy or too young or too socially inept to make my own way. I was rescued by a family friend who came to do a Teacher Training course at Homerton. She persuaded me to join the choir of Our Lady and the English Martyrs. It was just right for me: a small choir, beautiful music, rehearse on a weekday, perform on Sunday and move on to something new the following week. I've stuck with church choirs ever since. A couple of people in the choir were Early Music enthusiasts and somehow I got invited along to an evening of music making. It could have turned out a complete embarrassment because I didn't then know that treble recorders play in F not C, so my contribution to the chosen Purcell Fantasia was a fifth out from start to finish. Actually it didn't matter because most of the others were pretty ropey players and had smoked a fair amount of dope. When we all reached the end of the piece at different times I distinctly remember somebody leaning back and saying 'Wow! Far out!' in a way that was meant to be appreciative and not literal. After I left university I had some recorder lessons, took Grade 8, had more lessons and taught recorder for the local Music

Support Service for a while. Now I play in a group (guitar, violin / viola, cello) exploring C20 chamber music with recorder.

Emma Wheelock

I had always been excluded from school plays and choirs because I lacked talent, but I appeared in several productions in Cambridge: I remember "El Caballero de Olmedo" in Spanish, where I played opposite the man who later became my husband; also "Women beware women", where I had an incestuous relationship with my uncle. I also recall hitchhiking down to the Minack outdoor theatre on the cliffs in Cornwall, with the Fletcher players from Corpus, where we did the miracle plays and I cooked for 30 people on two rings in a cow barn. I also sang the Mass in B Minor and Faure's requiem - amazing experiences, both. I remember a concert for 100 flutes on a lawn outside King's or Queen's, I think, where we were each given a phrase and asked to walk around playing it at intervals in our own timing.

Penny Stirling

After an unsuccessful flirtation with the laddishness of CULES (Cambridge University Light Entertainment Society) I began stage-managing for GODS, the drama society run jointly by New Hall and Churchill. Singing in Trinity Hall chapel choir (women's voices being much in demand, atheists were acceptable) proved equally absorbing. As well as providing a crash course in sight-reading it involved occasional trips to sing elsewhere (St Albans, Peterborough, Ely). Particularly welcome was the post-evensong sherry, followed by an enormous (free) Sunday dinner. Luckily, I spent my first year in New Hall sharing C13 with Sue Addison (now Whitham), a famously energetic music student who introduced me to madrigal singing and to many new musical friends. Sue was a real force in getting music going within New Hall, and a highlight was her college choir's performance of Pergolesi's Stabat Mater. Her own rendition of Victorian parlour songs, especially 'Excelsior', was a triumph.

Maureen Bell

Music of all sorts was a huge part in my life during my first two years. I played the trombone, and as there was a shortage of undergrad trombonists, I somehow squeezed into CUMS 1 as second trombone. Under the beady but exacting baton of the famous David Willcox, we tackled the Verdi Requiem in that first term, performing it with top soloists in both King's College Chapel and Ely Cathedral. It was a sublime experience I shall never forget, even though I had some tortuous moments in rehearsal playing alone repeatedly, an especially difficult bit in the Sanctus. At the end of summer term 1972, eight brass players, including me, accompanied the CUMS Choir on a short tour of Belgian cathedrals, with David Willcox at the helm. I remember thinking how run down many of these cathedrals were, - but then in the summer of 1972, nearly everywhere seemed pretty run down, even bits of Cambridge. Now when we go to Cambridge, I have to pinch myself to reconcile the smart, prosperous city we see now. It wasn't like that in the early '70s.

I often met Sue Addison in college bands, music societies etc as nearly every college had some sort of music group, plus there were the cross-university music clubs. I must have clocked up miles cycling with my trombone on my bike, often in a compulsory long black skirt for performances. Pedalling up Castle Hill like this was I guess very good exercise on a bike with just 3 gears.

Charlotte Crawley (née Miller)

Does anyone remember being in the University Challenge team? I am pretty sure it was in our first year, probably our second term. Those of us who liked quizzing went to a meeting in the JCR President's room, I recall. She read out questions which we answered if we could. I was picked and, at some point, we all piled into a mini-bus to Manchester - it was filmed by Granada in those days. We were up against the University of Kent, Frances Moriarty (later Edmonds) was our captain. I still, after all these years, remember the three starter questions I answered correctly (and the one I didn't!). We were beaten, but not heavily, and then we got to meet Bamber Gascoigne, who was delightful. I remember we stayed on afterwards to see the next two teams play, by which time BG was wearing a different coloured velvet jacket, and talked about 'last week New Hall played the University of Kent; this week it's the turn of…'

Ursula Wide (née Buchan)

I also remember going to support our team from New Hall, in Manchester, at the recording of 'University Challenge' back in the day. Yes, it was very disappointing when we lost; however, there was one moment of big excitement: Frances Moriarty pressed her buzzer button at one point but it did not make a sound despite her conviction that she had pressed before any other player. She immediately interrupted Bamber Gascoigne to report this, but he tried to dismiss Frances, always a foolish thing to do, though he knew it not at the time! He explained, somewhat with disdain, I felt, that another contestant must have pressed their buzzer first, thereby cutting Frances off. Well, Frances was having none of this! She stuck to her guns; the recording was temporarily halted; and some technicians ran to the scene, eventually managing to fix the problem.
    Score: Bamber Gascoigne 0; Frances Moriarty 1.

Maryla Carter (née Ignatowicz)

Well, I also went to support, but my over-riding memory is of how unspeakably FILTHY the place was. Since then, I have experienced Unspeakable Filth in and behind theatrical stages in both private and state schools.... this was a shocking introduction!
I thought the whole show was contrived and took advantage of inexperienced young people. An eye-opener. Very disappointing.

Sue Whitham (née Addison)

Political action

New Hall was a relatively serene and safe place to return to after a day at the Economics Faculty where the post Keynesian economists and the neoclassical economists were having a bitter fight and hardly speaking to each other. On the one hand I was thrilled to discover an intellectual world where economic theories, model assumptions and the interpretation of empirical evidence were rigorously debated which was in sharp contrast to what had been taught as established theories and facts at A-level. On the other hand, it could be disconcerting at times. During 1972-73, faculty staff and students were involved in a debate about whether undergraduate students in Economics could replace two of their third year exams with a dissertation, a proposal voted down by the General Board, and which led to a student occupation of the Old Schools, and was the subject of a report by Lord Devlin. Eventually, the proposal was accepted, just in time for me to seize the opportunity to write a dissertation. I was grateful for that experience, as it led, eventually, to my academic career.

Diana Kuh (née Lewin)

Two things struck me about the Old Schools sit-in. First, during the evening, the OTC (Officers Training Corps) had a counter-demonstration outside. There was a crash, then broken glass on the floor. I noted (being a detective fiction fan) that the glass was inside the building, and so was caused by the OTC outside rather than us, but of course we would be blamed for it.
The other memory was the end of the sit-in. There was a court order to disperse us. There were rather silly speeches about how we would walk out one minute past the deadline "to show them", and shoulder-to-shoulder stuff, which didn't impress me much. But the speech ended "Will everyone please tidy up, and replace all chairs neatly against the wall". I'm not sure that Cambridge undergraduates were very good at anarchism.

Jo Edkins (née Dibblee)

I wasn't an economist but I remember the Economics sit-in because some of us from the English faculty joined for a short while in solidarity – I think because we were having discussions about changes to our Tripos grading at the time. I believe that in the previous year they had reconsidered all the English Part II exam papers, and found that whilst pretty well every First and Third remained the same, somewhere around 60% of the Seconds moved between 2.1 and 2.2, which suggested considerable subjectivity in marking. Students argued on the staff-student committee for a really radical reclassification of degrees to Research, Fail and Pass. Whilst this didn't get through, undivided Seconds were agreed. At the meeting where this was discussed the Chair asked what would happen if the Senate didn't agree, at which point Raymond Williams said he would personally lead the sit-in, and Lionel Knights said he would support him. It was agreed, and most of our year duly got Seconds. However, Miss Hammond told me later that they had noted which would have been 2.1s and which 2.2s and evidently the reform didn't last.

Pam Hilton

I can't remember which year it was that there was the occupation of the Old Schools – was it 1972? I remember a huge wintry rally-like meeting on the Sidgwick site at the end of which we 'voted' by a show of hands to occupy. I was incensed by this. I thought the vote perfunctory, and, more importantly, predetermined. I remember having a row with one of the organisers, who pointed out patronisingly that an occupation took a lot of organising and wasn't having any of my arguments about true democracy. In response to this arrogance, I stomped off, heading back to NH, underfloor heating and my own bed. I've often thought of this exchange since, and decided that both points of view are valid. However, I note from these reminiscences how few of us, myself included, had any inkling about what the occupation was all about – certainly the organisers hadn't made it clear. Were we just a watered down reflection of the 1968 generation, along for the ride? Or was it that without Facebook, Twitter and modem social media, not to mention an effective public address system, it was genuinely difficult to get points across?

Virginia Beardshaw

I can't recall how or when I first got involved with New Hall JCR, but I did, and in my third year I succeeded Phillippa King as JCR Secretary, hence sharing L19 with the Gestetner copier, and learning to type (after a fashion) to produce the template for JCR Newsletters. I'm not sure what New Hall JCR achieved, apart from the re-opening of the JCR Bar downstairs in the JCR by Fountain Court? There were several quite militant students involved, particularly Rosie Crafts and Cathy Marsh, who advocated lots of change within college. Tedious discussions about what the JCR Bar-cum-Shop should stock, dragged on. Shampoo, biros, Tampax and file paper were hot contenders. The college fellow assigned to this Bar Committee was the famous philosopher, Prof. Elizabeth Anscombe, who proclaimed the Bar/Shop should sell Kirby grips and Gee's Linctus cough mixture. I think I lost interest a bit after the Bar opened, but as L19 was my room, I couldn't back off! In my final year, Sarah Feilden from the year below us, and I were selected to be the first student members of the New Hall Council. Through that, I saw much more of Rosemary Murray, who turned out to have quite a jolly sense of humour on occasions, and called me Char, which was a surprise.

Charlotte Crawley (née Miller)

Enthused by the previous year's lowering of the voting age to 18, I soon made contact with the local Labour Party. When New Hall announced plans for a rent rise I joined the Rent Strike Committee. We opened a bank account into which students supporting the strike could pay their rent, to show good faith while withholding the money from the college. Strangely, though the experience of organizing is still vivid, I really don't remember whether we succeeded or not - though I suspect a compromise was reached. What I do remember is the meetings and leaflets, and especially (I was studying English after all) being given the job of turning the manifesto into something sounding less stridently Marxist, and therefore less likely to frighten both students and fellows. Finding less alarming alternatives to necessary words like 'capitalism' proved a demanding task.

In my third year I was part of a working group started by the two Kates – Belsey and Pretty – with the aim of attracting more applicants from state schools. We produced an illustrated booklet about New Hall, and some of us visited schools to talk to potential applicants. The photo-shoot for the booklet took place on my 21st birthday, and I remember dragging several male friends along to be photographed too, so as to make it clear that being in a women's college didn't mean total segregation. It's depressing, of course, to see that efforts to attract applicants from state schools are still necessary. We really thought that we were at the beginning of a genuine revolution in making Cambridge accessible to other students like us, and it's sad that we made so little difference. At least, however, Cambridge in the early 70s was waking up to the need to admit more women than could be accommodated in the three women's colleges. By the time I graduated three men's colleges were leading the way: King's, Clare and Churchill. Today's students would surely be amazed at the implacable resistance to female students exhibited by some colleges, and the weary round of discussions (usually involving the impossibility of admitting women because of inadequate bathroom facilities) which dragged on for years.

Maureen Bell

Politics played a large part in my experience. I was involved in several "occupations" (don't ask me what they were about!) including one at Senate House where I remember coming and going freely by squeezing through the toilet windows, watching all night-showings of very obscure films, and having intense, not entirely sober, conversations about changing the world. I'm surprised I didn't later take up climbing as a career or become a cat burglar. I seem to have spent awful lot of time at Cambridge climbing in and out of windows and over walls, avoiding curfews or gaining access, un-ticketed, to May Balls. And all in those long skirts!

By my third year, feminism had taken a hold and I got involved in a group of women based in Newnham some of whom I still see occasionally. I don't remember too much what we actually did except have a consciousness raising group and print off a lot of posters. I did have a 'feminist' tussle with the English academic board who tried to stop me doing a dissertation on women novelists of the 19th century on the grounds that it wasn't a proper subject for literature. Can you imagine how many dissertations have been written on that subject since!

Ros Coward

I took part in heady sit-ins at Sidgwick Centre and the Senate House, and numerous political activities including a couple of excruciating street theatres with top-hatted capitalists and cloth-capped workers. I attended a National Women's Conference in Oxford, which felt life-changing – and it was the Women's Movement that continued to feel most powerfully like finding home.

Helen Mayer

I remember a sit-in in Lady Mitchell Hall. What it was about I have no idea now, but it is linked in my mind with a sense that there was a lot in the Cambridge system that was ready for change. I had been to school at the French Lycée in London, and avidly followed the *évenements* of 1968. Their impact on my schooling were minimal as by then I had moved into the English section of the school, but it had meant an end to the annual prizegiving and many of the trappings I saw at Cambridge seemed to me to be ripe for a similar cull.

Mary Anne Bonney

I had the experience in Cambridge of meeting a wide variety of people with different views on life and enough like-minded people that I felt more at home than I ever had at school. There was also a quirky kind of humour that I recognised as Cambridge humour. I remember the first time I listened to "The Hitchhiker's Guide to the Galaxy", in 1978, I immediately recognised it as having been written by someone who was at Cambridge in the early seventies. I remember taking part in an enquiry on something which required a group of us to sit in one meeting in the town hall on Castle Hill. We took it in turns to attend and take notes. One of our rules was that each character from the town council was assigned a name from Alice in Wonderland and we had to remember who was the White Rabbit and who was the Queen of Hearts, etc. and enter them correctly in our notes.

Penny Stirling

THATCHER THATCHER MILK SNATCHER – I remember I hitched from Cambridge to London to join a demo against Maggie's policy to stop free school milk. [*Margaret Thatcher was Education Secretary at this time.*] I sort of sidled into the throng somewhere in Regent Street, I seem to remember, and shuffled along for about 50 yards chanting "Maggie Maggie Maggie, Out! Out! Out!". Then the chant changed, and I turned round to see this fist-pumping young woman pushing a young child in a buggy and shouting "Maggie Maggie Maggie Kill! Kill! Kill!". Her eyes were ablaze and full of real hate. I shuffled out of the throng and hitched back to Cambridge, very conflicted but full of thought. I didn't actually demonstrate again until the anti-Iraq war demos. I had no idea who that woman was, nor did I wish to – but she was a big influence on me in those formative years of political angst!

Lou Radford

In my second year I was elected as one of the two student representatives on the Student Staff Joint Liaison Committee of the Engineering Department which was interesting and I guess my first experience of committee work. I was fairly left wing and I remember two specific actions. One was taking part in a march going up Castle Hill to the County Hall offices. It was to protest about Margaret Thatcher who was the Education Secretary and we were chanting

'Margaret Thatcher milk snatcher' as I think she was responsible for taking away free milk from school children. I mostly remember it because when we were marching past Magdalene College we were flour bombed by some of the students there. We complained to the police who wouldn't do anything about it as it was 'private property' so I was deeply unimpressed! In February 1972 I joined the sit-in the Old Schools in protest at the Devlin Report which ended up being an enquiry into student representation and participation in governance, which I guess was dear to my heart because of being on the student staff liaison committee of the department.

Helen Morton

In the second year a group of us organised 'Cambridge Population week', highlighting the exploding world population (the concept then seemed to go into hibernation for 40 years). We had some good speakers, and produced a booklet, which we sold on Cambridge streets for 10p!

Sarah Watson (née Henley)

I joined the Socialist Society, remember the Senate House occupation, socialising with friends at Churchill College, and being persuaded somehow to be the person in the bed for the Cambridge to London bed race. This was a fund raising activity but my chief recollections were the freezing cold and the many repairs needed to the bed frame on wheels.

Liz Stafford

In the third year, I was living in college. When the power cuts started, for some reason the light bulbs starting failing in the upper corridor, which got darker and darker (that was - when they were on at all!) We thought that the porters had removed some light bulbs "to save power", and the rest got overloaded and started failing. The corridor was "wiggly" with rooms pushing in on one side and the bathrooms pushing in on the other, and we disapproved of the lack of light. At one point, bits of the corridor had no light at all. So I left the bathroom doors open, with their lights on, just to provide illumination. But this was obviously an even worse drain on power. (Yes, we did care about such things, even back then!) My boyfriend came up with a solution. He replaced some of the broken light bulbs with red light bulbs. The corridor was visible to the Huntingdon Road. Very quickly, the porters replaced all the broken light bulbs (and the red ones!) with proper white bulbs. How to manipulate authority....

Jo Edkins (née Dibblee)

I remember being given the opportunity to belong to and run student societies like Third World First and SCM and meet wonderful people who helped me to develop my lifelong commitment to social justice.

Wendy Spray (née Coulson)

In my last year I got involved in a women's group that did free pregnancy testing and provided advice on where terminations could be accessed. Hubris in someone so inexperienced really. I remember a meeting where we gathered with torches and mirrors to see our own cervixes. Radical times really.

Deborah Glass

I remember the intensity of those 8 week terms where life was lived at full tilt. As well as studying, I belonged to various societies of a political/social action persuasion. We often met at lunch time so there was the added inducement of a free lunch. Most memorable is the pregnancy testing service I was part of. I also stage managed a performance of Sergeant Musgrave's Dance which caused me to be walking along Trinity Street with a full human skeleton!

Alison Wray (née O'Brien)

I joined the Liberal Club. This was breaking out for me as my family and school expected me to be a conservative like them! The other Liberals were a characterful bunch and the only activity I remember was a trip to London where we went in the Strangers' Gallery at the House of Commons and also to the Liberal Club in London, which our leader described as "my club" in a Regency England / Georgette Heyer sort of way. After a year or so I gave up on the Liberals and moved my allegiance to Labour where it stayed for many years. These days I am a proud member of the Green Party.

I was active in the New Hall Union and managed to get elected as treasurer for the second year, possibly unopposed? As a union officer I was entitled to a room in college for the second year which was I think the reason I wanted to do the job. However it was a useful first experience of committee work. I used to enjoy the meetings and was inspired by the political passion of some of the leading lights mainly in the year above us. At school we were encouraged to do a bit of public speaking and there was a debating Society but this was on a whole new level and has probably been the basis of my political activity ever since. There were occasional demonstrations where we marched around Cambridge shouting slogans like "Maggie Thatcher milk snatcher."

Jane Mott (née Style)

At the start of the first year, I and two friends joined the Liberal society. As someone else has mentioned, they were a characterful bunch, and I made many good friends. But I hadn't thought through why I did that, as I'd had no experience of political thought or activity before Cambridge. I remember going on the occasional demo and sit-in, again without being clear as to why. But I found all of this really valuable experience in trying to figure out what my political values actually were.

Alison Litherland (née Hill)

Entertainment

I revelled in the enormous range of plays and concerts to choose from in Cambridge and especially enjoyed seeing Shakespeare being performed in some of the old courtyards. I also joined a coach trip for overseas students to go to London to see Götterdämmerung, an unforgettable evening.

Aileen Regan (née Kidd)

I heard Alfred Brendel playing a Beethoven sonata sitting about two feet away from me in Kettle's Yard. I was most disconcerted at all the snuffling, snorting noises he made through his nose! Nevertheless, it was really beautiful and it was so special to be able to listen in a gallery surrounded by all that wonderful artwork. I also remember being able to borrow a Ben Nicholson, I think it was and have it in my room for a term. I actually thought that was a false memory because it sounds so unlikely, but someone else had the same memory so it must be true. Jim Ede liked to be surrounded by beautiful young men and I was friendly with David and Andrew. Andrew had his own film theatre in an attic room somewhere all draped with ethnic cloth and strewn with cushions.

Penny Stirling

In those days the Lady Mitchell Hall was, bizarrely, the main venue for gigs – totally unsuited to developing any real atmosphere with its seats with writing-desk arms, but there were nevertheless some great events. The first time I ever saw Dr John was there, and he led a conga of the entire audience out and round the hall during the final number (Iko Iko I think) – I was near the front and as we came back in we met the tail going out. Lou Reed played there twice in late '72 – one time supported by Pete Atkin, which made for a strange combination. A friend of mine later married the guy who was Pete's manager at the time, who recalled the evening well; very cramped conditions backstage, Pete doing his usual warm up of singing Lady Madonna in Latin, Clive James wandering round nervously wondering how his songs would go down with a Cambridge audience and Lou Reed sitting, looking very stoned, wide eyed at what was passing in front of his eyes and ears. I saw John Martyn at the St Lawrence Folk Song Society in my first term – that gig was recalled in Cam a couple of years ago by someone who met his future wife that night. Gigs at the Corn Exchange (eg the J Geils Band) were for some reason less good. And at Kettle's Yard there were recitals by people like Hans and Ursula Holliger, or Cleo Laine and John Dankworth - those were like a drawing room event.

Pam Hilton

Kettle's Yard would lend out one of their collection to students for a short period of time. I remember having a Gaudier-Brzeska drawing. I thought it amazingly trusting of them!

Jo Edkins (née Dibblee)

I recall borrowing a succession of Ben Nicholson works from Kettle's Yard for my room - all small ones, some he had made for Jim Ede as Christmas cards, some in relief. I can't imagine the insurance implications now of letting people turn up, just sign their name and college and go off with an artwork like that.

Pam Hilton

New Hall friendships were a hugely important part of my life in our undergraduate years. It was amazing to find so many people who were interested in discussing serious topics (I hadn't had that at my girls' grammar school) and I probably spent far too much time pondering the meaning of life and how the mind and psyche work with Cambridge friends. Penny introduced me to Kettle's Yard, opening my eyes to the world of beautiful artworks, which astonishingly we were able to borrow - what generosity, and how honoured were we! Perhaps as a result, I've had many years of joyful appreciation of art, including collecting original artworks myself. Like Penny, I also remember well the concerts there, especially a fantastic Alfred Brendel Schubert piano recital, and helping clear up afterwards.

Lorna Robertson

Does anyone else remember going to all-night film-fests down in the Market Square?

Wendy Joseph

I have happy memories of the Red Balloon – New Hall's answer to a May Ball if I remember rightly - I think at the end of our first term. I also remember punt races between the different student Christian societies, where we got very wet!

Wendy Spray (née Coulson)

In comparison to Oxford (where several of us medics went to do the Clinical course), Cambridge was so wonderfully compact and university-orientated. I felt as if even the cinemas appeared to stop showing films once term was ended. We could bicycle everywhere and there just seemed to be so much going on: impromptu "bands", chamber music and recitals. One song recital was particularly memorable for the excellent rendition of Purcell; unfortunately, the performer raised her eye-brows with every high note and I had to listen with my eyes shut. It was such a pleasure to have the opportunity to attend such high-quality events by bicycle.

Joanna Watts (née Sloper)

Looking back, I'm astonished that I took so little advantage of the amazing cultural events all around me. A few films, plays and museum visits at most.

Helen Mayer

I remembered going to a play by Wole Soyinka, where he was present, in Churchill College. I looked him up in Wikipedia and this is what it says:

"From 1973 to 1975, Soyinka spent time on scientific studies. He spent a year as a visiting fellow at Churchill College, Cambridge University 1973–74 and wrote Death and the King's Horseman, which had its first reading at Churchill College." So maybe what I remember was a play reading.

Penny Stirling

I'm afraid that I didn't go to anything as interesting. I did attend performances at Churchill, including Under Milk Wood by Dylan Thomas, and the Jew of Malta by Christopher Marlowe. Neither was obscure, but I don't think that I would have seen them normally. I enjoyed both performances, very much.

Jo Edkins (née Dibblee)

I went to a lot of concerts, films, plays and operas and remember going to the Arts Cinema to see 'W.R. – the Mysteries of the Organism' which was thought to be quite shocking at the time though I can't remember much of the detail now. My other vivid memory is of seeing an opera by Francis Poulenc called Les Mamelles de Tiresias which was a short gender bending comic opera put on by a student group and very entertaining. It's not often performed partly because it's only 1 hour long but I highly recommend it!

Helen Morton

I went to the cinema about twice in the 3 years but otherwise all entertainment was University based and therefore quite cheap. There was excellent amateur theatre of course, discos at New Hall in the Dome dancing to The Rolling Stones, a folk club in the cellar at Clare College starring Jonathan Kelly once. The May Ball at Sidney Sussex was a highlight. I wore quite a pretty long mauve floral peasanty dress that I had made, with a lacy white shawl.

Jane Mott (née Style)

Socialising

My last memory of New Hall was a (slightly) drunken party with my housemates in the beautiful garden at Madingley Road to celebrate our graduation in May 1974. How lucky we all were to be at New Hall during those halcyon times!

Diana Kuh (née Lewin)

One of my summer term memories is of playing croquet in the garden at 69 Storey's Way. Not being remotely sporty, I appreciated the fact that it didn't demand great physical exertion; a keen eye, steady arm and ruthlessness were its principal requirements. An occasional bonus was catching a glimpse of Clive James reading or writing at a table by the house. He was then the TV critic for The Observer and married to the Director of Studies in Italian.

Sue Attridge (née Wood)

I still remember with some considerable embarrassment being invited for sherry by my Tutor and being left with her husband. Attempting to make polite conversation I asked him what he did, to his great amusement. I discovered later it was Clive James.

Siân Crisp (née Jenkins)

In our first week there was some sort of freshers' do at Churchill. I went with others, through the back way to Storey's Way. I left (probably early!) on my own, and realised I had no idea how to get back to New Hall. After a few false starts, I was mightily relieved to see a policeman across the road. I crossed over and asked him where I was. I remember him saying 'Madingley Road, Cambridge', and asked where I wanted to be. I of course replied New Hall; but the well-intentioned man sent me to Newnham... I'd walked quite away before it dawned on me it couldn't be right. When I arrived at Newnham, quite late and in a bit of distress, I found my way to the room of an old school friend who by then was a second year. I disturbed her with her boyfriend; they had to get dressed before they could open the door, but were remarkably kind to me in the circumstances!

Sarah Watson (née Henley)

Having thought I knew nobody, all sorts of people seemed to come and introduce themselves, having heard from somewhere that there was some vague connection to exploit. Does anyone else remember the College post? A miraculous way of opening and developing communication with almost strangers, prompted by the remotest links. And not just formal introductions. I remember Ursula and I tramping round Downing, publicising some cause or other, and to our surprise we were recognised from the Seeley, invited in for a drink, and coffee, and from then on we had another group of acquaintances.

Fiona Edwards-Stuart (née Weaver)

Like many of the others, my social life was mostly outside New Hall and with hindsight, I didn't take full advantage of the opportunities in

Cambridge. In the first term, I made costumes for the Footlights panto. I enjoyed Stephen Poliakoff and friends reading his early plays in the bar at King's. Some student politics, two sit-ins (no idea why) and many parties, including a memorable one in the clock tower above King's gothic gate.

Jane Dottridge (née Rooke)

Socially, it was mildly stressful at first, but it was also exciting to have so much and so wide a choice. And the broader education that was on offer was also available to us all. Many of us report making more friends outside college than within, but that was such a luxury too, to be able to take one's own decisions, to find one's own way, meet new acquaintances who became friends, in many cases for life.

Fiona Edwards-Stuart (née Weaver)

I spent much of my time out of New Hall, mainly because my boyfriend from home was also at Cambridge as were several of his schoolmates. That made settling in that much easier but perhaps didn't broaden my horizons as much.

I seemed to have to spend much of my time working to keep up. It was fascinating but so time-consuming and there were so many other activities I'd have liked to take advantage of. The terms seemed very short. We used to try and stop working by 9pm so there was time to have some time with friends in the bar.

Joanna Watts (née Sloper)

Like others I enjoyed the Sunday evening buffet. However, I don't think I was in College that much. I already had a boyfriend from home at St Catharine's and as I was studying Natural Sciences I was out much of the day at lectures and practicals on the Downing site or New Museums site. I think much of social life revolved around those with whom I shared practicals, with the notable exception of Di Kuh who was just down the corridor from me on the ground floor. We both came from Birmingham and shared a love of dancing. Other friends included

Debbie, Karen and Liz all of whom were, I think, on a field trip to Wales in early spring in our first year. It was memorable for my first moonlit walk along a beach.

Alison Wray (née O'Brien)

I do not have any memory of college events as such, but recall spending many an evening in people's rooms, putting the world to rights over cups of tea and coffee. Making occasional phone calls home or to friends involved standing at a pay phone which my memory places in a corridor at one of the corners of the building, otherwise, communicating with Cambridge friends meant notes stuck to or slid under doors.

Mary Anne Bonney

The archaeology students seemed to spend a lot of time in the pub discussing the finer points of a society lecture we had just attended or the latest theories or gossip of various kinds. We did not drink a huge amount, a couple of pints would last the night. I am not sure I should tell this story, but we used to drink in The Mitre. The landlord had put up blackboards and chalk in the loos with the aim, I suppose, of reducing graffiti. On one occasion, the guys in our group each came back giggling after visiting the gents. Eventually, one ventured the information that on the board someone had written "we who are about to, Di, salute thee". Only in Cambridge and only in those days could you get away with that!

Diana Murray (née Collyer)

Socialising was all wonderful but I hate to say some of the relationships took up so much time and energy. I remember a wet Sunday evening, walking up Castle Hill sobbing my heart out - no idea who that was over. We were completely spoilt by the number of boys/ men around and I feel that I spent so much time in men's colleges that I had fewer strong friendships with fellow New Hall students as a result. I feel sad about that. I had grown up with three brothers so often felt more comfortable in male company. It did however mean that I associated with several men's colleges whereas now Oxford and Cambridge colleges are mixed, I am told that students often spend much of their time socialising just within their own college.

Rosemary Grande (née Temple)

A lot of instant coffee was consumed in friends' rooms in New Hall and elsewhere as we discussed life and so on. Drinking was mostly, for me, in Sidney JCR where I progressed from cider to beer, which is still my preferred drink. I did not, however, enjoy watching the yards of ale being poured down throats and coming back up! After my cloistered boarding school experience, meeting people from other backgrounds and places was just great. Sharing a room with Catrin, I met most of the medics and some scientists who lived in our corner of the college in the first year, as well as the other mathematicians of course. So I think my social life was fairly equally divided between New Hall, Sidney Sussex (boyfriend and his friends), and other colleges where I made friends on my course and kept in touch with a few people I already knew.

Jane Mott (née Style)

It was pretty easy to be sociable. No pre-arrangements – people just knocked on one another's doors, within and between colleges. Or stopped to chat if they met in the street. 'How are you' was likely to be met with a treatise on the meaning of life. I also remember the gatherings in peoples' rooms (I always felt less comfortable in such groups), and frenetic dancing at numerous parties. How on earth did we arrange it all in those pre-phone olden days?

As my parents were still in South Africa, kind students sometimes invited me home over Christmas or vacations, or came to stay with me and my sister in the Oxford house my parents had bought for their retirement. This was nice, but I could have done with a bit more parenting!

Helen Mayer

Relationships

I think we need a survey of how many of us found future husbands while at New Hall. I did for one!
Living in single sex colleges meant you had to be more pro-active at socialising, so it was at a New Hall party that I met a Corpus Christi student who was completing his PhD. I was soon watching rugby matches and rowing bumps and learning how to punt. We both graduated in 1973, started working in London, got married in 1974 between rowing commitments and have made London our home ever since. We have two children, two grandchildren and still attend rowing regattas!

Aileen Regan (née Kidd)

So did I!

Penny Stirling

My then boyfriend, now husband of 46 years so far, another to add to the list!

Denise Phillipson (née Milburn)

I also married my boyfriend who was at Clare College and two years above. I met him at a Cruising Club outing the day after Dame Rosemary Murray in her introduction to Cambridge warned us of the predatory nature of the Third Years! Obviously, I didn't heed the advice.

Jan Sherman (née Phillips)

And, the Mr Whitham here is a Fitzwilliam man.

Sue Whitham (née Addison)

New Hall was a good place to start out. I ended up with a bunch of people whose surnames also began with 'B' on the B staircase. Some became life-long friends – I share an allotment with two of them.

And in 1971, introduced by one of those 'B's, I met my future husband, although we didn't start going out until he'd left. We married in 1976 and lived eventfully ever after.

Virginia Beardshaw

My boyfriend was from St Catharine's. We have been married for 47 years this summer so you can add me to the growing list of inter college partnerships.

Angela Bailey (née Webster)

I met my husband, John, fairly early during my time in Cambridge, he was in his final year at Selwyn, studying Economics. We started "going out" during my second term in Cambridge and quickly discovered a shared love of walking, spending a week of the Easter holidays walking a section of the Pennine Way. John then spent a year following a post-graduate course at Edinburgh University, and yes, it did seem a little as though he might be trying to get away from me but we decided that it would be "make or break" for our relationship. He showed his commitment during the first term of that year by travelling down to Cambridge by overnight train from Edinburgh. The highlight of his return journey was the need to request that the train, a mainline service, stop at Peterborough to allow him to board. Our relationship survived the year, and we were married a couple of months after my graduation.

Dorothy Cade (née Clark)

My boyfriend at the time was at St John's College - but I didn't find the husband for another 10 years.

Sarah Watson (née Henley)

I didn't marry my long-standing boyfriend from Queens' College; marriage came later through work!

Pauline Whitney (née Micklam)

My boyfriend at the time was at St John's, but I didn't find the husband for another 10 years...

I actually met my husband to be when answering a desperate plea from a friend who burst in while we were eating, to go and help out with the make-up down at John's where they were putting on Aristophanes' The Gods. My future husband had been roped in to be the philosopher because that's what he was reading. We made life-time friendships, with women and men, often formed within the first few days or weeks of term.

Siân Crisp (née Jenkins)

I too found a husband. He was at St John's, a fellow mature student who had done Part 1 of his degree in 1939, but then joined up and stayed in the army until he retired in 1971 when he returned to complete his degree, just for the interest. We married at the end of my second year and lived for a year in the semi-basement flat of Merton House, on the edge of St John's grounds. He was twice my age and, predictably, some people thought I was mad, but after our marriage in St John's Chapel in 1973 we achieved 41 years and two sons together before he died aged 95, active almost to the end.

Sarah Wilson (née Stallard)

I met John, my partner, who edited Broadsheet so introduced me to student journalism.

Ros Coward

I married a barrister, who became a judge and is now retired. We must be very unusual in not having met at Cambridge. He and Wendy Joseph were colleagues at the Old Bailey, which meant that she and I could reconnect after a gap of many years. My husband and I have lived for forty years in north-east Northamptonshire, have two children, four grandchildren and a cocker spaniel.

Ursula Wide (née Buchan)

That very first term I was in a cage outside the Squire Law Library, demonstrating on behalf of I think Amnesty, with I think Di Hills. A couple of lawyers from St Catharine's came over to mock us, but then realised we had already been briefly introduced a few days earlier, and so became very gallant, plying me with hot soup and sandwiches and chocolate, which was very embarrassing, completely missed the point of the demonstration, and irritated my new radical friends. However, reader, I married him, and I am still married to him.

Fiona Edwards-Stuart (née Weaver)

I was persuaded to come to New Hall by having already found a boyfriend who was at Peterhouse (we've now been married 46 years).

Wendy Spray (née Coulson)

I was struck by how many of you met your life partners in Cambridge, often leading to long (and hopefully happy) marriages/family etc. When you think about it, it's quite a tall order leaving school and going to university to study, while the hormones are champing at the bit and confusing the whole picture, isn't it? I didn't meet my husband at Cambridge, in fact I married much later, and remain happily sharing my life with the same lovely and interesting man. My aunty had a set of 1920s cocktail mats with little sayings on either side, I always remember one which, on the first side (pre-cocktail) was written "Marriage is a great institution…" and then after your cocktail, you'd turn over the mat and it said, "but who wants to live in an institution?" I always loved that! I was most definitely not seeking a husband. I agreed with that cocktail mat, but looking for love was a different matter and of course with sex on the menu too, well no wonder life after a strict school was so, well, different! And confusing! An all-girls school left me completely unprepared for the ups and downs and emotional catastrophes of the 'real' world of relationships. Who doesn't remember first love, but who doesn't also remember the pain of first rejection!

Lou Radford

I spent time studying in the wonderful light filled music library on the ground floor of the University Library. One afternoon in the summer of 1973 I was queueing in the tea room and fell into conversation with a friend, Andrew Cahn. We discovered that we both wanted to tour the USA that summer but had no one to travel with. We teamed up, found that we got on really well and have stayed together from that day to this.

Virginia Beardshaw

The freedom we had at New Hall and across Cambridge was extraordinary. I met so many fascinating and clever people from across the UK, and beyond, and New Hall was full of interesting folk. I had no regrets about coming to New Hall, apart from the fact that it had a somewhat dull name which got confused with Newnham. Like so many of us, I fell in love and met my husband at Cambridge. Conveniently, Henry was at John's. Like me, Henry hailed from Norfolk, but unlike most of us, he had actually gone round the world in his gap year. In anticipation of studying Arch. & Anth, (Archaeology and Anthropology) he had been to Samoa, Fiji and New Zealand! That was incredibly exotic back then.

Charlotte Crawley (née Miller)

Sexual behaviour was very different then from the previous generation and from now. We were in that period of sexual liberation, but I, for one, didn't quite know how to handle it, though I thought I did. In my first few weeks I lost my virginity in a very unedifying manner, which today might be considered as sexual predation if not rape. I was not entirely innocent, but it was not what I was expecting or wanting, and I didn't manage to extricate myself in time. After that I determined to take control of my own contraception so that whatever happened, I would not be at risk of unwanted pregnancy. I first tried a doctor who wanted to know whether I was in a long-term relationship, whether I was intending to get married etc. and refused to give me the pill. I think to be fair, doctors were not allowed to prescribe the pill on the National Health Service to unmarried girls. It was rather humiliating. I then found out about the Brook Advisory Centre which was in King Street. These centres were a forward-looking answer to the constraints of the family planning policy of the NHS and had been specifically set up to give contraceptive advice to young single people under the age of 25. The centre in Cambridge was well used.

Like others, in my second year, I met my future husband. He was an archaeologist who had just embarked on a PhD. It was ok at first and I joined him on excavations where he was supervising or directing in all my vacations. The relationship became very intense, and I gradually lost a number of my friends. I did, however, marry him in 1974 but it was not to last.

Diana Murray (née Collyer)

I was another who met my future husband, Jules Mott now known as Henry, at Cambridge. We met in the second term, in a very dull maths lecture where I was diverted by his charming smile as he handed me the next handout, and later by his amusing cartoons drawn to while away the hour! Coffee back at Sidney Sussex followed, and we still have the chipped mug he accidentally gave me! Our first date was at the Union Society when Lord Longford was the speaker.

Jane Mott (née Style)

Perhaps because I had not taken a gap year I was nowhere near ready to commit to a permanent relationship at Cambridge, but had several boyfriends from very different backgrounds, by which I mean serially of course, though if you remember that in was the pre-HIV era, it was our morals alone then that kept us on the relatively straight and narrow. I think the relationship with other students at New Hall is shown by this email trail: I have not been in contact with most of you for nearly half a century, but I feel a great accord with your writings, and look forward to meeting again because I know we have a great deal in common.

There wasn't a great college-centred feeling at the time, but I think we were, and are, prepared to help each other.

Sally Morgan

Relationships: Too many, which was not good for me. One of the downsides of being at a university where men so heavily outnumbered women.

Gillian Blessley

Cycling

I loved cycling down to lectures past the chimneys of Trinity Lane lurking through the mists. We used to judge whether we had been starving ourselves too much – worried about spending in the first few weeks – by whether we could cycle all the way back up Castle Hill.

Siân Crisp (née Jenkins)

Castle Hill was a struggle on my ancient and heavy bike, especially as I had a penchant for Fitzbillies Chelsea buns.

Deborah Glass

Cycling. Like most students my bike was the major means of transport. I was tickled by the (obvious) need to have it registered. My number was NH 620 and I left it on my mudguard for years afterwards. One day, when cycling to the UL laden down with a basket full of books, I was lucky not to have been killed. My specs had broken in half the week before and I had taped the pieces back together with Elastoplast – great look! – whilst waiting for a new pair. As I rode along I realised the Elastoplast was failing and the specs were sagging down my face. I was in the process of turning right when they fell off and I nearly ran into a car, which screeched to a halt. I apologised profusely to the driver and he was amazingly nice about it all. A narrow escape for me; another pesky student on a bike for him!
I also remember someone hauling a bike – not mine – onto the roof of New Hall during Rag Week.

Anne Muir (née Borrett)

Cambridge was a beautiful town as well, a lovely place to grow up in. A novice cyclist, I found Magdalene Street rather intimidating, and went along the Backs to the Seeley rather than through the town.

Fiona Edwards-Stuart (née Weaver)

When I arrived someone suggested getting a bike from the police auction. I got a heavy old Raleigh for £10. Once it was stolen, and I had to get to one of the outlying villages to rescue it when the police told me it had been found. However the real insult was when my lock (a combination) was stolen but not the bike. Several years after I left someone offered me £10 for the bike, so I felt that I had got my money's worth.

Pam Hilton

I have vivid memories of the high speed, death defying bike ride down the hill with a somewhat slower return.

Ros Coward

I also cycled a lot in my first year of course (as I was living in New Hall) and enjoyed cycling out into the countryside to the west and south of Cambridge for a bit of fresh air.

Helen Morton

Cycling was so much part of the Cambridge experience: King's Parade jammed with bikes going to 9 o'clock lectures, the wind always against us going up Castle Hill, but so thankful we didn't have to go all the way to Girton!
I don't remember damaging the hems of my flared trousers so I think I must have worn cycle clips or tucked them into my socks. I also had a skirt protector on the back wheel and did cycle in a long skirt. And probably a short one too with one hand holding it down!

Jane Mott (née Style)

I spent my third year back in New Hall, in my own room on the ground floor and was happy to rediscover walking into town through gardens to Storey's Way and across the playing fields to the Backs and cycling up and down Castle Hill, with my books and shopping precariously stacked in the unbalanced bag on the back of my Raleigh Shopper bike, catching the hems of my flared jeans or my long (homemade) Laura Ashley skirts in the chain.

Mary Anne Bonney

I was quite worried about overspending the money that I had and tried very hard to keep accounts, I'm still not very good at it. I do remember thinking that taxis were a huge luxury and not in my league of expenditure. On one occasion, it must have been in my first term, I remember manhandling a trunk all the way from the station by balancing it on my bike. Pushing it up Castle Hill nearly killed me.

Diana Murray (née Collyer)

Cycling back up Castle Hill late at night at full speed to get back before midnight. Always tricky when the men's colleges chucked guests out at 2am. I always found cycling up the hill exhausting at whatever time of day. I still live in Cambridge and sometimes still cycle up the hill; it's still exhausting but I never ever do it at midnight now.

Alison Litherland (née Hill)

In the second year of my first term, I was having a race down Castle Hill with two chaps - they were on foot and I was on my bike. They tried to bar my way to stop me and I collided with them and broke my right wrist - so I then had the next six weeks in plaster. A real pain, especially as it was the time of the black outs. One of the boys, Simon, felt so guilty that he kept bringing me up beautiful bouquets of flowers.

Rosemary Grande (née Temple)

I didn't own a bike during my first term in Cambridge and among my friends had a certain reputation for walking everywhere, including one cold day, to afternoon tea at Homerton. (I'd ridden a friend's bike occasionally during the first couple of years at secondary school but I think my parents had been loath to encourage me as my best friend at primary school in Sheffield was almost killed at the age of six when a lorry rolled back on to her bike while she was out cycling with her Dad.)

During the Christmas vacation I managed to convince my Mum that I needed a bike and she said that she knew someone who might have an unwanted bike. One day in February the second-hand bike arrived at the Porters' Lodge and the following Saturday afternoon I might have been observed in the road round the back of college doing my best to ride a few yards without falling off! I soon got the hang of it and joined the masses riding up and down Castle Hill for nine o'clock lectures and doing my best to get to the top of the hill without getting off later in the day. Just before the Easter vacation my new boyfriend (now my husband) suggested that, now I had a bike, we ride over to watch The Bumps. All went well until going round a roundabout I was spooked by a van on my outside, wobbled and we both ended up in heap, luckily on the pavement (or verge?) side of the road. Handlebars straightened, we continued on our way. My only other mishap was, in a later year, riding one evening along the road in front of King's College with a male on either side. As we chatted they both turned inwards but travelled on leaving me wobbling to a heap in the road. Thank goodness there wasn't the traffic there is now and they did realise and wait for me to pick myself up!

I loved my bike and the freedom it gave me. The thrill of speeding down from college to lectures, a supervision or one of the other colleges. I convinced my then boyfriend to cycle to Huntingdon and back one Saturday afternoon - something I think I felt happier about than he did! My trusty bike was used in Cambridge and at home for the rest of my three years. A really valuable skill learnt and perfected in Cambridge!!

Dorothy Cade (née Clark)

I had a nasty cycling accident in my first term, turning right out of New Hall onto the Huntingdon Road during rush hour on a rainy November evening. I did not see a motorcyclist coming up fast in the middle of road between lanes, and he did not see me. He hit my rear wheel, narrowly avoiding my leg. I did a dramatic somersault and landed flat on my back in the road near the opposite kerb. Mercifully no car hit me either, and I escaped with only a few bruises. I was taken to the medical room at New Hall and my parents were summoned from London. I suppose I was in shock but remember thinking everyone was making a fuss about nothing! After that I think I made the extra effort of walking my bike to the pedestrian crossing when leaving New Hall after dark, but don't think the experience made me a more cautious cyclist otherwise!

We were teenagers, and therefore immortal. Brakes were often not well maintained. I cannot forget the regular spectacle of hordes of bikes descending Castle Hill for morning lectures, red traffic lights at Kettle's Yard, and several people bracing their feet to the road to supplement their faulty brakes!

Bikes were frequently stolen, and often abandoned at the train station. Combination locks were easily hacked. At one point I had a bike stolen. A few weeks later I made a day trip to London and found my bike at Cambridge station, and happily stole it back again!

Gillian Blessley

To me it was one of the joys of Cambridge that everywhere was so easily commutable by bike, even by my second-hand, 3 gears only variety. I had never previously owned one at all, and there were of course no helmets, or knee pads. Others have mentioned flared trousers, but I also had to contend with Oxford bags, long and flared skirts, and platform soled clogs: 3" of cork to manoeuvre onto the pedal. I still marvel that I didn't fall off more than I did. My particular nightmare was coming out from a 9am Maths for Scientists lecture in DAMTP, and as everyone was rushing to the Downing site a huge phalanx of cycles would emerge from Mill Lane and turn onto Trumpington Street, with absolutely no room to wobble as you set off, and complete ignominy if you did knock into someone else. I had no idea how to mend a puncture, and I think back with shame of taking advantage of my roommate's engineer friend, who obligingly dealt with my bike problems, and yet we evermore called him Mike the Bike...

Sally Morgan

Food

Learning to cook on one electric ring with Katherine Whitehorn [*Cooking in a Bedsitter*]; she said you could use any vegetables to make a vegetable curry –we came back with Brussel sprouts from the Market and proved it's not true. A friend's bedder taught us how to make watercress soup: pour a glass of whisky, discard the watercress... We did have a surfeit of Fen delicacies – celery and rabbit - in Hall.

Siân Crisp (née Jenkins)

New Hall room showing sink and electric ring.

We had grants, and parental contributions, but money always seemed tight. I went into Hall for the first evening, but I thought that this would cost too much money as a regular practice. Lunches in Hall also didn't seem worth it, but breakfasts.... You paid for breakfasts for the whole term, and it wasn't very much, if you managed to get up and actually eat them.... Well, I did, and fed well each morning. The college had been paid for a certain amount of food, and so provided it, even though the numbers eating it decreased throughout the term. There was a fair amount of choice, and nothing to stop you eating everything rather than choosing, or going back for more, or, indeed, taking away rolls or yoghurts to eat later.

I skipped lunch after such a large breakfast. I taught myself to cook, from Katharine Whitehorn's *Cooking in a Bedsitter*. The cooking equipment was a single electric ring supplied in the room, which took ages to heat up. There were fridges in the corridors, but I stopped using those after my food got stolen.

Jo Edkins (née Dibblee)

I do remember the big fridges at the top of the staircases and their disadvantages. I decided to store cold items on the windowsill after I "lost" some food. My brother and his friend came to visit me and I tried to impress them by buying lots of cheeses and cold meats from Sainsbury's and made chocolate mousses, all of which I put in the fridge. Unfortunately when I came to serve the feast everything had gone but the empty ramekin dishes were still there! It turned out well though as I was treated to lunch at The Anchor instead. I hardly ever ate in The Dome as like most people my budget was limited. I tried to manage with the one ring in the room using a book called *The Paupers' Cookbook* by Jocasta Innes which I still have. After I met my boyfriend/husband to be we cooked together in a proper kitchen in Clare

Jan Sherman (née Phillips)

I came to New Hall knowing nothing about cooking. I think my room mate recommended KatharineWhitehorn's *Cooking in a Bedsitter* and I learned a few simple recipes from there (well, I say a few. I think I lived on cauliflower cheese and spaghetti bolognaise).

Alison Litherland (née Hill)

The solo cooking ring in every room was a gadget which I relished and I loved experimenting with recipes. I've lost my *Cooking in a Bedsitter*, but still sometimes use my 1971 copy of *Poor Cook* by Caroline Conran & Susan Campbell. Making new friends was one of the best bits of year one, and then offering them some rather basic supper seemed immensely exciting.

Charlotte Crawley (née Miller)

Particular memories include the market – especially the cheese stall and the flowers. The Chelsea buns from Fitzbillies were delicious and I loved exploring the restaurants on the few occasions I ate out. Breakfasts at New Hall were wonderful as were the rolls and yoghurts we took for lunch. Sunday night dinners were also a grand occasion and often led to competition, particularly amongst the male guests, as to who could get the most food on to their plates. Mostly I cooked on the two ring electric stove in my room using the Paupers cook book.

Karen Greenwood

The breakfasts cost £7 a term and like many others, I made the most of them, always taking a bread role to munch at lunchtime.

Sarah Watson (née Henley)

I remember the Sunday salads in hall. The fen celery still seems special. I used to take a fresh bread roll and a carton of milk from breakfast for my lunch most days. Recently I discovered a Vietnamese bakery near me which produced dinner rolls that have exactly the taste and texture that I remember. Excellent!

Deborah Glass

Although I always had breakfast in college as it was good value and for me it was wise to have a motive to get up in the mornings! - and like most people regularly attended Sunday suppers, I mostly learned to produce a limited number of dishes which would cook on a single ring in my first couple of years, and became slightly more adventurous in my year in Fountains Court.

Denise Phillipson (née Milburn)

I also remember queuing for groceries at various counters around Sainsbury's before it became a self-service supermarket. I might be romanticising my memory but I recall a comfortably old-fashioned feel to the place.

Sue Attridge (née Wood)

I remember that strange New Hall smell of cork and cooked food, and the space station serving hatch in the dining hall.

Ros Coward

I remember my friend particularly liked Blue Mountain coffee that we bought in a lovely coffee shop in town. We liked the BBQ pork dish from the Chinese take away to the south of town.

Joanna Watts (née Sloper)

Even though I'd always cooked at home, my improved cookery skills, learned as an au pair, were put to good use at Cambridge for cheap meals, cooking for friends (despite the one hot plate) teaching fellow students, mostly men to cook, and contributing a home-made cake to parties. It certainly helped to eke out the grant money supplemented by delivering Christmas post.

Jane Dottridge (née Rooke)

Food: Scotch eggs you could buy at the cafeteria on the Sidgwick Site, the free-for-all eat-as-much as-you-can once-a-week at college, the cheese counter in Sainsbury's with more cheese than I had ever seen before and no money to buy it with ...

Wendy Joseph

I made a lot of omelettes and spaghetti bolognese and sometimes The Dish, which was a very nice stew out of Katharine Whitehorn's *Cooking in a bedsitter*. Sometimes in my room and sometimes at Sidney Sussex with my boyfriend. From Sidney we used to frequent the Corner House where on Tuesdays and Thursdays you could have a delicious moussaka for 35p with chips but unfortunately slices of potato instead of aubergines. For a proper moussaka with aubergines in it and rice you had to go to the Eros I think, and spend at least 50p. Occasionally I got to go to Formal Hall at Sidney, where grace was said in Latin. The best was the Sunday evening buffet in the Dome at New Hall though.

Jane Mott (née Style)

I rarely ate in hall partly because of our timetable and partly because I enjoy cooking. My New Hall friends cooked and shared meals with me: Isabel introduced me to cooking spaghetti that was not out of a tin; Alison prepared interesting dishes such as kedgeree and ratatouille and Maryla baked something really tasty using tinned mackerel.

Hilary Martin

I remember a very nice Greek restaurant called Eros, in Petty Cury off Market Square on the first floor which was a very popular place to go to with my friends. Plus lots of pubs, especially the ones on the river.

Helen Morton

My parents took me up to New Hall the first year, I couldn't wait for them to leave, especially after my father remarked loudly, looking at the college "Humph. looks like a public lavatory". This was after a very late lunch at the Eros upstairs on Petty Cury, chips peas and toms with everything - 36p for the cheapest item on the menu, Spaghetti Neapolitan.

Deborah Glass

Mostly I cooked in my room in the first year. Eros was an occasional treat, mostly at lunchtime as it was cheaper – I'd never previously come across moussaka. There was also an Italian place on a back street which had as the first item on the menu 'spaghetti without chips' I never ventured to the exotic 'spaghetti with chips' which came more expensively further down and sounded terrible. In the second year we had a shared cooking rota in the house I was in – the hobby of one of the people was cordon bleu cookery, so we did very well every fifth day, rather less so the others.

Pam Hilton

Someone mentioned Eros in Petty Cury. I do remember the moussaka from there. The sailing team used to entertain rival teams there after matches and it was the first time I had eaten such "exotic" food.

Jan Sherman (née Phillips)

I only spent one year in College, and usually managed to get lunch in one of the other colleges or very occasionally the Mill; after that I shared a flat near Parker's Piece, with Ursula Buchan and Emily Smith, which we found for ourselves without help from college. I don't remember breakfasts at all. I can't have gone to them. I remember regularly sharing a Mars Bar and a coffee with Ursula in the Seeley, and the cheese scones in the UL. Shopping in the market stalls. I remember seeing a group of Chinese tourists in Mao uniforms taking photos of the bread queue outside Fitzbillies. I think the fact that we were not obliged to always eat in Hall, (were meal tickets optional or restricted, I can't remember), also helped us to be more outward looking than many of the other colleges, although it probably meant we dispersed more quickly as a group. As a guest in any of the male colleges' formal hall, you could fall into conversation with anyone. Our JCR was very dull, until Charlotte Miller (now Crawley) took it over.

Fiona Edwards-Stuart (née Weaver)

When Sue Addison (Whitham) and I shared a room in the first year, we cooked some appalling meals (hope you don't mind me saying so, Sue). Inviting a couple of people to dinner in our first term, we opted (in our sophisticated way) for doing Vesta Chicken Curry. The problem was that we needed 2 packets for 4 people (one packet served 2) and, never having done this before, we debated whether having twice the amount meant that we had to cook the packets of rice in the same saucepan for twice as long... and made the wrong decision. I also remember an attempt at a stew and going to the butcher halfway down Castle Hill to ask how much meat we'd need. He supplied the agreed amount and we added veg and set it to cook on the ring...but had little idea of how long stewing meat would take to cook. The result was horribly chewy (even the veg). And eggs went off too soon because of the underfloor heating. Acquisition of *Cooking in a Bedsit* and a student cookbook sold by another university (Warwick?) was a step forward. Presumably we did occasionally cook something edible. Pancakes, I think?

In the 2nd and 3rd years, in Neville House on Thompson's Lane, Sue Wood (Attridge) introduced me to the decadence of duck pate, a real treat, bought in small quantities from the deli opposite John's. We cooked together often, but would tend to cook the same thing until we could bear it no more. Much experimenting with, I think, something resembling a jumbled up Spanish omelette and a rice dish with peas (copied from our stay with Sue's French friends) which was sometimes improved by the addition of a tin of pilchards.

Maureen Bell

I remember eating lots of sandwiches and buying small granary loaves from a bakery near St. John's. It was the best granary bread I've ever eaten and never lasted long. Towards the end of term, I'd resort to eating porridge, occasionally incorporating an egg in it for extra nutritional value. All those carbs! Thank goodness I cycled everywhere. In a later year, in Neville House, Maureen Bell and I used to cook rather haphazard risottos, with whatever we could find in the fridge. We called it 'rice mess' which sounds pretty unappealing though the results were usually quite tasty.

Sue Attridge (née Wood)

I remember cycling regularly from our Chesterton Road house to the little bakery opposite St John's to buy a warm melt-in-the-mouth soft white milk loaf or a delicious granary loaf to share with others in our house. Someone else mentioned the granary loaf from there was the best ever, and I agree - moist, malty, chewy, super flavoursome... yum!!

Lorna Robertson

I nearly always ate breakfast in hall, and enjoyed the Sunday buffet suppers, but otherwise it was mainly self-catering. I discovered that tinned mackerel and rice made a tasty combination, and was a keen market shopper, mainly for the small sweet, coxes that were plentiful in autumn. There were occasional forays to the Gardenia in Rose Crescent for a treat, Tesco's was good for over-ripe exotic fruit and Arjuna for wholefoods.

Mary Anne Bonney

Urgh Omelettes and coleslaw were our standby evening meal. When entertaining, we rose to the dizzy heights of beef stroganoff with rice. The recipe was amazingly quick and easy, chopped beef, a carton of yoghurt, a tin of Campbell's condensed mushroom soup and a spoonful of tomato puree (or possibly ketchup). So tasty. At one time, I resorted to cooking up heart (never to be repeated) and also had a few weeks of 'black pudding' - I had no idea what it was.
I loved dinner in the men's colleges and was also often taken to lunch in Queens' college - the days of chivalry. My friend would push my bike and carry my books too.

Rosemary Grande (née Temple)

Because I didn't have my interview until May I was first told I would have to arrange my own accommodation, but then I was offered a room in Beaufort House, the college property across the garden in the corner of Storey's Way, by the back entrance to Fitzwilliam. I kept the same room for two years and it was quite adequate with a washbasin and gas ring as well as gas fire. There was a communal bathroom and a kitchen with electric cooker and fridge, but that was really the domain of Maureen Whittaker, a college secretary who had a bedroom and sitting room. A friend gave me a multi-steamer and I got quite proficient at cooking fish and several vegetables over the one gas ring, but actually in the evening I think I usually had soup or a boiled egg, having filled up with lunch in the University Graduate Centre, the one perk allowed to Mature Students. There was a posh restaurant, but the food in the canteen was subsidised and very good value. It was also handy in second and third years, being just along from the Land Economy lecture room and library in Laundress Lane. I still went there in my last year after I was married and living in Merton House belonging to St. John's where my husband rented the semi-basement flat and then I cooked in the evening (devoted little wifey, but he did always do the washing up!).

Sarah Wilson (née Stallard)

My memory is that the lunches in college were really good value. If I didn't need to stay in the centre for a supervision or meeting someone I'd feast on the display under the dome. Think it was the first time that I'd encountered sweet corn and the combination with chicken drumsticks is a lasting memory. Otherwise, apart from the occasional meal out or when a group of us cooked for each other in our final year in the house in Thompson Lane, I generally catered for myself. Cambridge market was great source of fresh food (celery still covered in dirt straight from the fens), topped up by trips to Tesco or Sainsbury's all precariously balanced on the handlebars.

Dorothy Cade (née Clark)

After a Biochemistry practical assaying vitamin C levels in a white cabbage, I frugally carried the 95% intact cabbage back to college with me for supper. I had no carrier on my bike, so this had to be done with one hand for the cabbage and one for the bike.
For some reason we were convinced the price per unit of alcohol was least for ginger wine, so would stop on cold winter evenings half way up Castle Hill at a pub that served it. I have never touched it since. Philippa and I had a joint birthday tea party one year, and I am astonished that I thought I could cook a cake for this. Luckily both

Philippa and friends obliged, and by the end of the party the whole function room was still full of sticky cakes and sticky people as everyone else at New Hall rolled up with delightful cakes, scones, etc.. Apart from the pleasure of watching the servery rise up through the floor in the NH dining room, the breakfasts were a great idea; Miss Murray, of course, set them up to ensure we all went off to work on a good meal. Did I really eat cereal, prunes with yoghurt (still a favourite), bacon and eggs, toast and coffee every morning? Yes.

Sally Morgan

I shopped in the market, and I too fondly remember the celery with black soil direct from the Fens. I also bought rabbit from the market and made stews. There was a health food shop called Arjuna on Mill Road which I think was started by some recent graduates, and where I often shopped. Originally they had a big cheddar wheel displayed on a wooden chopping board, and would cut pieces off to order with a big kitchen knife. One day the board and knife had been replaced by a wire and ceramic cutter such as you would see at Sainsbury's, which was much less appealing. Apparently the Health Inspector had decided the wooden board and knife were unsanitary. This sticks in my mind, since we have subsequently been told that wooden chopping boards have antibacterial properties and are actually safer than plastic ones.

Gillian Blessley

This was the era when Councils went about razing neighbourhoods to the ground to build modern housing, multi-storey car parks and shopping centres. To them, the Kite looked ripe for redevelopment. A hotly contested plan was produced for it. The fight over its implementation resulted in planning blight which meant its streets were locked in a 1950s time warp. There was a corner grocer's at the end of Warkworth Street with a huge bacon slicer where they would adjust the thickness of the rashers to your precise requirements. This kind of shop was vanishing fast in the rest of the country. There was also the Free Press, a tiny pub in Prospect Row round the corner from Warkworth

Street, with a cosy snug where we sometimes went of an evening. All plush covered furnishings and mirrors. There were also junk shops where I ferreted out treasures. I still have a pair of pretty blue pottery arts and crafts vases I bought in one of them.

Virginia Beardshaw

We rarely went out to eat - I think meals featured less strongly than they might today. Mine changed yearly alongside my accommodation. First year - lentils boiling over on my electric ring; the wet smell of scrambled eggs on that rising servery at breakfast; Lou Radford's lovely omelettes to cure all-comers' woes. Second year in that so-called commune: collective meals, someone imposing an industrial-scale granola-making rota, and an ensuing revolt. Third year in my dreary bed-sit kitchen – various brown rice concoctions. Fourth year in my lovely all-women house –splendid salads (by others!); Holly's morning upset when her egg didn't fry just right. Oh, and a weekend of stale crusts alone in Oxford, having spent my last pennies on a second-hand LP of Bach Preludes (I suspect some romantic posing there).

Helen Mayer

Clothes

I can still remember the outfit that I wore (at my New Hall interview) so clearly, as I had sewed it. A lovely Vogue pattern sewn in bottle green baby fine corduroy. Reminds us how money was tight and we often made our clothes. This was obviously my one 'smart' outfit. I wore it to a school friend's wedding which was in 1974, so four years after my interview.

I can still remember the few clothes I wore at Cambridge clearly. A gold and cream coloured striped, rather tight polo neck jumper. I must have looked like a wasp. Some very elegant (although I say it myself), just below the knee home-made corduroy skirts, knee length brown suede boots, Loons, my sisters beautiful floor length red check wool coat, lots of people in moth-eaten fur coats, floor-length flowery skirts which were dreadful for getting caught in bike chains, home-made thin cotton ball dresses for May Balls.

Rosemary Grande (née Temple)

I was interviewed by Kate Belsy and another young woman (whose name I don't remember) both of whom were not only casually dressed but were wearing jeans. I remember feeling simultaneously disconcerted and relieved.

Sue Attridge (née Wood)

I remember exactly what I wore for my New Hall interview: tweed maxi skirt in heathery purple with matching coat and a Jaeger jumper in a deeper purple.

Virginia Beardshaw

Several people have mentioned what they were wearing for their interviews and I have no recollection of that, only of coveting the chestnut brown fine corduroy skirt Esther Goody (the interviewer) was wearing.

Sarah Wilson (née Stallard)

I remember at a play at Churchill, I met the actors afterwards and one of them was wearing a long yellow dress made out of a striped Indian bedspread. I admired it and she agreed to swap dresses with me. I was wearing a red Indian kaftan. I loved that dress and kept it for many years until my mother decided to clear out my wardrobe in my absence and threw it away.

Penny Stirling

For my New Hall interview, I wore a green tweed suit that I had made myself (why green I will never know as it is a colour that really does not suit me).
Brian, our tutor, led us on a field trip to Wessex – Stonehenge, Avebury, Silbury Hill, and Glastonbury. I recall that we got quite tiddly on cider, which we were not expecting to be so strong, and having to sleep in the bus because no-one had bothered to tell some of us that we needed to book up accommodation. At the time I was wearing long skirts and floaty blouses, long hair and, more often than not, bare feet. Very Hippy. I was thrown out of a café in Glastonbury for not wearing shoes.

Diana Murray (née Collyer)

At my interview I wore a lemon yellow Donegal tweed dress with a matching tailored jacket, which I made specifically for university interviews. They didn't get much use afterwards!
I made almost all my clothes myself. I had some orange and black bell bottom trousers made from a William Morris curtain fabric purchased at Liberty's. My first yearmaster at the Architecture School thought that these were very cool, partly because he owned a jacket made of William Morris fabric himself! I have always hated wearing skirts but those were de rigueur in those immediately post flower child days, so I made a long flowery skirt with ruffles at the bottom which I wore much of the summer. Jeans were a bit of an extravagance, but patched jeans became fashionable. I had a pair that lasted me about eight or nine

years, patched when they wore out, and then patched again over the patches. I finally had to burn them after a camping trip to France where I picked up a (human) flea in a public bathhouse. There were too many places in my jeans for a flea to hang out!

I went barefoot one summer term, but gave up after a few weeks when my feet cracked horribly.

Several of the male students wore Afghan sheepskin coats that had the fleece on the inside and were elaborately embroidered on the outside. I don't recall that women ever wore them. In winter I wore the standard boiled wool duffel coat, but also later on my mother's hand-me-down fur coat.

Indian hand printed cotton bedspreads were all the rage. There was an Oxfam shop at the bottom of St. Andrews Street that sold them. The usual price was £1. I lusted after a particularly beautiful dark red one costing £2, which seemed a frightful extravagance. It took me a few days but I finally bought it, and never regretted the decision. I would still be using it if I had taken more care washing it, but it acquired holes.

Gillian Blessley

And what did we all wear? Freed from the constraints of school uniform, I bought several pairs of brightly coloured Loons (which soon developed oily ripped bottoms where they caught in my bike chain) and a couple of long patchwork skirts (also sadly bike chain fodder).

Angela Bailey (née Webster)

I had a pair of clogs that I was very fond of wearing with a long skirt. One clog fell off as I was turning in front of Johns on my bicycle. Fortunately not much traffic as I retrieved it unscathed but with a face as red as the clog.

I had made myself a yellow jacket (that my daughter now wears) which I wore with some yellow loons (a fiver as I remember, my whole weekly allowance). While in this outfit, outside the Natural History Museum, waiting for a lecture, a Porter told me that I reminded him of a hymn he used to sing in Sunday School... 'Jesus wants me for a Sunbeam'!

Deborah Glass

I had absolutely no money for clothes, and no idea about them anyway. I had always wanted to wear Levis but they just didn't fit my shape, I think the expression is "too high in the waist"! I wore an Indian bedspread type long dress a lot and mercifully have no photographic evidence of that. I think I wore a lot of big jumpers and long skirts, completely impractical for the bike of course. I was saved from being a complete sartorial train wreck by a French friend who was pregnant and gave me her hand-me-downs, and I became more chic!

Lou Radford

I knitted myself (with king size knitting needles and very thick maroon wool) a scarf to wear on my bike at Cambridge. It was so long that I could wind it round many times. It WAS cold. I also bought an old black lacy dress from the market which was cut on the bias and hung beautifully. It was very fragile and required frequent mending. I had a long white and green summer dress which I decided to wear while punting; inevitably it did not stay white very long...

Joanna Watts (née Sloper)

My school uniform was grey (in the psychedelic coloured sixties!) and then there was "dress smartly at work" for six months. Skirts were compulsory for both. So at New Hall, I was delighted that no-one cared what I wore, and I spent the entire time in trousers. One pair were red, I remember. Other clothes were strictly functional. The thickest coat I could find, and sheepskin mittens from the Market. These were not a luxury - I wore them while trying to take notes in Maths lectures in an unheated room with doors open to the bitter Cambridge winter.
Trousers were better than skirts for bikes, of course (in the sixties I tried to bike in a mini-skirt, and it ended up round my waist!) but these

trousers were flared, or even bell-bottomed, and they suffered from getting caught in the chain. Ragged trouser bottoms were common.

Jo Edkins (née Dibblee)

The early 70s were not a high point for fashion ... but
Does anyone else remember a little shop tucked away in the streets behind Castle Hill, on the way to the church which is now part of Kettle's Yard? It was on my frequent route between New Hall and St John's where I was in a couple of plays and where my boyfriend was a student.

The shop sold hippy-ish smocks - a real early 70s fashion item - made out of Liberty-type material or possibly even out of old dresses and aprons. I loved them and had a couple which I wore over the proverbial bell-bottomed jeans which, as many people remember, had the inconvenient habit of getting tangled up in bicycle chains. I once had to borrow a pair of scissors from a shop in the town centre in order to free myself.

The shop survived for a few years after we all graduated - I used to spend quite a bit of time in Cambridge when I lived in London and retraced those steps often. Then on one visit I saw that it was no longer there. There is something about that unique little shop that crystallizes my memories of that first year at New Hall.

It is fascinating what different people remember of the same time - Lorna Robertson remembers that she and I swapped winter coats for a while, but I have no memory of that!

Nicola King (née Brown)

I had a small room of my own on G staircase, which was great during power cuts, as it warmed up very quickly when friends came round with candles in jam jars. The room didn't have much in it, just a narrow bed, a desk and one armchair, but we wrapped ourselves in blankets and rugs and all squeezed in to keep warm. A prized possession of mine was a cream goatskin rug from Primavera, opposite Kings, very soft for those who had to sit on the floor! I recall also trying to sew flowered triangles into the bottom of my old jeans legs to make them into bell-bottoms - not so easily done by candlelight!

The little shop selling smocks that Nicola mentions rings a bell for me - how we all loved our smocks!

Probably my favourite shop in Cambridge was the silver and leather shop on Castle Hill which I used to browse in frequently. It had the most wonderful scent of leather, and beautiful handmade silver jewellery. My purchases there were extremely rare, as I hardly ever had spare money. So I was over the moon when some New Hall friends joined forces to give me a 21st birthday gift in May 1974 of a stunning hammered silver ring necklace, still a favourite and treasured piece.

Lorna Robertson

My favourite dress was a long purple and red kaftan. Until the weather got too cold I was barefoot. I'd been to France in the summer, where my sandals broke on the first day, so I just carried on without any footwear. When the weather got too cold for bare feet it was usually desert boots, worn with the kaftan. I also had a black and white mini-kilt bought from a friend, which I teamed with a charity shop purple jumper and green woollen tights – don't ask me why! Also a pair of the inevitable bell bottoms and a smock top. I had a maxi-coat, which had been my mother's in the late forties, which I had to pin together to cycle.

Pam Hilton

I think my clothes reflected the changes in my life each year.

In my first year I almost lived in two outfits my sister had helped me to buy: a maroon Biba dress, a multi-faceted long brown and white Biba skirt and little white jumper, and long slim brown suede platform boots. In my second year I started to explore the vintage stall in the market - I still keep a rainbow-striped cardigan with maroon edging which I wore regularly over black trousers and top. I also sailed about in an ultra-light pair of platforms I'd painted luminous green – the only comfortable heels I've ever worn, and almost the last. During my difficult third year there were some flowing vintage dresses – black or flowered and rather shabby. All this time I had a mushroom of long curly hair. During the safe landing into my fourth year, I restrained it safely into pigtails and wore rather plainer trousers and tops.

Helen Mayer

It was a time of long hair, loons and long skirts. For some reason, inexplicable to me now, I went through a phase of not wearing shoes even when cycling! And of course, expanding horizons and new experiences including punting; May balls; learning to cook for myself etc

Alison Wray (née O'Brien)

I wore a terrible pair of corduroy trousers with triangles inserted to make them into flares. And a khaki jacket from the army surplus shop. And plimsolls. I used to make some of my clothes during vacations at home. Skirts were either very short or very long and I wore both sorts.

Jane Mott (née Style)

Cambridge was then, and still was in the 1980s, completely lacking in student type clothes for women. Loons from the market stall were available in an amazing array of colours, but May Ball dresses were definitely thin on the ground, and I found myself wearing the same one as at least one other woman. Another year I resorted to a rather stylish nightdress, which had a extended life as beachwear when I went with Di and Siân round Europe with an Interrail ticket - I think it was the very first year such a thing was available, and we went everywhere, specialising in longer trips overnight to save on hotel bills and covering all the countries which were then open (in the Iron curtain period of course, and even Spain was a bit uncertain!) We had some rigorous discussions en route, fuelled by my book (Alvin Toffler - Future Shock), which I have never finished as one of them threw it out of the window to curtail the discussions! Not a very NH approach.

Sally Morgan

Instead of intense studying, I threw myself into college and university life. Cambridge was just brimming with so many things to sample, and I know I was like a child in a sweetshop – dazzled by choice and exciting opportunities.

There were plenty of challenges. After our first month, I managed to irrevocably shrink four jerseys and cardigans in the college Laundry. I had done virtually zero washing of clothes, so that was an expensive lesson in how not to wash wool garments.

Charlotte Crawley (née Miller)

Punting

My first punting trip was in the first few days of the first term with a young man who was very keen to impress us. Unfortunately, the pole stuck in the mud by St John's College; he held on to the pole as the boat continued and was slowly lowered into the water. When he struggled out onto the bank, his home knitted jumper sagged way below his knees and he never spoke to us again.

Siân Crisp (née Jenkins)

Ah! Punting! I went on the river a couple of times with friends, and I too came unstuck as I veered towards the bank and was knocked into the water by a tree! I recall going to Cats (St Catherine's College) for a cuppa afterwards and having a bath there (antique plumbing), borrowing some oversized jeans and a shirt before cycling back up the hill to New Hall. Quite an afternoon!

Anne Muir (née Borrett)

The first time I went punting was with a group of friends, and most of us couldn't punt. The pole has to be lifted vertically out of the water and then pushed downwards to push you along, but beginners tended to push sideways or even backwards. You also have to avoid the tree branches overhanging the river. One of the beginners was getting into a flap handling his pole, and we shouted to him "The tree, the tree!" He said, "What tree?" And we yelled "The pole, the pole!" and he said, "What pole?" (Yes, he got the pole stuck in the tree.)
Bridges were a problem as well. You had to get up enough speed before going under a bridge, because you couldn't use the pole once underneath. And if you lifted the pole too quickly once through, a mischievous person on the bridge could just seize the pole and take it from you, leaving you and the punt stranded.

Jo Edkins (née Dibblee)

I loved your punting story. I do hope my husband who was at Clare and two years above us didn't take your pole as you went under Clare bridge. It was a pastime of his and his friends although he insists they gave them back and no one fell into the river.

Jan Sherman (née Phillips)

I went punting with friends a lot and rather fancied my technique.

Helen Morton

Once when we were punting on the upper river, someone mentioned that it was possible to stand up in a punt, climb onto one of the foot bridges, and then climb down back into the punt again on the other side. One of those stupid things that students do.... One person in the punt promptly wanted to try this. He managed to climb onto the bridge all right, but his friend, who was punting, tried to punt as fast as possible to leave him stranded on the bridge. So the climber rapidly jumped down into the punt without looking where he was going. He landed on the shoulders of the punter! They both stood there, one on top of the other, swaying from side to side, and I really thought they were going to be OK. But no, into the river they went! They surfaced again, both blaming each other, and most annoyed at the rest of us for laughing at them.

Jo Edkins (née Dibblee)

After some good punting experiences with tall men in the first year, in my second year a group of somewhat shorter women decided on a Sunday morning to take a punt out, thinking it couldn't be that hard. We soon discovered that if you're only 5'3" there's a great deal of pole above you when you lift it up, so problems with the centre of gravity. We tacked our way embarrassingly towards Grantchester, staggering around on the end of the punt, somehow magnetically attracted towards every fisherman on the bank. We took it in turns but were all equally useless. There were audible groans as they saw us returning later and hastened to get their lines out of the water before we reached them, still proceeding bank to bank in a zigzag. Then I got a postgraduate boyfriend who had spent six years perfecting punting, with tricks such as end over end poling, using one arm only… Reader I married him (mistake).

Pam Hilton

I was very lucky that one of our group of medics (Sarah) linked up with a John's student, who had access to a college punt. In our long vac August term, we only had one subject so many afternoons were spent punting to Grantchester with picnics. I think we all learnt to punt reasonably competently, though not without unexpected swims. I don't think anyone even knew to worry about Weil's disease in those days. I will never forget the mother of one of us joining a punt trip, attired in a very smart and expensive dress. She was standing up in the boat with her hands on the college wall as the boat slowly drifted out into the water. We watched in horror as she descended frontwards into the muddy water. She had a wonderful sense of humour!

Philippa Evans (née Taylor)

I never mastered punting but had friends in Churchill who had access to Churchill's kayaks. We went kayaking down to Grantchester and would often retrieve lost punting poles for stranded souls. Sometimes this resulted in free glasses of champagne by way of thanks!

Gillian Blessley

Money

I was pretty self-reliant, able to manage my money and affairs. Talking of which, I was eligible for a full grant from the county council (remember those?) but the first instalment was late, so I had to go to ask kindly Miss Hammond what to do. She lent me £10, and told me to keep a note of my outgoings, which I always did, anyway. Meanwhile, I lived on boiled eggs cooked in my room, which must have seemed stand-offish but I couldn't afford to get into debt.

Ursula Wide (née Buchan)

Having a grant meant that I needed to take paid work only in vacations, enabling me to be a full-time student in a way which would be impossible now for young women like me.

Maureen Bell

I hardly ever ate in The Dome as like most people my budget was limited partly because Devon County Council were not very efficient at processing my grant on time.

Jan Sherman (née Phillips)

I remember my bank account being at a branch in Burton and having to have an 'arrangement' with a Cambridge branch to allow me to draw out £5 a week. I guess it must have taught me about budgeting in that I never spent very much money at one time because I couldn't. I think I felt I was frugal all the time but I never felt I was broke.
I didn't join the Union (at £12 a year it was far too expensive).

Alison Litherland (née Hill)

Tuition was paid for, but our living expenses were covered by a council grant, and parental contributions. These varied on our parents' income, but presumably we all ended up with roughly the same amount of money. It would depend on whether the parents added more (or less). My parents scrupulously handed over the precise amount, as a cheque, at the start of term, and that was it. I was an adult, wasn't I? It was up to me to make it cover everything. I managed to live within it, but I did look at every penny spent. I remember budgeting £5 a term on something I wanted, but didn't need. A book, perhaps, or a cassette tape. The rest was spent on my rent, the cheapest clothes, worn until they were in holes, and food, cooked by me because it was cheaper. Society subs, but they weren't much. Plus booze, of course, but little of that, and drunk in college bars because it was cheaper. (Night clubs? What are those?) My friends ate at the Corner House, in King Street, and I would have double fried eggs and chips, as the cheapest thing on the menu (39p, I think). Perhaps I was just mean with money!

Jo Edkins (née Dibblee)

I don't think we all ended up with 'roughly the same amount of money'. Holiday jobs were essential I do remember that, as things were very 'tight' and I remember wondering how on earth some people could afford to buy records and new (yes NEW not thrift shop!) clothes! But I did enjoy a pint and a game of darts at the local pub when I lived in Grantchester, so things weren't that bad! I did have a very small Baby Belling oven in my NH room for a time, that was great and enabled many souffléed omelettes!

Lou Radford

I lived on the standard grant, and I remember spending everything I could scrape together on clothes. I ate the Sunday buffet in college and I think there was another cheap night, I went to bread and cheese lunches associated with some society I joined and apart from that, lived on bread, curried baked beans and eggs. I don't think I ever went drinking and I used the library for books. But I did buy a wonderful second-hand coat and hat at the market, which I was very proud of, and good jeans. Does anyone else remember the Arjuna restaurant? I went there a couple of times in my last year and had my first taste of brown rice, which I thought was delicious and a dish called "oodles" which was seasonal veg au gratin. That and the UL cheese scones were part of my family cooking repertoire for years.

Penny Stirling

I had enough money to survive on but I felt many of the luxuries and outings came as a result of friendships with boys who had much more money that I had. I often hitched to places in holidays - so money must have been scarce. I hardly ever bought books but worked in libraries so I didn't need to. I just felt lucky to be in Cambridge, and never worried about not having money.
I think the prudence I developed then has stayed with me all my life. The idea of food waste, or any other sort of waste, appals me. I still use libraries lots and love them. I drive an old battered Skoda, use my daughter's 20 year old bike - I love the simple life.

Rosemary Grande (née Temple)

I was lucky enough to have almost a full grant, and my parents made up the rest so I never felt particularly short of money. For my 21st birthday I asked for a sewing machine (which I still have and it still works brilliantly, in fact rather better than the expensive all singing and dancing machine which I bought a few years ago!) and after that made many of my clothes. I found that in the long hours spent reading it was hard to stay awake so I always had some sewing on the go, and a 20 minute burst of that was enough to get my attention back on track.

Denise Phillipson (née Milburn)

I received a full grant and found the first year very hard as I had no reserve from summer work, which I had in subsequent years.

Sue Attridge (née Wood)

I think I, like a lot of people on maintenance grants, just assumed I'd make do. My parents also handed me termly cheques for the required amount and I never asked for top-ups. Having said that, when they came to visit they brought food, took me out for a meal and slipped me the odd fiver! I was generally very careful, although in the final week or two of my final year apart from my New Hall breakfast tickets, I remember surviving on apples from the market, sliced bread and edam cheese - and finally just bread and ketchup sandwiches - for which I developed quite a taste!

I also remember the Corner House and Eros as places to eat for special occasions. The Buttery at the Seeley was also a favourite re-fuelling station during revision sessions in particular. I didn't buy many clothes at all, but did buy some key books. Train fares were an expense - especially as my boyfriend, whom I went to see at least once a term, was at Sheffield University. One advantage here was that I could borrow books from Sheffield which were often more freely available due to the different syllabus.

We also had the option of student rail cards which helped a bit.

Anne Muir (née Borrett)

Finding free or at least cheap sources of food was a skill worth honing. I sang in Trinity Hall Chapel Choir for 4 years and at least one of the attractions was the free sherry plus reliably generous Sunday dinner. A parental visit every half term meant a meal out for me and a friend (usually Berni Inn) and a delivery of food supplies from home. By the end of term, though, I had usually run out of both supplies and money, and I remember once living for a few days on dry white cobs with beetroot. I liked beetroot but couldn't afford the usual cheese or butter.

(And yes, I mean 'cobs'. Now I'm further north again I can use the word and be understood. The first time I went into a baker in Cambridge and asked for some cobs I was met with blank stares. I soon learnt that 'rolls' was the word needed...)

My boyfriend once got a food box from home and at the end of term we had several days of cream crackers and marmalade. There was a place whose name I can't recall, run by a Greek Cypriot (I think) family, which was affordable and less crowded than the Eros. It might have been on King St but I really can't remember! The food was pretty much chips with everything, but exotic to me e.g. chicken chasseur, and even curry (with chips or rice). Lovely!

Maureen Bell

I couldn't have taken up my place at New Hall without the university scholarship from New Zealand, so am very grateful for that opportunity. I worked to pay for my airfare and received no other funding so I had to budget very carefully, as most of you did. I had an extra complication in that my tutor Kate Belsey had to write a letter twice a year confirming that I was still in residence and was working satisfactorily so I could claim my next instalment. I then posted the letter, which took a week to arrive in NZ, who then posted me a cheque, which took another 2 weeks usually, then I paid it into the bank and waited a week for it to clear before I could pay the bursar. Luckily he was very understanding and happy to be flexible with timing. I did point out to the funding committee that sending instalments 3 times a year to match the termly payments, instead of twice, would make life much easier for the recipient but I'm not sure if they ever took that on board. I mostly used my single ring in college to cook and looked for bargains in Sainsbury's and the market like many others. The once a week graduate dinner in college was a treat, especially with free sherry beforehand. I hardly bought any clothes but I had to buy some basic crockery and cutlery from Woolworths as I couldn't bring anything from home on the other side of the world. I still have one plate that has survived 50 years as a souvenir. As an overseas student I was allowed to stay in my room for extra weeks during vacation, which was a great help but I also had the luxury of being able to foist myself on an aunt in Scotland and an uncle in England when I needed to escape Cambridge and enjoy some free home-cooked food for a week or two. I used to ring my aunt once a week putting 2p in the slot on the college phone and then she would ring me back and pay for the rest of the call – a lovely aunt! After graduation, I got a job in the University Library for a couple of months doing very basic unpacking and stamping but it paid the rent for a room with a friend of a friend in Cambridge while I was applying for jobs in London. Luckily, I landed a job and a flat share in London with two kiwi friends, so managed to start an independent life without any debts, unlike my children, despite the huge contributions we made towards their university education. I think we were quite a fortunate generation in many ways.

Aileen Regan (née Kidd)

I mostly remember that I always had some money left at the end of each term whereas in the case of my brothers who were at university at about the same time as me, one of them was always overdrawn and one of them about breakeven. I guess I was the one who was a bit more cautious and careful with my expenditure.

Helen Morton

I was on a full grant in the first year as my father was made redundant about the time I went up. I think it was about £500 for Oxford, Cambridge and London, and maybe only £450 elsewhere. Did we only pay about £100 of that for our rooms, including heat? I used to draw £5 a week out of my new bank account for food, and it seemed to be enough – I loved the piles of sweetcorn in the market in the autumn and ate a great deal of that in the first term. With money saved from summer jobs it seemed ok.

Then I suddenly found myself rich: my grandmother died and left each of her three grandchildren £5000, which was a total surprise. This was enough to buy a house, which my parents urged me to do and to let out all but my own room – I guess they feared what a nineteen year old might otherwise spend it on. My older brother used his money to spend a year travelling in South America. So my experience after the first year was very different from that of others, as I had my own place in Grantchester Meadows, shared in part with people in their mid-twenties.

Pam Hilton

I was very lucky in that I had a full grant which covered both academic and college fees. Apparently this was because I had been in full time employment and had paid more than the minimum three years of income tax, so Somerset County Council was landed with me. I think it may even have allowed me to stay in my room in Beaufort House for part of vacations so that I could get to grips with essential reading. It was just as well because I came back from my travels down to my last shilling (and then had to adjust to decimal coinage which had been introduced while I was abroad). I seem to remember that apart from food my occasional expenditure was on clothes because some of the little Cambridge shops had quirky items I hadn't seen elsewhere.

Sarah Wilson (née Stallard)

Money was tight but we were so lucky to leave University debt free in those days. The maximum grant was around £460 of which my mum had to contribute a small amount. It included a book allowance which I think was about £50, but you could get many of the books second-hand.

Jane Mott (née Style)

I had a full grant, and £1 per week clothes allowance. so really was quite well off. I certainly had no clear idea about budgeting, and I think we were all particularly mean with food.

Sally Morgan

I was fortunate to receive a grant, and money wasn't an issue. I drew £50 a week from the Midland bank machine in Market Square, and took on a range of menial jobs in the holidays. A long shot from so many students today who have to work to survive during term time.

Helen Mayer

Holiday jobs

In my first summer vacation I worked as a nursing auxiliary in a local 15 bed cottage hospital, which had a wonderfully caring and friendly atmosphere. There was a high staff to patient ratio. Most of the patients were geriatric cases, although there were two women who'd had brain tumours and were slowly recovering. The permanent staff were kind to me as well as the patients and I did master 'hospital corners'.
For the next two summer vacs I worked in an old people's home, run by the local authority. It was pretty soulless, although the staff did try to inject some compassion and humour into the place. From both the hospital and the home I learnt that good working relationships could transform difficult or unpleasant tasks into bearable situations. Camaraderie made all the difference.

Sue Attridge (née Wood)

I had one paid job in the summer holidays, working at Tiptree picking fruit for 3 weeks, and managed to earn £45 more than my board and lodging there. I was rather proud that I could do manual work well enough to get paid!

Jo Edkins (née Dibblee)

Vacation jobs were an interesting mix: working in Ladbrokes for several weeks (quite an education); six weeks at Butlins in Skegness (horrendous); a stint with the Sales Forecasting section of BT (great fun) and finally working in the Council audit department in the year of local government reorganisation (1974). As part of this I was stuck for over a week in a huge stock cupboard, having to climb up on top of the shelves and perch there counting forms and tickets etc. My boss said I looked like a pixie sitting cross legged on the top shelf. I was not amused. Health and Safety would have banned it these days! I had a dust allergy too and sneezed continually while I was there. Being a Christmas Postie was another high-risk venture, never knowing when a large dog would accost you in the garden or a small snappy one take your fingers off as you pushed stuff through the letter box. Still - it kept me in pennies, and I still have all my fingers.

Anne Muir (née Borrett)

I worked during most of the holidays. I usually worked as an orderly at the local hospital and had similar experiences to Sue. I worked alongside many great and very entertaining characters. We worked on the old, long Florence Nightingale wards, serving up patient's meals with food freshly cooked and delivered from the kitchens, tidying up the vases of flowers (remember when that was allowed) and generally talking to and supporting both the patients and the nursing staff. It was a wonderful training for becoming a doctor.

However, I did several other jobs too, often secretarial/admin, but without a doubt, the best job I did was working in Botham's bakery in Whitby. Up at 4am and working from 5-12, and then off to the beach for the rest of the day. It was always sunny (or so I remember). I even reached the dizzy heights of 'gingerbread maker'.

Rosemary Grande (née Temple)

I was very fortunate in many ways with my holiday jobs. My first summer I went to the USA under the BUNAC scheme, which helps students find vacation jobs abroad, where they obtained a working visa provided you left the USA by October. My father worked in the food science industry and had given me the names and phone numbers of several friends, so I arrived in New York, rang them up and managed to land myself a two-month job in the research lab of ITT Continental Baking testing food samples and earning $40 per week which was really good money in those days! I then spent three weeks travelling around the USA on the Greyhound bus really enjoying myself and making lots of new friends. My second summer, I went to Australia under a scheme run by the English Speaking Union where they found you a job related to whatever you were studying. I had a two-month engineering job at a firm called EMAIL in Sydney which produced air-conditioning equipment. The big advantage for me of going to Australia was that I was able to travel on to New Zealand for two weeks to meet my father's family for the first time - my uncle and my aunt and lots of cousins - which was really good. My third summer I worked as an *au pair* in Geneva because I wanted to practise my French and I found a lovely family with whom I'm still in touch, including the little girl I looked after who was 2 years old when I first met her and who is still a good friend 50 years on!

Helen Morton

I did the usual Christmas post – I was deemed too short to be sent on rounds, so spent my time sorting letters, which was warm and dry. My best holiday job was in 1973. I taught in a Hounslow junior school which stayed open through the summer to improve the English of Ugandan Asians who had been expelled by Idi Amin the previous summer. A teacher dropped out at the last minute and I stepped in. The progress these kids made over the period was astonishing. One day a week we took them on expeditions to places such as the Natural History Museum, and I also accompanied other classes on visits, as I was the least qualified 'staff' member. Even in my dreams I was counting heads frantically; inevitably we seemed to lose someone temporarily each trip. Worst was when a small girl said during lunch at Windsor Safari Park: 'Miss, Rajinder's climbing into the hippos.' I did the run of my life, though by the time I got there someone was holding him by the scruff of the neck and telling him he could have been killed. I recently found a photo of the class, which brought it back. The pay seemed astonishing: £25 a week for five relatively short days, whereas the year before I had earned £10 a week for longer days in a department store sale.

Pam Hilton

I was lucky that I had a reasonable maintenance grant with my parents topping up the rest so don't actually remember any problem with money during term time. Holiday jobs did help to top up for a few student style holidays away and were a great opportunity to see something of the rest of life.

It was fun "playing" at being postman for a few days before Christmas during my first year. Unfortunately for the students my sorting office was well organised, and our employment was terminated as unnecessary after three days.

During the summer at the end of my first year I spent a month working at the small local hospital along with a number of other fellow students from my secondary school. We all got together in the staff room to eat our packed lunches and reminisce! There were two wards and we were employed as "general cleaners" on the geriatric ward. A variety of work from serving and clearing up after drinks morning, afternoon and evening (depending on shift), helping with the serving of food, loading and unloading the dishwasher, dry mopping the ward floor and cleaning the bathrooms! How things have changed in these days of health and safety!! Was I really left to serve drinks and biscuits to a ward of geriatric patients without any reference to special diets?

The following summer my future mother-in-law found six weeks work for me at St James' Balham where she worked part time in a social work role. The other two students taken on were both medical students and we spent most of our time in a shed in the grounds going through and discarding the files of the deceased - something of an eye opener for me. I think I was somewhat relieved that our boss never followed up on his offer to show us round the morgue!

Dorothy Cade (née Clark)

I suppose vacation jobs were the work experience of our day as well as being essential for buying clothes and paying for holidays. I worked in Marks and Spencer's and learned how to return things successfully by sounding disappointed rather than angry. I went strawberry picking in Sussex but it rained so I went home to Ipswich and down to the labour exchange. They sent me to a local factory where I helped pack glacé pineapple into boxes for a few weeks and met some great characters as well as learning about clocking on and off and losing pay if you were late. Christmas post of course was fun with free buses all around the town, and finally a job at Fisons Fertilizers in the library where they wanted me to summarise magazine articles for their index system.

Jane Mott (née Style)

Before going up to Cambridge I had a summer job working in the local SPAR supermarket. It was incredibly boring – we three women had to restock the shelves and put price stickers on all the items. If the restocking was complete, we had to tidy the shelves, and when that was done, we had to do it again just so that we looked busy. The young men worked at the butcher counter and were paid about 50% more than the women. I used to look forward to Saturdays, our busiest day, when they put me on the tills because I was fast and could remember a lot of the prices. The other people who worked there were all permanent employees. There was a girl younger than me who had had an abortion, which rather shocked me. The other woman was middle aged and tried to befriend me because she knew I was interested in books. Except that she was reading romance novels whereas I was reading The Origin of Species! Although the job was very dull, I am very glad I did it – it gave me a window into the lives of people I would otherwise never have got to know.

I also worked the Christmas post at the Watford sorting office, which was wonderful fun since most of us were university students. I suspect the men were paid more than the women because they were allowed to go to the train station to pick up the sacks of mail, which the women weren't and also that's just how things were. People liked to send clotted cream at Christmas. Often the labels would come off so one of the perks of the job was taking home orphaned jars of clotted cream. Probably that wasn't legal, but nobody ever tried to stop us!

During summer vacs I was incredibly lucky to have the opportunity to work in an architect's office in London, so I was building professional experience before I even graduated. I think very few of my fellow architecture students had any work experience at that stage.

Gillian Blessley

In the Summer vacations, I had three jobs, each one worse than the last, filing vehicle tax forms in the local council, washing old women in a care home and plucking chickens, which was piece work. On my final day, I earned 29p for 6 hours work, then quit.

Penny Stirling

Social attitudes and external events

I clearly remember how strange it was to have such an unbalanced number of male and female students. I became an active feminist in those 3 years with an increasing awareness of sexism towards female students.

Karen Greenwood

Reflecting on the immense cultural change today; there was virtually no ethnic diversity and very little acknowledged gender diversity in Cambridge when we came up. And I don't recall any discussion about it. Women were still very much in the minority, as were state educated students, and we concentrated on the former issue. I remember being really appalled at the sexist attitudes of many male students, that women were their intellectual inferiors or needed looking after because they were pretty incapable. This was not something I had ever come across before and presumably related to private, single sex education. I also sadly recall several young women who were devastated at not finding a boyfriend instantly on the premise that if there were 10 men for every woman (the statistic bandied around) there must be something wrong with her.

Siân Crisp (née Jenkins)

After Cambridge, I was glad to escape the 'ivory tower' mentality and the arrogance of privilege which I came across. I held a small party when I graduated for some friends including my tutor. I shall never forget that he said "It's a shame you only got a 2:1. Never mind, you are a good cook."

Diana Murray (née Collyer)

I surprised a man exposing himself in college one afternoon, he'd entered by the door to the road at the carpark end. It got locked after that. I didn't see what was going on until I was quite close (because of the corridor wiggles and my lack of attention). I laughed (from surprise mainly at such a ridiculous activity) and went back to the Porters' Lodge and Mr Ellis chased him away.

Deborah Glass

Owing to a teacher training year, I was still a student when the Cambridge rapist was at large. I remember the irony of colleges suggesting that women invite their men friends to sleep in or near their rooms, and mattresses being dragged around the corridors. There was real apprehension and I used to carry a pot of pepper and a small vegetable knife around with me. No doubt quite useless, it made me feel less anxious at the time.

Sue Attridge (née Wood)

Other random memories surface. There was the time a gang of us decided to break into one of the fellows' gardens late at night. We sat around talking quietly for a while till suddenly everyone else got up and melted into the bushes. They didn't immediately come back so after a minute or two I set off to look for them. One of the bushes whispered 'get down, there's somebody coming'. It turned out to be a false alarm, as did my brush with the Cambridge Rapist. I'd stayed on for a fourth year and had a Saturday bar job. One night I was walking back up the hill towards college at the end of my shift. The road was deserted except that behind me I heard heavy footsteps gradually catching up with me. Eventually a young man drew alongside and announced rather portentously 'Some people think I'm the Cambridge Rapist'. I said I didn't think he was; he went on ahead of me up the hill and that was that.

Emma Wheelock

We had power cuts in the first year, lots of candles or darkness several days a week.

Deborah Glass

I remember the power cuts too which I think came in rotation around Cambridge so that friends on other colleges would have power when we didn't have any at New Hall. When our power was off, I used to go and visit my friends in Corpus or Queens and take advantage of their lights being on to do my studies!

Helen Morton

I remember power cuts, both when I came up for interviews, and stayed in Newnham, and I also have a memory of cycling to the other end of Cambridge on Shrove Tuesday with a screw top glass bottle containing pancake batter in my bike basket, because we had no electricity so I went and shared my pancakes with someone who did. How did I know they had electricity in the absence of text messages?

Penny Stirling

I was reading Anglo-Saxon and Old Norse. During the miners' strike I remember thinking how appropriate it was to be reading these old texts by candlelight in my room. Shopping in the small Sainsbury's store in town when it was lit by candles and lamps also had a certain old-world charm. The university was divided into blocks with power cuts in different time slots, so it was always possible to find somewhere else to study if you were desperate.

Decimalisation was a very hot topic when I arrived in the UK and I was surprised and slightly amused to see how divided the country was on the merits of this changeover and how long it took to be accepted, as New Zealand had managed the process overnight four years earlier with hardly a murmur of dissent.

Aileen Regan (née Kidd)

During the miner's strike in 1974, because our flat in Warkworth Terrace was opposite the police station, we (Emily, Ursula and I) never had our electricity rationed, and so lots of people came to use our very large kitchen to study as well as socialise. It was all extremely convivial, not difficult at all. External events, which were tumultuous in many ways in our day, hardly seemed to impact very much on our hectic but ivory tower life. When we went up, there was the state of emergency in Pakistan, throughout 1972 was the height of the Irish Troubles, Bloody Sunday, bombs in London and elsewhere, the Munich Olympics, the Bader Meinhof menace etc.; the UK joined the Common Market on January 1st 1973, the Arab-Israeli war was under way as we started our third year, and after the misery of the 3-day week there was a hung British parliament in February 1974. I think I was aware of all this, but somehow analysing the contributing causes to inflation in Tudor England, or the role of the frontier in the American Myth, or whether Justice was Fairness seems to have been a more immediate preoccupation. Extraordinary really. I have just noticed that the notorious photo of the Napalm Girl was taken on June 8th 1972. We were in the middle of our first ever May week then.

Fiona Edwards-Stuart (née Weaver)

It's easy to forget how far social attitudes have moved in fifty years for women. In relation to race and economic background there's a long way to go, but at least women now can expect to be treated much the same as their male peers in many respects. When we went up, it was less than twenty-five years since Cambridge had actually deigned to award full degrees to women. We now take it for granted that women are as likely as men to have senior roles throughout the university. 1971 was the last year of totally segregated colleges and nine times as many men as women; however 'male' colleges still felt able in 1972 to put a cap on the number of women they would admit. Our second year was when the cracks in the male establishment started to appear and the first five male colleges finally let just a few women in. In the summer term of our first year I had just joined the JCR committee and I recall a rather odd meeting with the Churchill JCR who seemed to think a completely alien species, for whom they would need to make many special provisions, was about to arrive in their college. They were planning tampon machines in every bathroom and seemed amazed when we said no one had bothered to do that for the women in an all-female college.

Things have improved in employment practices. In 1977 I asked why I hadn't even been interviewed for a job for which I was better qualified than the successful male candidate and was told that this was because I was married and so 'of course would not want to travel', which was a requirement of the job. We were the tail end of the generation who went to consciousness raising groups and began to understand about patriarchy. We were the generation who adopted 'Ms' – I've always used that, and I have also kept my own surname, when marrying, divorcing and then remarrying.

In 1978 when joining the Civil Service I was asked about my plans for marriage and child rearing (the psychologist did back down when I checked with him that he asked the men the same). Women made up only about 20% of my cohort of Fast Streamers. When I joined the Ministry of Overseas Development, later re-named ODA (Overseas Development Administration) and then the much lamented DFID (Department for International Development), there wasn't a woman in the Ministry above Head of Section, even though we were advocating 'Women in Development' to the rest of the world, telling them that they must enable women to play their full part in society. Things were changing more rapidly elsewhere in the civil service, but ODA was curiously slow. The best civil servant in the generation above me was always promoted several years after her less able male peers. I'm glad to say it started to change rapidly in the later 90s and there was soon a female Permanent Secretary in the Department.

Pam Hilton

How it was different, back then

There were computers - I did Computer Science, after all! But no-one used a computer for their personal life - just for academic purposes, and it was paper tape and punched cards, rather than keyboard, mouse or touch screen. Nobody owned their own computer. No-one even had a calculator.

Everything was hand-written - essays and assignments. We wrote letters! No emails, no social media. We could phone home using the phone in the corridor, but home couldn't phone us. Meetings were carefully arranged, or you dropped in on people to see if they were free - no mobile phones!

We bought the (printed) Reporter to see when lectures were. We read notices on notice boards, or leaflets in our pigeon holes - no other way to see what was going on.

Everything was paid using cash or by cheque. Cash meant going to the bank when it was open, as there were no cash withdrawal machines.

Music was on LPs, or cassette, or you listened to the radio (or recorded off the radio onto cassette, illegally!) The news was on TV, or radio, or newspapers.

Jo Edkins (née Dibblee)

So interesting to read about Ancient Computers, Jo. Great behemoths, weren't they? And all that paper they gave out, piles and piles of it, with the little holes either side, and the print so small and generally illegible.

It makes me think of what we have now.... and though the I-pad is, like the "Pickwick", the "Owl" and the Waverley pen, "a boon and a blessing to men", these later developments have their drawbacks. At New Hall, we had no fear of our privacy being intruded upon day and night by these modern devices which track your whereabouts. We were not suborned by social media, by influencers, by the Fear of Missing Out. Even, the News had to be sought out. (I gather that Fitz did a deal

on the "Times" for students. Only someone as boring as my own Mr W of 47 years, faugh! would take this up, scuse me whilst I yawn.)
And I think we were the better for this. You had to make quite an effort to be made to feel inferior, or not "trendy", or to be excluded, to be criticised, dissed, etc.
We called in on people, we barged in, we came away if they hadn't yet got up, or a Man was there! ..... we weren't taking photos incessantly; we were living the moment without that. It's not like that now.
Also, because we did not have this easy access to "knowledge", we had to look up stuff in books. We couldn't immediately read a compendium of criticism of "Sense and Sensibility", for example (not that Eng Lit was my subject). We had to search. Everyone knows that a thorough Study of the Text is the key. Just like (in my subject) mastery of scales is mastery of the instrument..... btw, I wasn't much good at scales.
Negotiating one's way through the "Reporter" was itself an art. What strange titles other disciplines' lectures had! "Zoonoses" sticks in my memory! Whatever were they? And were they Zoo Noses? Elephants' trunks etc ....the inexperienced and ignorant mind boggled.
Also INK! You could not take ink into the UL! They inspected your gear on entry, and confiscated ink. It seems centuries away. (I hope the UL tearoom is still serving up those amazing cakes!) and "oh! stands the church clock at ten to three? and is there honey still for tea?" Happy days.

Sue Whitham (née Addison)

The trunk!
I remember that we'd have large trunks to take our stuff between home and parents. At least I remember my parents buying me a large trunk and all my worldly possessions being shunted about in it three times a year. (And I still have it, at the far reaches of the loft). I remember the time I put all my books in it at the end of term and was surprised when no one could lift it.

Alison Litherland (née Hill)

I don't remember many non-white British students back then - and there were so few women compared to now. I think there is even more pressure on students, both academically and socially.

Rosemary Grande (née Temple)

Some memories of the pre-technological world. It had its advantages! There was a wonderful feeling of freedom in the pre-social media world, that I think has been lost now. We could do as we liked without anyone taking pictures or posting tweets or checking up on us on Facebook. There was no pressure to send texts or make regular phone calls to keep family informed and it was almost impossible for anyone to ring you. For me, making a phone call home to New Zealand was a major event that only happened about once a term and had to be arranged through the porter's lodge in advance for a specific time to suit both hemispheres. It was quite exciting to send off an international telegram with every word carefully counted when we received our results and receive a congratulatory one back. I looked forward to checking my pigeon hole for the blue aerogram letter in my mother's handwriting every week, with news of friends and family. My weekly letters home were much appreciated and I discovered years later that she had copied out every letter by hand into a large scrap book as a record. Now, I am scanning and digitising many family papers for the archive which can be shared internationally at the click of a button.
If you wanted to see someone, you just had to take a chance that they might be in their room or leave a message under the door or in their pigeon hole, if needs be. My boyfriend did realise that we could phone each other for free on an internal university line when he was in one of the science labs but it was hardly private and only useful on the odd occasion. Otherwise, the next date was usually arranged at the end of the previous one in the form of "I'll be in a certain pub from about 8pm after our rowing training."
I doubt if I could write anything longer than a shopping list by hand these days and certainly not in a legible script. I had to find a typist for my dissertation, which proved a slight challenge, as she had to cope

with odd Anglo-Saxon and Old Norse characters. I remember having to fill in a few by hand before submitting it but she did a pretty good job. I'm sure we had to be more thoughtful in our writing and take time to phrase things in our heads before committing to paper, without the luxury of computer editing. Obviously, we were totally reliant on real books for research without the internet so libraries were my second home. Now, language students can get anything translated on Google in a matter of seconds, even dead languages, and while that definitely saves time, I do wonder if our hard slogging actually gave us a deeper understanding. I remember struggling with a biblical text in Old High German (my modern German was pretty basic), but because it had been translated directly from the Latin text on the opposite page, I just about worked it out (having studied Latin to university level) and learnt a lot in the process. I'm not sure a quick Google fix would have been as beneficial!

I had one of those little transistor radios that was my link with the outside world for news bulletins, listening to music and a range of interesting programmes. The poor thing got dropped from the upstairs part of my room on more than one occasion but luckily my boyfriend understood the inner workings of such devices and managed to fix it for me. Now, he fixes electronic devices for the grandchildren.

Aileen Regan (née Kidd)

My parents-in-law lived on Storey's Way, so I've been back to Cambridge many times, but didn't visit New Hall often. The last time I did was International Women's Day on 7 March 2020 just as Covid was beginning to strike. I visited the special exhibition about education for women in Cambridge at the UL. This had been co-curated by a Murray Edwards don, who was young enough to be my daughter.

The exhibition was humbling. It took so much effort for women to gain a foothold in the 19th and 20th centuries. It was well over 100 years from the time the first women students were admitted to Girton to get to anything approaching equality. I was reminded of a conversation I had at a party in John's in my first year when a man told me that no more women should be admitted to the University because if they were there would have to be two levels of courses and exams, since women would only ever be able to meet a lower standard than the men. This was presented as a self-evident truth. Views like his were not unusual in the early 1970s.

On this International Women's Day visit I was struck by the new entrance to the college, so much more welcoming than the one when we were there. The gardens were lovelier too, bringing back fond memories of sitting in the sunshine in Orchard Court. The International Women's Day programme was really impressive involving talks by Murray Edwards graduate students from Africa, India and South America about women's issues in their countries. And there was a spectacular athletic/gymnastic display by a team of accomplished and supremely confident Cambridge women wearing fetching sparkly costumes. Not a blue stocking in sight! I was amazed and so proud of them. I couldn't have dreamt of anything like this when we were there. Nor would I have been capable of joining in, then or now!

Equally striking was the way that the Women's Art Collection enhanced the buildings and really lit them up. The paintings and sculpture add such a dimension to the college and its modernist architecture. What a brilliant combination.

Shortly after this visit we were plunged into the first lockdown and our worlds shrank. Little did we know then how long the suffering from the pandemic would last. Initiatives like this conversation over email which has brought our year at New Hall together in such an unexpected way have really lightened the darkness. Thanks to all of you who have prompted so many memories of Cambridge in our time there together.

Virginia Beardshaw

Of course, we would never have been able to write this book, in this way (via email), back then. During lockdown, too!

Jo Edkins (née Dibblee)

Reflections

A range of memories: the candle-lit essay writing, the wiggly top corridor, St John's disco, the traditional Sainsbury's where they cut cheese, bacon etc. all by hand at different counters, the whole place beautifully tiled, my first demo round the Market – and being kicked by a policeman, which really shocked me.

Siân Crisp (née Jenkins)

I really loved the fact that we were women and men, not girls and boys!

Jane Mott (née Style)

My impression was that lots of people at Cambridge came from very 'well-to-do' backgrounds and had travelled the world and lived abroad. Many people, especially outside of New Hall had been boarders at big public schools. They were often so self-confident. Not necessarily clever. Some people were studying such exotic subjects like Japanese and anthropology.

Overall I loved my years at Cambridge.

It was the only part of my education that I ever felt really stimulated and could discuss ideas and thoughts with my teachers. I think the supervision system was fantastic if you had good supervisors as we did. I echo Philippa's thoughts that, at the time, I didn't realise just how much time and energy they all had for us and our education. Looking back and reflecting on my education and early years of being a doctor, it stands out as the time that I was inspired by successful, phenomenally clever and inspiring female role models. There were very few female doctors in hospital medicine in the 1970s and early 1980s and it was a world where the macho rugby playing, beer swilling man would often succeed and be loudest. I believe that Cambridge gave me the education and confidence to cope with that world, and that having a Cambridge education on my CV helped hugely, especially in those days when we had to keep applying for the next job every 6 to 12 months.

It was also the time that I formed many of the close friendships which have given me so much over the last 50 years. Not necessarily friendships made during my time at New Hall, but often friends or contacts of friends made while at Cambridge, including my husband.

Rosemary Grande (née Temple)

I, like many, found the undergraduate experience at one and the same time wonderful in terms of learning/teaching and, equally, hard to find my way through, coming from a state school and more relaxed social setting.

I was a medic/GP and I learnt so much from "salt of the earth" fantastic and unsung people I worked with and patients I met in the NHS and in life in general. Living still in Cambridge, I realise that, among the unassuming colleagues and friends to whom I am so grateful, some are in fact outstanding in their professional or business lives - far from unsung in their work, but equally kind, courageous and working with integrity and dedication.

I rather thought that everyone at New Hall, except me, had gone on to the top echelons of life. Evidently many of us had less stellar journeys, though still of value. I didn't realise, when I was young, how much hard work and thought the New Hall Dons put in to create the New Hall I experienced. Living in Cambridge still, I am very impressed by New Hall/Murray Edwards and very grateful.

Philippa Evans (née Taylor)

I have very happy memories, despite the hard work as a medic (I don't think I realised we worked hard, until I read the contributions from some others!). Actually, I have no regrets at all about the work. I know I would have been completely lost trying to do some of the courses which people have been describing, with no clear idea of what I was meant to be doing and, in some cases, inadequate supervision. Give me a jam-packed timetable, with little time to think but great supervisors, any day!

One of the good bits of our weekly 'timetable', as Philippa reminded me, was the toasted crumpets in my room after biochemistry practicals on Thursdays!

But I think I will select as the greatest bonus, the opportunity to do a Part 11 in pharmacology in the third year (at that time, medics could choose anything they wanted; Philippa was much more enterprising!). At school, I was still uncertain about following a medical career; I enjoyed science, and my other choice would have been a science degree. This is one thing that encouraged my application to do medicine at Cambridge, where I could get my science degree and follow a different route if I chose.

I was extremely lucky to do a final year project with Mike Waring on the structure of DNA, whose existence had only been confirmed a few years before. The project involved a lot of hours sitting staring at test tubes and measuring sedimentation rates, sometimes late into the evening. I didn't mind and was fascinated. The best bit was the results: beautiful curves emerged (how lucky was that?) and we got a paper out of it. It was a great experience for which I have always been grateful. However, for a long time afterwards I pondered the words of a PhD student in the lab who advised me 'whatever you do, don't be a GP!'

I was lucky not to experience the trauma and anxieties that a number of people described. One episode stands out though. A good friend from the year below us went missing for several days during exam time. She was finally found, thankfully, safe and well, but had only a sketchy recollection of events in those days. It was a genuine amnesic episode, brought about by the stress of the exams. None of us had had any idea of the stress she was under, but I suspect it may strike a chord with some people. There's no doubt that some of us found things, especially exams, very stressful at times.

Sarah Watson (née Henley)

Life at Cambridge all those years ago:

When I arrived at Cambridge in October 1971 it was seven years since the discipline of a school timetable. In 1964 I spurned the idea of university, even though I had friends who were getting excited at the thought of going to recently established places like Sussex, East Anglia and York, because I was keen to get out into the world and earn my own living. It took time for me to realise that spending a further three years studying actually opened up far more opportunities, although the delay was to my advantage in that I would never have achieved a place at Cambridge at 17 whereas at 24 my singular lack of high grade 'A' Levels was overlooked.

However, it also meant that my brain had become used to dealing with the practical problems of survival while working my way round the world and had become positively atrophied for academic work. In the middle of my first term I descended into a deep slough of despond and almost came to the conclusion that I had made a big mistake in thinking I deserved a place at all. Ros Morpeth was another mature student who had a room in Beaufort House and we occasionally walked together to lectures (I seem to remember she wasn't too confident on a bicycle). She always appeared to be totally on top of essays and background reading and my confidence wasn't helped by having supervisions with Sian Jenkins, who was a really bright spark. Fortunately Esther Goody, who originally interviewed me, must have noticed my despondency because she was immensely supportive and encouraged me to battle on at least till the end of term, before I made any drastic decision. Then I must have written one or two acceptable essays because the gloom eased and I realised that I should stop being defeatist and make the most of all the opportunities.

So, the best bits. Having been born and bred in the country I loved the open spaces, walking through John's or King's to the Backs, the carpet of crocuses under the trees, the tracery of frozen snow on bare branches (as long as the icy wind had dropped). And the music. I really had not expected the diversity in various colleges and the West Road Concert Hall. Reading how some people were enthusiastically welcomed into the chapel choirs of male colleges I wish I'd had the confidence to do that, but I did get into the habit of attending Choral Evensong in St.

John's most Sundays because I was captivated by both the ethereal singing and the awesome thundering of the organ.

Altogether those three years at Cambridge stand out as one of the bright threads in the weft and warp of my life. If I could relive that time (but only if it was still fifty years ago) I hope I would make even more of the amazing opportunities on offer, but it is no good having regrets with hindsight.

One last "best bit" - lying outside in the sun the day after Finals, reading a NOVEL.

Sarah Wilson (née Stallard)

My experience of Cambridge was a series of extraordinary and wonderful experiences, interspersed with periods of working really hard on my own, somehow trying to crack the big questions of life through the authors I was reading: Tolstoy, Gabriel Garcia Marquez, Neruda, which made me feel quite introverted and isolated. In my third year, I went on the contraceptive pill, and the doctor prescribed a very high dose oestrogen pill which made me very depressed. My boyfriend was writing a long essay on Beckett and asked me, "Are you not happy? Answer yes or no". This was not helpful. I went around asking friends with a car if they could take me to see a hill because the flatness of the landscape was unbearable.

Penny Stirling

New Hall gave me: the chance to be at Cambridge without taking time out after A Level (in retrospect I would have benefited, but I didn't realise it then): two relaxed final terms at school thanks to its policy of offering on the basis of two Es at A Level; the chance to live in one of the most beautiful cities I know (I loved walking along Trinity Street late at night, or Grantchester Meadows early in the morning): the chance for a grant to read literature, which seemed amazing at the time (and even more so now, as students build up huge debts and focus so much on employability): the chance to make mistakes - I've made plenty, but have also fallen into many fascinating things in an unplanned way, without ever being particularly ambitious, so I don't regret any of it. The only really bad bit was in my second term when my then boyfriend ended our relationship suddenly and I realised I really hadn't taken advantage of getting to know others as I should have.

Pam Hilton

At the time those three years at New Hall seemed to last forever, but looking back they were over really quickly. I was still only 20 when I graduated and, similar to the experience of others, I was far too young and immature to have fully benefited from the experience, although what the experience did do was to enable me to grow up and widen my horizons.

Alison Litherland (née Hill)

In retrospect it turned out to have been a very formative three years at New Hall. But when I left I was pretty much drifting and hadn't learnt much about myself. I look back at that 18 year old arriving at New Hall and feel a bit sad. There was a lot on offer that I didn't fully explore mainly, I suspect, because insecurity made me defensive.

Ros Coward

Unfortunately, the thing that shaped my New Hall days, and really my subsequent life, was the mental instability and then death by suicide of a very dear friend from another college. He had been unstable and depressed for a long time, and had made several attempts on his life. His friends all tried to help him, but we were out of our depth – nothing had prepared us for that. His eventual suicide completely shocked and shattered me, and put me quite off the rails for a long time. It was very traumatic and I lost my compass on life. Such grief and loss and confusion, I'd never had to deal with anything like that in my life. My ensuing erratic behaviour also lost me a very lovely boyfriend as well as my own personal direction. I wish I had known at the time about the student equivalent of Samaritans. Although Miss Hammond (Director of Studies) was very sympathetic, having a separate 'personal tutor' was no use at all, she barely knew who I was, and I battled with depression for a long time. As a young student I was completely unprepared for the insults of mental distress, and completely lacking in any personal support, and most importantly, I didn't know how or where to seek help.

There's no point regretting these things as they cannot be undone, but it's certainly a reminder of how life's unexpected events can alter one's course and present new challenges. Several years later, when I lived in London working as a journalist, I trained to be a Samaritan. The training was absolutely brilliant, and as well as enabling me to be on the end of the phone for people in distress, it also gave me an insight into my own issues about losing a loved one to suicide. My work now, as an acupuncturist, often brings me into contact with distressed people, and my training and life experiences have enabled me to be more useful to them than I could be to my friend all those years ago.

Lou Radford

I am grateful to New Hall for a couple of very good friends, to the University for the concerts and plays I attended, the Arts Cinema for the films, and the pubs for facilitating many wide-ranging discussions, as well as games of bar billiards. And I am particularly grateful to my supervisors for enforcing a reasonably rigorous training of the mind, even if I had quickly to unlearn that dreary essay style we had been advised to adopt, when I started to write for the general reader.

Ursula Wide (née Buchan)

Although I was technically a mature student I don't think I was in any way prepared for life as a female Cambridge undergraduate. My problem was that after seven "gap" years I found it incredibly difficult to get my brain in gear and half way through my first term wondered if I hadn't made a big mistake in coming at all, but I suppose a streak of stubbornness/pride came to my rescue.

Then nearly three years later my feeling of inadequacy surfaced again at 9 o'clock on the end May Bank Holiday when faced with the first of the six exams for Finals. When instructed I turned the page over and went absolutely blank. After what seemed an age I looked round and saw all the boys scribbling away. I had switched to Land Economy and was the only female in a very small department - and thought "Hang on, half of these have been borrowing my lecture notes for the past two years" so somehow got started, although even so, halfway through one of the questions in the Economics paper I realised I had mixed up macro and micro so put a line through everything, wrote something for two other questions and then only had time at the end to draft the headings of what I would have attempted. Unsurprisingly I was awarded a 2:2, but that didn't seem to matter in my future career.

Sarah Wilson (née Stallard)

I was always unsure how I had managed to get into Cambridge. As so many have said, it was easy to feel that all those around me were brighter and more confident, something which began probably with the first meeting of the whole group of MML students with Dorothy Coleman. Socially it also felt such a different world, but I did realise fairly quickly that there were lots of people whose company I enjoyed and felt comfortable with, and that I could cope with, if not excel at, the work. I appreciated the opportunity to sample such a wide variety of literature and the challenge of making some sense of what I was reading.

Despite the workload it did feel in some ways like a 3-year break from reality. Everything in the short terms was intense, and the availability and sheer variety of things to occupy your time was wonderful. Music of every kind, theatre performances, playing croquet in Storey's Way, even walking around Cambridge itself, all of this felt like an enormous privilege. I wasn't a cyclist but loved walking along Queen's Road or Grange Road to the Sidgwick site, especially in autumn when you could crunch through the leaves.

Denise Phillipson (née Milburn)

And what have we learnt from these shared reminiscences? That we are survivors! That New Hall provided us with a start. That we have not lost our youthful idealism...we haven't, have we? And that all lives are valid. Some lived in the spotlight, others.... well, here is a quotation from Middlemarch: "the growing good of the world is partly dependent on unhistoric acts; and that things are not so ill with you and me as they might have been is half owing to the number who lived faithfully a hidden life....." But it is a New Hall "hidden" Life!

Sue Whitham (née Addison)

My happiest memories of Cambridge are of the place – its buildings and gardens, frosty mornings along the backs, ducklings in the Botanic Garden, browsing in Primavera. It took me a while to build a group of friends but once I had found them, there were discussions on all kinds of subjects, and bonding over Fitzbillies' chocolate cake. I was disappointed in aspects of my studies: I had probably not given enough thought to what I was letting myself in for, in a course so focussed on detailed scrutiny of literature and where it might lead me and much of the teaching did little to inspire. I regret not spending more time on extracurricular pursuits – there always seemed to be so much to read and digest for the next essay. My grumbles, though, are more with Cambridge and its systems than with New Hall, which I remember as warm, welcoming, nurturing and open to all kinds of people and ideas. I have been back in recent years to see the Women's Art Collection, which I think is a great addition to the college and the distinctive New Hall aroma still evokes a sense of promise and new prospects.

Mary Anne Bonney

I think the whole experience of Cambridge undergraduate life was a huge privilege. I have realised this more, recently, particularly after discussing snippets people have sent in with my husband. His tertiary education was very different, at a technical college (which later became a university) doing an integrated course in engineering (leading to what subsequently became an MSc). It was very hard work and an excellent training; the academic content was rigorous and the equipment excellent. But there was none of the 'broadness' of Cambridge, of the opportunity to branch out, both academically and in so many other ways, and none of the camaraderie; just a constant hard grind. Food for thought! Yes, we were lucky.

Sarah Watson (née Henley)

I just loved the city, the beautiful buildings, but also the abundance of open spaces and the river, and the Botanic Gardens, all within easy reach. I loved the market which I frequented at the end of the day for bargains, and the small independent shops such as the little tobacconist in the market square that exotically sold snuff. I loved Heffers – I spent too much money on books and stationery, the cafes and especially Fitzbillies. I loved the music and theatres and didn't at the time appreciate how privileged we were to be able to enjoy such a high quality of performance from the day-to-day chapel services, to the highly professional concerts and plays put on by University societies. I loved the academic discussion which, even in Edinburgh, I have found hard to replicate.

Diana Murray (née Collyer)

I'd do it all again! A great experience.

Sarah Watson (née Henley)

Best bits and Worst bits

Best bit was the place itself, which struck me (from a Midlands mining town) as like living in a dream or a film set: buildings ancient and modern, bookshops, the Backs with sheep, the river, cycling to Grantchester. Just walking around it was a daily pleasure.
Worst bit: feeling lost and out of my depth - especially when faced with small talk over sherry.

Maureen Bell

Best bit(s): The romance of it all. Beautiful buildings, wonderful choral music, art, love affairs, magical happenings. My wonderful tutor Lorna Close, who gave me permission to study what I wanted how I wanted to.
The worst bit: I worked really hard and spent a lot of time alone, trying to think in a way that was almost beyond me. I remember the release after finals, almost like a pressure cooker.

Penny Stirling

Best: a chance to be independent and start shaping my own life
Worst: seeing the grim reactions to pressures of Cambridge life in many friends.

Karen Greenwood

Best bit: Cycling to lectures past Kings Chapel, against a bright blue sky, vivid green lawn and glowing autumnal orange of the chestnut tree.
Worst bit: getting only an ordinary pass at Maths at the end of year 2, so no honours degree for me.

Jo Edkins (née Dibblee)

Best bits: Making friends for life and cycling all over Cambridge.
Worst bit: Constant 'Fear of Missing Out'

Virginia Beardshaw

The best bits. So many interesting people to talk to; staying up until the small hours discussing anything and everything. After being shunned as a boring swot at my grammar school, I really appreciated actually having friends, and friends who were cleverer than me and who had more experience of the world, and who introduced me to so many interesting things that I had no idea about.

The worst bits: definitely the cold. Freezing hands on cycle handlebars until I discovered sheepskin gloves. And the exhaustion of cycling up Castle Hill at the end of the evening.

Alison Litherland (née Hill)

Not many people have commented on the absolute beauty of Cambridge; cycling down along the Backs on an early summer morning, under those magnificent trees with bright green young foliage, is an outstanding memory. Coming back via Garret Hostel Lane and the arched bridge over the Cam just for the sake of the view from the top. Working in the Wren library as they had the only copy of a particular Wittgenstein manuscript I needed. I remember nothing of the text, but just to be there, in such a wonderful building and collection of books was simply extraordinary.

Worst bits were feeling lonely; I think mobile phones would have been a godsend. Also a sherry party in my first week, not the saintly Janet Moore I should say, but I was ordered by the host to open a bottle with a weird contraption that turned out to be a corkscrew of sorts: I had no idea until then that sherry even came in bottles with corks, and certainly couldn't control the weird object to effect that. Something I learnt from Cambridge I guess, along with how to write an essay (thanks Siân), continued to be useful throughout my career, as has the corkscrew.

Sally Morgan

(One of) the best bits: the way we all used to leave notes for each other pinned or Blu-tacked to our doors. How nice it was to come back from a lecture to find a note inviting me for tea, or offering me a part in that

play at St John's ... a custom long swallowed up by the vortex of the internet and Whats App, no doubt.
(One of) the worst bits: the scratchy static blue nylon sheets at our 2nd year house in Chesterton Road (which I can almost still feel on my skin), and the hyper-vigilance of our landlord watching out for men leaving the house early in the morning, matched only by the beady eyes of my boyfriend's landlady in St John's Road. She had a mirror above her kitchen sink lined up directly with the front door so that she could keep an eye on all comings and goings.

Nicola King (née Brown)

Best bits: being intellectually stimulated and enjoying lots of singing and lengthy late night discussions when we sorted out the world. Plus of course walking along the backs on a spring day through a field of flowers
Worst bit: getting glandular fever in my second year and missing out on 3 weeks of lectures.

Helen Morton

My best experiences: drinking in the beauty of the place, crocuses in bloom along the `Backs; the willows on the Cam coming into leaf; yellow stone against blue skies and also the sense of history and the feeling of life opening up, full of possibilities.
My worst experience: drying up in the viva on my undergraduate project, an experience which was humiliating, scary and knocked my confidence significantly.

Alison Wray (née O'Brien)

Best: the place! Not only the architecture, and the Weight of Centuries, but the ambience, definitely not being "buried with inferior minds" (Jane Eyre)
Worst: the appalling helpless turmoil of an ingenue's growing up, and, amidst study and intellectual discoveries, also discovering the vanity,

selfishness and perfidy of Men! These ghastly memories have never left me.

Sue Whitham (née Addison)

Best bit: Looking back fifty years on, I think I enjoyed more freedom and independence during those 2 years than any other time of my life.
Worst bit: The History of English Language exam paper which seemed to bear very little resemblance to anything we were actually taught in lectures.

Aileen Regan (née Kidd)

Best bit: Being able to study History of Art and be a humanities student for a year - although it probably wasn't the best thing for my medical career.

Rosemary Grande (née Temple)

Best bits: Being involved in student societies like the Student Christian Movement (SCM) and Third World First, often meeting over cheese lunches and feeling we could do things to make the world a better place. I've tried to hang on to that commitment and optimism and I'm still in touch with life-long friends from those groups.
My 21st birthday punt party, jointly with a friend from Homerton, including a wonderful picnic on the riverbank.
The confidence and resilience Cambridge helped me to develop.
Worst bits: Not getting enough sleep when the next door neighbour to the house in Chesterton Road wanted to play music when I needed to go to sleep!
The cold, cold wind straight from the Urals, felt so keenly when cycling.

Wendy Spray (née Coulson)

Best bits: As a medic, being allowed to do an arts subject in the third year of my time at New Hall.

Worst bits: As so many others have said, feeling lost and inferior to other students who seemed so confident in the Cambridge environment.

Philippa Evans (née Taylor)

Best bit: just being in Cambridge, and becoming independent as a person and as a learner. I feel so sorry for those who have missed out this year on that freedom.

Worst bit: the MML (*Modern and Medieval Languages*) course. I admit I enjoyed the topics I studied, but the standard of lectures was not high, and language skills were relegated to a very unimportant role; the only oral exam was before the course began, and the colleges/department did nothing to encourage a year abroad. As a result, hardly anyone pursued this option, although theoretically it existed. I believe this has since changed, but at the time there seemed to be an assumption that just reading lots of French/German, etc, would be enough to make you a fluent speaker too. I'm not sure this is a great approach to language learning...

Denise Phillipson (née Milburn)

Best bits were extraordinary; worst bits were depths of despair. I think the 8-week terms were such a hot house with so many things to learn about myself, let alone the academic sphere. By the holidays, I was exhausted and spent the first week at home in bed ill having (as my mother put it), burned the candle at both ends. I met lots of people but didn't keep in contact with many. I was too gauche, naïve and socially at sea. I would enjoy it all so much more now!

Deborah Glass

The best: This was definitely the long vac term. As scientists we had to return to Cambridge between each academic year for practical work during the long vac. It was a wonderful time to socialise, go punting and enjoy Cambridge with far less pressure of supervisions and exams.

The worst: Shortly before exams I was revising in New Hall library and when I went out briefly, my lecture notes were taken from the table where I was working.

It was very upsetting especially as it was my best subject and I was hoping to do well. Fortunately a good friend Dave at Queens kindly lent me his notes.

Hilary Martin

Best bits and Worst bits: The worst bits were the lack of academic support and struggling with my portfolio, plus the constant churning of boyfriends due to the imbalance between numbers of men and women. Neither was good for me, but they also had upsides in that I had an incredible amount of free time to pursue anything I wanted, and I was rarely lonely!

I adored being at Cambridge. The best bits were being able to go to any lecture anywhere I wanted, plus just generally being around so many smart people and soaking up so many interesting ideas. That truly changed my life.

My favourite memory of Cambridge is walking through Kings at sunset during Michaelmas Term, hearing the choir practising for the Carol Service. Glorious ethereal music floating to the heavens, absolutely magical.

Gillian Blessley

One of the best bits was meeting and being amongst so many interesting and often friendly people, in such a beautiful place, and in times when so much felt possible.

A flip side of that was being in an ivory tower, remote from the real world; the famous gap between town and gown.

Another best was the freedom we had to explore and question – although for me that also fed into the worst, a sense of being lost at sea and alone.

On the whole it has been a huge and worthwhile privilege.

Helen Mayer

After New Hall

Being a new college in a new, unadorned building, New Hall carried no accumulation of tradition that I might have found intimidating or stifling. I was the first in my family to go to any university, and only the third pupil from my school to get to Oxbridge, and was initially rather overwhelmed. New Hall's informal atmosphere, and the presence of other girls from state schools, helped me to feel that I belonged there as much as anyone. I remained socially awkward though and many opportunities passed me by. Despite that, I enjoyed being at Cambridge and left with a much greater sense of self worth than when I started. That enabled me to recognise and accept that I was in no way ambitious. I had neither desire nor temperament to be a 'go-getter' or a leader; to make a mark on the world or to make lots of money. I trained to be a teacher but left after a year, realising that I wasn't conscientious enough to not begrudge the hours of marking and preparation that left me with virtually no time for myself.

Thereafter, at a modest grade in the Civil Service, I rarely had to take work home, although its content was far from stimulating. Working part time enabled me to do a two-year diploma course in humanistic counselling and then to develop a small practice from home. Counselling was worthwhile, stimulating and satisfying; and I continued with it for about twelve years until, having taken early retirement from the Civil Service and done an RHS course in horticulture, gardening became the focus of my enthusiasm and time. It was only at the end of summer 2020 that I stepped back from being the gardener for a charitable trust, whose three acres had become 'my' garden for ten years. I loved the work, could do as I pleased, and knew that I was improving and increasing wildlife habitats for insects, birds, small mammals and amphibians. I added trees, shrubs and innumerable herbaceous perennials to the ornamental areas and, whilst I wasn't seeking praise, it was gratifying to know that staff and visitors found the gardens beautiful and uplifting.

New Hall encouraged alternative and diverse approaches to thinking and, by extension, life. This fed my self-belief so that I've been confident in the choices I've made.

Sue Attridge (née Wood)

My Cambridge degree almost certainly helped to open more career doors in the UK than my New Zealand degree (in English) would have done on its own. I started out as a lowly editorial assistant for the Royal Society of Medicine then spent a few very enjoyable years with The British Council before moving into teaching in both adult and further education, which allowed more flexibility in juggling work and childcare. In those days, your UK degree gave you 'recognised' teacher status so I made the most of it and concentrated on the post-16 cohorts, who were relatively civilised. (I did acquire a selection of teaching certificates along the way to improve my status!) Although Anglo-Saxon and Old Norse may not seem to be the most vocational area of study, I enjoyed using my knowledge of the History of the English Language when teaching more advanced students, both first and second language speakers, from a range of different countries. It was particularly relevant in my last role as a teacher trainer, delivering an ESOL specialism qualification. Since retiring from a 'proper' job I am still involved in giving occasional private tuition to ex-students by request and really enjoy the teaching without the soul-destroying paperwork. Lockdown encouraged me to learn how to teach on Zoom for both my adult students and my grandchildren! My husband was at Cambridge for 7 years as both undergraduate and PhD student so my Cambridge friends are almost entirely through his network and we've attended many reunions over the years. There is no doubt that my two years at New Hall helped to shape the rest of my life.

Aileen Regan (née Kidd)

I never did do anything with my degree. I did a teacher training course but didn't immediately land a teaching post so I took on a couple of temporary part-time jobs as gardener and nursing auxiliary. I enjoyed both so much that I ended up spending my working life as part-time district nurse and part-time gardener. It's been impressive, but irrelevant, to have been able to put M.A. Cantab as my highest qualification on job application forms.

Emma Wheelock

Over the years I taught English in Turkey, worked as a TV journalist, and wanted to study medicine as a mature student, but actually decided instead to study Acupuncture, which I have been practising for many years now, and which I absolutely love.

Lou Radford

Towards the end of my first year, I contemplated leaving my Economics course, as neoclassical economics did not inspire me, and losing my father was painful and destabilising. By chance, my life was changed by an offer through a New Hall postgraduate to be a nanny for the summer of 1972 for two US economists (Joe Stiglitz and Charlotte Kuh). The experiences of that summer were instrumental in deciding to complete my degree, and then marry Charlotte's younger brother, Peter. I have been grateful for the career and life opportunities that these decisions opened up for me.

I remember my male postgraduate supervisor of my third-year dissertation telling me what a mistake I was making, going to the US to get married as soon as I graduated, rather than continuing with economic research. Little did he or I know that I would end up as an epidemiologist at UCL several years later, and eventually become the scientific director of the oldest British birth cohort study and establish the MRC Unit for Lifelong Health and Ageing!

Diana Kuh (née Lewin)

I haven't used the economics all that much, although not being overawed by figures and analysis has often helped me. I trained as a community worker, spent time working in Lesotho and Botswana in development, was a community worker in London for 10 years and then moved back to Oxford. I taught for a few years at Oxford Brookes University, but otherwise worked or managed community development mostly in social housing until 2016 when I set up as a freelance life coach and love it, particularly working as part of a project, helping ethnic minority women to find employment, volunteering or training.

Wendy Spray (née Coulson)

In my third year, my boy-friend gave up his post-grad studies and got a job at Pye's, the local electronics firm in Cambridge, as a computer programmer. We married a few weeks after I got my degree, and I joined him at Pye's. I mentioned at the interview that I was about to be married to him, and was immediately given the job. An interesting version of nepotism.

Jo Edkins (née Dibblee)

After New Hall I moved into a succession of squats in London with some friends who had finished Cambridge the year before. Another friend had a job in Islington Housing Department, who'd tip us off about houses that they'd bought but weren't yet ready to renovate (when we would need to move on). I remember pushing Sally's piano down the road to the next house; ritual post-move meals in Brick Lane, paraffin heaters; the Hornsey Public Baths on Sunday mornings for our weekly wash.

After my year out I went to Central London Polytechnic for my Part 2 (post-graduate diploma) in Architecture, as by then I was in love with Steve, (my partner of 40 years), who I'd only known vaguely at Cambridge.

Part 2 at Central Poly was a striking contrast to Cambridge. It was, of course, much less elite, and there was no campus and far less social life. But perhaps the greatest difference was the prevalent tendency to unquestioningly accept and comply with the tutor's word. There was almost none of the freedom around studying that had been so liberating and also bewildering at Cambridge, and which may now be increasingly rare.

After struggling through my Part 2, I mostly practised in local government architecture departments, which back in the 80's were still at the forefront of public social building. For the first time, really, I found my strengths and passion in design, contract administration, working with end- users, and over-seeing it all take shape on site.
I retired around 3 years ago, and am very fortunate to be doing many of the things I care for most. I volunteer with the wonderful Women for Refugee Women and am active in Climate campaigns. And enjoy, amongst other things, running (lots), a poetry discussion group, and time with my family and grandchildren.

Helen Mayer

After Cambridge, I spent six months working in private gardens in Oxfordshire, then a year as a trainee at the RHS Gardens at Wisley in Surrey, then several months in a bulb nursery in Holland, and in an arboretum in Belgium. From 1976 to 1979, I studied for the Diploma of Horticulture at the Royal Botanic Gardens, Kew. When I went for the interview, they did not ask about my degree, being more concerned by my lack of science 'A' Levels. I loved Kew, and found the study comparatively easy, probably because I had learned how to work at Cambridge. I had been given a full grant by my county council to go to New Hall but, mercifully, Kew pays its students, since they work much of the year in the gardens. Afterwards, I pursued a career in horticultural journalism and books, of which I have now chalked up 20, 18 on gardening, and two on social history, the latest of which is a biography of John Buchan, a copy of which I have given to Murray Edwards library. Sadly, I was too late to send Zara Steiner a copy, but I hope she would have approved of my reversion to history late in my career.
I have in the past also been the gardening columnist for a variety of national publications, including, inter alia, The Observer, The Sunday Telegraph, The Independent, The Daily Telegraph, The Spectator and The Garden. I was a magistrate for ten years and am now chairman of a charity, the Finnis Scott Foundation, that gives grants to horticultural

and art-historical projects. I spend a great deal of my time in my garden or other people's.

Ursula Wide (née Buchan)

I felt proud of gaining a place at New Hall and, like many others, rejected an offer from Oxford (Somerville) in favour of New Hall, which combined the academic kudos of Cambridge with a delightful and very dynamic modernity. I wouldn't have swapped my time at Cambridge for anything else, despite having a mini 'breakdown' in my final term and coming unstuck in the finals. Having totally frozen, I walked out of my first exam. Helen Clover, my lovely Director of Studies, scooped me up, dusted me down and enabled me to continue. I limped through the remaining papers and came out with a Third. It took quite a long time to work through the resulting demoralisation and dented self-confidence. Someone talked of imposter syndrome on coming up. I got a bad case of that going down, especially when I came to take my MA. I then struggled to find some direction and a career that satisfied. However, after having my children I began to work for Relate as a couple counsellor and realised this was a career I really wanted to develop. I re-engaged with academia to get further qualifications in the field and finally confronted my demons. Phew! I could do it after all! Nobody else doubted it – just me. I started working full time with Relate, counselling, supervising and teaching. I finally became a Senior Practice Consultant before I retired in 2016.

So the Cambridge experience was a highly ambivalent one for me, but very valuable as a non-standard springboard into personal possibilities. There was also the Growing Up, the fun and especially the lifelong friends I've made. Cambridge has never defined me or given any 'assurance of competence'. Instead it administered a necessary jolt so that I could find competence in other ways. New Hall was, and remains for me, a very special place.

My parents had high career hopes for me which I clearly disappointed in comparison with my brother, for example, who became the senior partner in a dental practice. Marriage and motherhood was hardly a career, they reckoned, merely a standard part of life. When I became a counsellor with Relate and gradually expanded my work there until I was full time, they thought it was a bit 'new age' and hardly a proper career – not like medicine, the law or engineering etc. Don't get me wrong – they were always loving and supportive, but the subscript was clear! When I started training other counsellors and supervisors, and then became a member of the Senior Practice Team which had managerial components, that fitted their template a bit better. I mention all this because 'success' contains many assumptions, and a hierarchy of attributes, which are sadly, if unsurprisingly, patriarchal. Parenting, mothering in particular, comes very near the bottom, even though it is arguably the most difficult, complex and important job of them all. In Relate the workforce was predominantly female. It was, nevertheless, interesting that a disproportionate number of supervisors and senior managers were male, as in many of the 'soft' professions.

Anne Muir (née Borrett)

I finished up as a GP in Windermere for most of my career, having married an engineer in Kendal. I'm still here. Since retiring as a GP in 2012, I have very much enjoyed voluntary medical work on several occasions both in Nepal, with PHASE (www.phaseworldwide.org), mentoring health workers in very remote rural mountain communities; and similar work in Peru with LED (www.lighteducationdevelopment.org). I'm not sure where this fits in with New Hall, but I'm sure it helped me to learn to continue to take opportunities that present themselves, and to go on learning!

Sarah Watson (née Henley)

As I was completely clueless as to what I wanted to do after graduating I ended up having a late gap year: half the year on a kibbutz in Israel followed by the other half of the year as a bus conductor in London. I then worked as a research assistant for a couple of years, followed my husband to the US for a year, then did a PGCE at Homerton. Teaching was not for me though, and after having my children I decided I wanted a job with a desk and pieces of paper. I started freelance editing and worked in publishing for the rest of my career, seeing the pieces of paper gradually give way to digital information. Alongside this I have always drawn and painted, and now I am retired I can concentrate on my art.

Alison Litherland (née Hill)

What have I done with my life after Cambridge? I have been a Teacher. I have worked for 40-odd (some have been very odd) years in various primary schools, "doing the music"...a morning here, an afternoon there. I have had "orchestras" and "bands", and taught so many recorders that I need a hearing aid now. I've done singing, music festivals, Infant music (arrgh!). I had a great time, and touched a lot of lives.

Some of my pupils have gone to music college, but many have just had real enjoyment. Young children, trailing their clouds of glory, are like Dogs - it's always "My Favourite!" They are as "keen as terriers round a rat-cage" (Conan Doyle). As they get older they become Cats, with "you want me to do WHAT?" and "what's in this for me?". N.B. Never become a Cat!

The so-called "assurance of competence" gained from getting into New Hall has been a bulwark for me throughout my lowly teaching career. The Cambridge card has rebuffed arrogant "specialists" seeking to show me my business, and Ofsted inspectors, who have melted away in the wall. If I am dealing with some prat, I find that to put it at the head of the notepaper works very well. It simply is the Ace. I am very grateful to New Hall for this.

Sue Whitham (née Addison)

I have been very encouraged to realise that many of us have had fulfilling careers without being the high fliers that some people seem to think follows automatically with a Cambridge degree, although there have indeed been plenty of those among our number. I loved Susan Whitham's comment how satisfying it had been to use MA Cantab when dealing with some prat. The only time I can remember really making use of it was when trying to get information from the old Ministry of Agriculture when I thought they were being dilatory. I tried using MA Cantab and had a reply by return, which perversely then annoyed me because I felt a hard-working moorland farmer was just as deserving of a quick response as I was

Having achieved a Land Economy degree I was able to qualify as a Chartered Surveyor without doing any more exams, just two years' practical work which I did with the local District Valuer and Valuation Office in Taunton, followed by a TPC (Test of Professional Competence), so for a few years I was actually a civil servant, after facing a rather alarming interview board immediately following my farewell to Cambridge. Then I found more and more of my time was taken up managing (and occasionally being hands on) our 200 acre farm on the edge of Exmoor, to say nothing of coping with two very energetic sons, so I retired from my salaried job. That also then gave me time to type, edit and proof read for my husband.

Sarah Wilson (née Stallard)

I graduated, newly married to a lecturer in Economic and Social History at Hull, who had just finished as a Cambridge post-graduate, so I moved there for an MPhil. I started a second-hand bookshop in Beverley with friends and worked in it part time. I also lectured for Hull University Extramural Department and the Workers' Educational Association plus doing an adult education teaching diploma part time. My first assignment was a class in Goole. When I got there, I discovered that the previous lecturer had been Richard Hoggart in 1952 and four class members had gone along as young mothers, now with adult children the same age as me: they said they had been asking the WEA ever since for another course.

By 1978 my husband had fallen in love with someone else, so we divorced and he moved to S.Korea. I had become really interested in development issues and wondered who might employ an English Literature graduate in this area. I applied to the Civil Service Fast

Stream and stated boldly that my only interest was in joining the Ministry of Overseas. To my amazement I got in and spent seventeen years there, with diplomatic service postings in Kenya, New York (UN) and Brussels (EU). On the latter two postings I was accompanied by my second husband, a musician – this time I got it right.

At 42, I became pregnant and discovered that, despite having a female Minister, they couldn't actually countenance a job share at Head of Department level (now quite uncontentious). So I left and started chairing Civil Service Selection Boards part time. I still work freelance for them (now FSAC) - our focus is on widening participation to have a Civil Service which reflects the country. When I joined, the issue was to bring in women. The hardest area to make real inroads in now has proved to be lower socio-economic groups; overall ethnic minority success is now not bad, though within this we still struggle to attract good candidates from some specific groups. I also assess for medium to high-level posts in UN agencies in developing countries.

There was a thread on what Cambridge did for our lives. It certainly prepared me for the largely male environments in which I have often worked, and for being the wage earner throughout life, having married a folk musician and produced a musician son. It probably opened a few doors, though Civil Service application was strictly merit based. Cambridge still carries a cachet in international UN circles.

However, now it is a bit of an embarrassment in the Civil Service, which has worked hard to get away from Oxbridge domination: when three of us who wrote the Fast Stream exercises for eight years from 2010 realised that we were all Cambridge graduates, we played it down. Have others found that it's now something to keep quiet about?

Pam Hilton

I studied for a PhD in plant biology in Leicester. Whilst I was there a Swiss professor did a sabbatical in our lab and I was the only person who bothered to try to talk to him in French. He offered me a teaching and research job at Lausanne University and I have remained near the shores of Lake Geneva ever since.

After some time in biology research I turned my hand to environmental work, acting as a consultant for various UN organisations.

Later I was offered contracts doing technical translations from German and/or French into English as well as editing technical writing on a wide range of topics.

Hilary Martin

When I left, I found it quite hard to adjust to life in the "real world". I was pregnant within a year, which was another whole education in itself. After 10 years or so, I decided to train as a homeopath. I still work with people in that capacity and I am continually fascinated by how many different kinds of people there are in the world, each speaking their own language and with their own unique viewpoint, connected to their own words, which you can never quite translate. I love to ask questions that enable me and the other person to really appreciate their uniqueness and to enquire what does or would make their life sing. So maybe what I learned in Cambridge was something about the endless variety of language and experience, how you can never exactly translate, which enables you to keep questioning.

Penny Stirling

And after New Hall? Loads of job offers before we had even taken finals (do you remember the milk rounds?) I wanted to go into Industry, so chose a graduate traineeship with the BAA, with a day release to the Polytechnic of Central London for an MBA, having been advised that I needed a more "proletariat" qualification to support the Cambridge one. This was the mid-seventies after all. The BAA was fun, I was in the Industrial Relations section. The PCL was okay, seemed a bit flabby, but I did pick up the hard skills of statistics and accounts, which was useful. We bought a house in Islington, where one day I bumped into Wendy Joseph, then living in the next road. I had 3 more children, and moved into employment and public policy analysis, for the EU, the ITBs, the Design Council and others, as well as getting immersed in lots of local parish-pump voluntary work. I slowly built up some independent consultancy expertise in small businesses, governance, charities and social enterprise; nothing stellar, but very satisfying. Looking back, it has been an utterly normal trajectory from bright young thing challenging the status quo to wise-woman warning of unintended consequences. Antigone to Cassandra? But I prefer to keep below the radar. For many different reasons, Cambridge was probably the seminal experience of my life, and it was New Hall that got me in there. Or that famous entrance paper anyway.

Fiona Edwards-Stuart (née Weaver)

What did I get from New Hall? It's hard to differentiate from Cambridge in general. Certainly both moulded who I am today and what I did.
I read Arch/Anth and then Social Anthropology. After a year at the LSE on Social Administration, I worked in Social Housing in Liverpool. I was writing a lot of reports for the Government on why/how the legislation for Housing Associations wasn't working on the ground; and realised I needed a doctorate to be taken seriously, so went back to Cambridge and studied Italian migration. - great fun if not very apposite.
I then had 2 children and worked self-employed for various charities/NGOs creating interactive education packs mostly for schools – on environment, history etc. I found I really enjoy applied academia; finding out masses about a subject and then distilling and sharing it. And I became very interested in how children learn and focused on that. We had moved by then to this area south of Oxford and I met up with academics there and became involved with the Ethnicity Seminar and the International Gender Studies Centre, as a Research Associate, which has been interesting and frustrating over the years. This led to some teaching/projects in Oxford and in Myanmar, Armenia, with Roma/Travellers etc.
My husband's public role by then made it difficult for me to accept funding for the Education projects and I followed the path of what my Oxford colleagues term 'a trailing spouse'. This sounds so derogatory

but can give one amazing opportunities; I had the opportunity to work with projects with Plan International with street children in Ethiopia, Delhi, Ghana and Malawi; met many fascinating eminent people at the WEF at Davos; stayed in Embassy Residences round the world; meals with Desmond Tutu, Nobel prize winners, staying at Chateau Lafite with the German Chancellor – the first time Germans had been there since the War; events at palaces, in China, the States and so on. All with my anthropologist's hat on. I found the 'Cambridge card' helped my self-confidence and gave me some validation in all this. And now my husband is an Honorary Fellow of St John's and various friends are Heads of Houses its nice to feel I'm there in my own right as a New Hall alumna – with many discussions about the change of name of our college.

(It's been brought to my attention that I should have pointed out that we met all my costs on any trips!)

One major life lesson I took from New Hall came from a friend; we were discussing dissatisfaction with some things that NHU were doing, and she said that one shouldn't just complain but do something about it. We stood for election and tried to do what we thought right for the next few months.

This came back to haunt me recently at Oxford with a bullying situation. I felt obliged to live by these high standards and stand up for right, with far reaching consequences but definitely something I'm pleased New Hall gave me the confidence to do.

Siân Crisp (née Jenkins)

I must confess I do what you have been calling Public Realm stuff. At least I do it in front a lot of people, sitting as a judge at the Old Bailey. It was the culmination of a lot of chances and mischances. It certainly wasn't ever a choice I made. I was happily reading English and changed to part 2 law because I had a boyfriend who was doing that. It led me to the Bar and finally to the Bench. Of course it is fascinating and I'm incredibly lucky. But a job like teaching, where you can make a child's face light up with knowledge, or medicine where you can make a child well, or mothering where you can make a child, all might be thought a lot better than looking into that child's eyes and sending him to prison for 15 years. So like everyone else, I reckon it's the unsung heroes who really count.

Wendy Joseph

My time at New Hall was one of the most intensely lived experiences of my lifetime. I loved it, and feel it was deeply formative. Socially, I gained confidence in myself as a young woman, a friend and a loving partner. Intellectually, it gave me endless ongoing cause for thought, reflection and new learning, not to mention an entrée into my first job as a junior academic at Murdoch University in Perth, Western Australia (my family had migrated to WA in early 1973). From there I moved to a career in research management at the University of Western Australia where I worked for 32 years (some part time while I had two gorgeous children), and retired in 2014. I'm now enjoying living life at a more leisurely pace with lots of fun activities including helping run a community youth music program, and a big band which performs for monthly dances to raise funds for charity. I'm very happy living in Western Australia, and feel incredibly fortunate to have spent my undergraduate years in Cambridge at New Hall.

Lorna Robertson

In my third year I calmed down, forgot some of my prejudices about a career in medicine, and applied to London medical schools. I cut my hair, and 6" off the bottom of a wonderful Biba midi dress to look the part for interviews. It worked, but meant I had to earn all the money I could in the holidays as I had no grant. I did a 4-day typing course, and went to an agency in London. The best job I had was typing for the BBC; I think they liked me because I was happy to type into a computer, which had put off most professional typists. Eventually I worked as a nursing assistant in a mental handicap hospital outside London. It paid less, but gave great experience of life at the other end of the NHS.

I've never regretted starting medicine after Cambridge. I found the science easy after Nat Sci tripos, and I knew how to organise life by studying efficiently. I've gone on to specialise in oncology, be the first part-timer in the department (half the consultant staff were less than full time by the time I retired), and head of department. I retired when I realised I was no longer 100% committed to my patients, but up to that point I loved it, and still feel it was the greatest job in the world (well, perhaps after wildlife camera woman, for which I have no skills at all).

Sally Morgan

I realise now how fortunate medics were not to have difficult decisions at the end of our first degree. I went on to clinical training at Oxford with three other medics from my year and then back to hospital posts in Cambridge, having by then married an academic. After ideas of oncology, I discovered general practice and that what I liked most was working with people. I spent nearly 35 years as a GP in Cambridge, in a practice where we had our own lists in the old-fashioned family doctor way, a huge privilege.

Throughout my medical career, I have been massively grateful to New Hall for giving me access to the outstanding scientific training and academic rigour of our medical course. It enabled me to appraise and use the ever and rapidly-changing body of knowledge required to be competent as a doctor.

In the late 1980s (amidst the frantic battle against the NHS reforms of 1990) I became involved in a small way in the development of counselling in general practice, which opened my eyes to the way understandings of mental health could transform the experience of working with people and enhance the outcome. In the late 1990s, still being a GP, I trained as a psychotherapist and hoped to be of some use in medical education.

However medical work in the 2000s seemed to me to be taken over by management and by a culture of only recognising things which can be counted numerically. This left me and many other doctors overloaded with management duties and feeling that the human side and the integrity of medical work were being devalued. I retired in 2016, exhausted, but understood from the farewells I received that I had been able to contribute as a GP something that was felt to be of value, a working life to which New Hall gave me the key.

Philippa Evans (née Taylor)

I, too, like others have been "just a GP" working mostly part time to fit in and follow wherever my husband's career took us and bringing up our family. I found general practice challenging at times but very rewarding in being part of the local community and being privileged to closely interact with families in a way that Consultants may not. It was wonderful to see the babies that I helped deliver grow up and become mothers themselves.

Jan Sherman (née Phillips)

I stayed in Cambridge for a while working for one of my former teachers. Then I drifted to London and got a job in Covent Garden working for a different former teacher. My boyfriend and I decided to go to the south of France to help with some building work that his friend was doing. I had the job of rewiring the place and had the interesting experience of shopping for electrical supplies in French! French wiring was all single insulated conductors in conduit, as opposed to English twin + earth. I occasionally had nightmares about multi coloured spaghetti, or that I had found another circuit whose purpose was entirely unknown! During that trip I read about Landscape Architecture as a career and decided that was what I really wanted to do. So I never went back to Cambridge or anywhere else to do my Part II. I worked for architects in London who also did some landscape projects, and was given an extraordinarily free rein to do some very third rate planting design! Plans to apply to a MLA program (which I am not sure I would have got into anyway, given my 2:2) were put on hold when the boyfriend and I made another adventurous trip to Los Angeles, where I was able to work for landscape architects under the table. The boyfriend and I split up, none too soon, and eventually I met my future husband. We have been together since 1980, and I have been living in LA ever since. Due to a lucky break in the licensing procedures in the US, I was able to obtain a Landscape Architecture licence here without ever going back to full-time education. I spent most of my career working for the same small firm, doing mostly commercial work such as office buildings, hospitals and especially colleges and universities, mostly in California but occasionally in other states too. I went on medical leave in 2018, but have never gone back, since I found I was so much happier and healthier without the stress of constant deadlines. So I am now technically if not also officially retired.

Gillian Blessley

After graduating I decided to apply for teacher training and was pleased to discover that a fellow student from New Hall was on the same course at Leicester University. We became good friends and both then worked in our first schools in Sheffield and shared houses for many years. After a few years I decided to leave teaching and was lucky to work for 4+ years as a research officer in the Sheffield Applied Psychology Unit. From there, I got a job as a research officer in Birmingham Social Services, so that I could be with my boyfriend Mark, who I married in 1984. (I had met him through old Cambridge friends, so there is a link back.) Later, I worked as a planning and research manager in the Probation Service and subsequently spent about 15 years as Chief Officer of Probation first in Warwickshire. I retired in 2015.

Liz Stafford

When we graduated in 1974, just before equal opportunity legislation, there were few jobs for women in geology, as North Sea oil and coal were men only. But with my degree and an MSc in hydrogeology, I've worked in consulting and academia since 1976, initially in an entirely male dominated world but fortunately now much more inclusive and flexible. When I first asked to return to work part time after my first child in 1980, it seemed to be a new idea and potential career blocker.

Now it appears to be acceptable for everyone to have a better work-life balance, so I've been part time for the last 8 years. I'm involved in professional activities beyond my day job and quite disappointed that after 50 years, I'm still the first woman to take several senior roles. Not rich and famous, but always ready to speak out, network and do the voluntary jobs. Is that the New Hall or Cambridge influence? Maybe, but it might go back much further to a 'girls can do anything' head teacher at primary school. Perhaps that's what New Hall was looking for with their innovative exam paper?

Jane Dottridge (née Rooke)

I carried on with my engineering and qualified as a civil engineer in 1978 after working with a couple of firms of civil engineering consultants (Rendel, Palmer & Tritton and Halcrows) on projects like the Thames Barrier and then joined BP for 13 years initially as an engineer on offshore projects before moving into corporate planning while doing a part-time MBA. I did various other jobs in refinery management and refinery negotiations plus I was Secretary to the BP Oil Board for a year which was fascinating. I spent a couple of years in Australia working at the Kwinana Refinery for BP and then back to a corporate HR job.

They had a big voluntary redundancy programme in 1992 and I decided I wanted to leave and do something that was more worthwhile. I thought the charity world would welcome me but it turned out to be not quite like that. In any case, I worked for three charities in succession (VSO, Marie Stopes International and Trinity Hospice in Clapham) but by 2000 I had decided I wanted to get away from London because I was fed up of the noise, the traffic and the crowds of people. A friend who sang in a choir with me encouraged me to apply for the role of Bursar in Oxford and Cambridge colleges, because she thought that my skills and experience would be perfect for that. The job of Treasurer (Finance & Estates Bursar) at Somerville College Oxford came up and I went to the interview and met the Principal, Dame Fiona Caldicott, who I knew of from the hospice as she had created the role of Caldicott Guardians, who protect the confidentiality of patient data. I really enjoyed working with her and we achieved a lot to improve the position of the college including new student accommodation buildings plus improving the finances and investments.

I left Somerville at the end of 2012 taking early retirement so I could do some more trustee and non-executive roles to build on the trustee roles I already had. I've spent the last eight years working as a trustee for various organisations including Chair of Trustees of Ark T (a small arts charity in Oxford), Chair of Trustees of the University Women's Club in London and Chair of Governors of Pipers Corner School near High Wycombe plus a trustee of 2 other music charities. It's been a challenging time to be involved with all these organisations because of the impact of Covid but I've enjoyed it. I have also carried on doing lots of singing in chamber choirs until Covid struck and all singing was banned - Zoom rehearsals really aren't at all the same thing!

Helen Morton

I loved my time at New Hall although I didn't have time to join in much. After graduating I did a year at Homerton, not at that time a member of the University, to obtain my PGCE. I taught English at the school then known as Manor Community College on Arbury for twenty-five years, loving it. I became Head of English and each Christmas delighted in directing a performance of 'Oliver', 'West Side Story' or whatever, where the pupils could play in the orchestra, sing, dance, make costumes or props of whatever - education! Local people delighted in paying and filling our hall.

Alison New - SRN MA (Cantab) PGCE and a former City Councillor in
all that too!

My Cambridge degree in psychology paved the way for my future career as a Clinical psychologist working with children. Although not the most comprehensive psychology degree because of it being within the Natural Sciences tripos, it enabled me to gain a place on the M. Phil in Clinical psychology at Edinburgh university. I went on to work in child mental health and latterly in paediatric psychology. It has been a rewarding career which I have enjoyed and found satisfying.

Alison Wray (née O'Brien)

When I graduated, I stayed on in Cambridge and started looking for a job (no milk round for us). I signed on at the local dole, having no other immediate prospects. Having just got a 2:1, I was rather surprised that I only qualified for clerical work. How arrogant can you be? Still, I joined the Post Office for a temporary job. We sat in a large room in rows of desks with a supervisor on a raised platform at the front. We were all given a pile of index cards, each with the account of a telephone number in the East of England district. Our job was to cross out the total, add the price increase, which I think was something like £1.60 per telephone line, and rewrite the total at the bottom. The highlight of my time there was working out the new bill for the Sandringham Estate. It took a team of about 10 of us all summer. A job which can now be done in minutes, and probably more accurately, by computer. Still, it taught me a lot about the importance of working with a team of people from all sorts of backgrounds, some of whom could do the job better and faster than me and with more patience. It was back to the world outside the ivory tower with a bump.

My husband, meanwhile, was recruited to the Inspectorate of Ancient Monuments in the Department of the Environment. In those days, you were 'deployed' wherever the Inspectorate wanted you, and he was sent to Scotland to join what is now Historic Environment Scotland. I followed and was lucky enough to be taken on as a Research Assistant with the RCAHMS (Royal Commission on the Ancient and Historical Monuments of Scotland), an independent, but government funded organisation carrying out fieldwork and research to create an Inventory of monuments in Scotland. I presented for interview in my lucky green tweed suit. I joined in 1976, when there were 26 staff, I became CEO in 2004 and had 110 staff. We had remained independent from 1908, but the Scottish Government decided we should be amalgamated with Historic Scotland and my final years before retirement in 2016 were spent bringing these two organisations together to form Historic Environment Scotland. What of my husband? He became more and more controlling, and I became more and more isolated. I managed to escape the marriage in 1978 and we were subsequently divorced. I met my lovely Scottish husband in 1985, we married in 1987 and have two lovely daughters and two beautiful granddaughters.

I left Cambridge as a very changed person. I was much more confident and knew a lot more about myself and what I could achieve, although the Archaeology department was not highly regarded, the Cambridge degree has been a passport to opportunities and is widely respected. I don't use that card very often, but it is sometimes useful. Above all, I have never been intimidated by a room full of men, a male dominated committee or a senior male colleague. We have all been part of that generation that have helped break through the glass ceilings or into male dominated professions and helped pave the way for those that follow. Even so, I do still get that 'imposter syndrome' feeling that someday I shall get found out.

Diana Murray (née Collyer)

I spent my working life in social housing – policy, management, and finally teaching on a BSc/MSc degree. I learned to write properly working in local government; and I learned to study properly doing a MSc at the LSE in my forties. The most important legacy from New Hall for me was the friends I made there, still my friends today.

Rosie Boughton

I had a place to go to Oxford for clinical, but at the last minute I turned it down to go to London, as my boyfriend was going there and I wanted to keep having ready access to the art world. Probably not a wise decision. My clinical training was not good, but I think I grew up in London. I saw the diversity I hadn't seen in Cambridge. I worked in many of the teaching hospitals in London and also went to Oxford, but especially loved working at the Royal London hospital in the East End.

I went on to do research in Cambridge into Type 2 diabetes and then became a consultant endocrinologist at the University hospital in Norwich. I was our department's lead for teaching the medical students and loved that.

I loved my career and feel I was only able to be successful, and to make the most of my career, as a result of the excellent education in Cambridge and particularly the wonderful supervision system provided by New Hall.

Rosemary Grande (née Temple)

I got through the exams in one piece and then went on to the London School of Economics for a year to study Social Administration – this really meant the workings of the welfare state. This led to an interest in health policy that resulted in a job at the Department of Community Medicine at Oxford under Richard Doll. Andrew and I got married in 1976 in order to move to Brussels where I was a *stagiare*, or intern, at the European Commission. Then eventually to the King's Fund where I was a Founder Fellow of the King's Fund Institute and then was lucky enough to lead the Fund's work on the future of health care in London. Barbara Stocking was a very supportive colleague at the Fund and then again later when I followed her into the NHS, where the management culture was brutal. I managed to keep my end up but was much happier when I moved to the voluntary sector, where I had a happy period at the British Red Cross. My final job was running I CAN, the national children's charity, where it (mainly) felt good to be in charge.

Virginia Beardshaw

Teacher training, really just a way of intersecting with the known world, almost all my relatives are teachers on both Mum and Dad's sides. I went to the career counsellor saying that I didn't know what sort of job I might get. They suggested career counselling, which was odd as I had just said that I didn't know much about what the world had to offer. It felt like they needed to tag someone before they could move on. I taught for 4 years but left because I realised that I didn't like (other people's) children enough. I did an MSc in occupational health, worked at Boots in Nottingham as an occupational hygienist for 4 years than went to Birmingham university to be a consultant occupational hygienist for local industry, bringing money into the Dept. and doing some teaching. I got into research, trying to get better occupational exposure assessment for epidemiology. I moved to Australia in 1995, finally did a PhD and have worked on benzene in the petroleum industry, firefighters' cancer, silicosis and pneumoconiosis, among other things. I think I found my metier, picky stuff on my own but part of a team for a worthy outcome.

Deborah Glass

I had left school wanting to go into teaching and, having married during August, joined a PGCE course at The Institute of Education, London University. How much easier than for those following teaching courses now: our year was neatly divided up so that we were not expected to do "academic" work during our two spells of teaching practice. My teaching practice was at Mary Datchelor School, a girls' grammar school in Camberwell Grove.

After completing the PGCE I taught at Putney High School for three years before our move out of London to the Southampton edge of the New Forest. I taught in a Hampshire comprehensive school for a year before our first child was born. The school had already asked me to take on their Maths 'O' level night school course a direction which was very valuable in enabling me to "keep my hand in" through the births and early years of our first two children.

A move up to Edinburgh saw the birth of our third child and although I never broached the Scottish education system I was able to keep in touch through a small amount of tutoring and work with the PTA of our children's primary school. I clearly remember the discussions which took place when the idea of governing bodies for schools was being introduced in Scotland.

A Cambridge maths degree meant that I never had a problem finding work. After moving back to England and the West Midlands I initially became a School Governor at our son's primary school and in fact for a short time helped with some of the governor training in Birmingham primary schools. As the family became more independent, I moved back into the field of maths education with both tutoring and work in Adult Education. Both great areas for flexibility: I could change from daytime teaching to evening teaching depending on the needs of the family. My final role within Adult Education gave me the chance to support the maths department through an Ofsted reinspection (then successful) and to move on to supporting (mainly GCSE) maths tutors in the Birmingham Adult Education Service. I continued to teach my own classes and really enjoyed the variety of this work across all areas of the city. The Service became involved in the government backed scheme for "Improving Learning in Mathematics" and I was able to use and encourage a more collaborative approach to learning: so well suited to over-16s. Fun and generally successful.

Dorothy Cade (née Clark)

My ambition by the third year was to leave the ivory tower and work in industry, and luckily there was a demand for graduates at the time so people came especially to recruit us. It was called the Milk Round. Many companies had Graduate Trainee Schemes for people like me with little idea of what my role could be, and I joined Imperial Metal Industries in Birmingham. I found the heavy industry quite exciting with the furnaces and the piles of shiny copper rods and pipes, and after 6 months was offered a post as a Systems Analyst / Programmer. The computer took up several rooms and input was by punched cards. My boyfriend Jules had also found a job in Birmingham, and we soon got married and bought a small house for about £6500. A few years later we moved to Burton-on-Trent, where the beer was much better. I worked at Pirelli, had a longish break for childcare, then started a new career as a lecturer in the local FE college where I taught ICT to adults and youngsters until I retired. We moved to Shoreham-by-Sea in 2016 to be near our daughter, and now there is an adorable grandson too.

Jane Mott (née Style)

I was ready to leave Cambridge after four years there and I arrived at the Courtauld Institute in London to start a two year Art History MA in September 1975. I thoroughly enjoyed The Courtauld and London was marvellous in many ways, but I quickly came to appreciate that very special gift that Cambridge gave us: the opportunity to try almost anything within an easy two-mile radius of the Market Place. Participating in music or sport in London was much more complicated, even social life was more challenging due to the distances involved, particularly as Henry and I lived in then not so trendy Peckham. After The Courtauld, I plunged into the art world via working in museums and galleries, and there I stayed, even after we returned to live in Norfolk back in 1983, and our three children were born. Although I am now retired, I still have fingers in various 'arty pies' in Norwich and beyond. Living in north Norfolk did seem pretty remote for the first 15 or so years. but as the internet and mobile phones homed in on our horizons, we have become ever more connected.

Charlotte Crawley (née Miller)

By the end of the three years, I was determined not to pursue any course that required exams, desperate, though ill prepared, to enter the real world and eager to put whatever skills I had to some practical use. I moved back home which was in central London and I was pleased to find that a number of my Cambridge contemporaries ended up not far away. Among them was my husband to be who I had been aware of as a friend of friends at Cambridge but did not really get to know until we met again at a mutual friend's party in January 1975. My ambition was to work in publishing, but, having progressed smoothly from school to university, I did not appreciate the work I should have done to make myself ready for the next steps. I ended up getting a job as "girl Friday" at Punch magazine. It was not what I had had in mind but I appreciated the long lunch hours and various opportunities to review exhibitions, restaurants and even books, the company of some very smart and funny people. Being in London, I took full advantage of the evening classes offered by the ILEA, in the practical pursuits I craved, like pottery and printing which continued to sustain me as hobbies, when taking time out to look after my two children and later when I worked part time in administrative roles for charities in St Albans where I now live.

What did I gain from New Hall? A measure of confidence in my own judgement and a sense of the variety of people, their interests, attitudes and values, which has been borne out by the diversity of the contributions to this volume.

Mary Anne Bonney

Deaths

Kate Belsey died a short while ago. I think the people who read English would remember her, and perhaps others too. She wasn't long at New Hall but (with Kate Pretty) did a lot with us English students and for the college in general (e.g. interviews, trying to get more applicants from state schools, setting up seminars) and as far as I was concerned was the best supervisor I had. She did her PhD at Warwick, on English morality plays - and was so enthusiastic about them that a few years later I did a modernized, outdoors version of The Castle of Perseverance (epic production) with upper school students in Ampthill. It was a real pleasure to meet her again later in life when I returned to academic work. She was by then in Cardiff, had made a great contribution to critical and literary studies, and came several times to Birmingham University to lecture (where on one occasion we needed an even larger lecture hall to accommodate the vast audience she drew). She was a humane and fun person too, and I remember her very fondly indeed for her personal as well as academic support all those years ago.

Maureen Bell

I was so sorry to hear of Kate Belsey's death - I remember thinking of her as a role model, with a style of feminism to which I aspired - and it has been fascinating over the years to follow the critical insights she has published. In our first year she organised joint supervisions with a group of boys from (I think) Trinity Hall, saying to us that she thought they needed to meet some women who were neither their mothers nor matrons. They looked very nervous at finding a formidable woman like Kate directing their learning, along with a group of opinionated girls their own age.

Pam Hilton

The beginning of my journey through these memories started when, in response to Wendy's first email, I phoned Lynn Millward's (Beardsley) home to pass on the information as Lynn did not have an email address.

One of her two sons answered informing me that she "was certainly not available" as she was in hospital. Shortly afterwards I discovered that she had only just been rushed into hospital the day I phoned. She died, in hospital, on the following Thursday (28th January 2021). (Not from Covid). Such a sad way to start on this memory journey.

I shared a split-level room with Lynn during our first year and have kept in touch, mainly with Christmas cards, since we left Cambridge. After I moved to the West Midlands we did manage to meet up a couple of times and I'll try to share some of my memories here. I know that other people have different memories and I've found it interesting to discover more of Lynn's interests.

I think Lynn and I had possibly been chosen to share a room as we had a few things in common. We both came from "the North" - Lynn from Belper near Derby and I had lived in Leeds since the age of 11. We'd both come from state schools, even though I now discover that we were by no means unique in that way. We were also both very much the youngest of our respective families - Lynn having two older sisters. From my memory, we got on well as room-mates (well, I don't think we ever fell out!). We didn't do a lot together. I remember Lynn as being quiet but very thoughtful. She "came to life" during the afternoon coffee sessions with her friends from the English course (and a few historians). As a mathematician I was privileged to join on a number of occasions. Lynn came with me to a couple of social events with the Baptist group of which I'd become a member. I remember an early Christmas party in our first term where we went as a couple of Santa's Helpers! During our second term we took part in an organised cycle ride to Ely. Was it organised by Churchill College? My outstanding memory is the return journey when Lynn and I were together cycling through dark and rain. Of course, the lights on neither of our bikes enjoyed the rain and gave up the ghost. It wasn't long before we were stopped by a policeman and told in no uncertain terms to ride into Cottenham (I think) and get our bikes sorted. We decided to get back to our warm college room!!! I remember another outing we made by bike to enjoy a picnic in the Gog Magog Hills - I think that might have been at the end of our third year, just after finals.

After leaving New Hall, Lynn returned to her home in Belper, near Derby. My moves from southern England to Edinburgh meant that Lynn and I didn't meet after summer 1974 until I moved to the West Midlands.

I learned through Christmas cards that Lynn did some work for the Workers' Educational Association. She also spent some time delivering post and became involved in local politics. I knew that she married Richard Millward, a local farmer's son, who delivered milk (from the family farm?) He was also the Mayor of Belper for at least one term. Lynn was a very caring mother to their three children: Beatrice, Malcolm and Ian. Richard died a number of years ago.

The last time I saw Lynn was nearly five years ago (was it really that long?). We met on a day in June for a coffee at de Bradelei Mill in Belper followed by a picnic on a hilltop somewhere nearby. (See attached photo) It was a sultry day as we lazed on blankets and reminisced about New Hall days and life since. I asked Lynn how she had met Richard and she said that as a member of the local Labour Party friends had persuaded her to stand for candidate in the local council elections. Richard stood against her (I assumed as Conservative candidate). Richard won the election but the outcome was their marriage!! Their son was unable to corroborate this when I spoke to him recently so maybe I'd need to contact Local Council to authenticate this story.

Lynn and I parted intending to meet again soon - the years fly by. What I do know is that Lynn was always a reliable and kind friend of whom I have fond memories.

Dorothy Cade (née Clark)

I really appreciated Dorothy's words about Lynn Millward. When Wendy sent out her first communication, Lynn was one of the people I hoped I would soon see again, then she appeared on the list of those who had died. She came to stay with me sometimes in the late seventies, but then I moved to NY for a while and had my address book stolen from my bag - she was one of the people I sadly never managed to re-establish contact with in those pre-internet days.

Lynn had the knack of sitting quietly throughout a discussion and then throwing in a comment slowly and quietly, which made the rest of us completely rethink where we had got to. As well as coffees in each other's rooms, we would sometimes go down to the pub by the Silver Street bridge and sit with a pint, listening to bands like Slade on the juke box when we felt the need for a bit of 'normal' life.

I'm not sure how she actually met her husband, but I do recall taking her to visit one of her sisters (in South Norwood, I think) when she was staying with me in the late seventies and there being a certain awkwardness between her and her sister about her having married a Conservative.

Pam Hilton

Marguerite Kickler (née Kemp) arrived at New Hall as a Natural Scientist but realised quite soon that she wanted to be a doctor and managed to change to Medicine in the first couple of weeks of term. We shared a split-level room for our first year. She was a delightful, vivacious and talented person with distinctive curly red hair.

She was an interesting mix of thoughtful seriousness together with a light-hearted humorous side. We had many interesting discussions late into the night with her perched on the notorious stairs in our room. We went to Christian Union "bread and cheeses" lunches together and she introduced me to Judo at the University Judo Club. She was an accomplished Brown Belt which is just one level below the highest level of Black Belt.

She played both the oboe and the guitar and was involved in several musical ventures including busking around Europe during one summer vacation.

After leaving Cambridge she went to London to do her clinical training and house jobs and also worked in Truro. She then moved to Germany where she met and married Holger. They had a daughter.

We lost touch for a while but a few years later I received a phone call from her as she was attending a medical conference in York and wondered if she could visit. We spent a wonderful afternoon catching up before she returned home.
She sadly died at the early age of 53 years in 2009.

Jan Sherman (née Phillips)

I got to know Judy Tyrell in Sheffield after teacher training in Leicester with Liz Stafford. She was in a share house with some other ex-Cambridge people. She was kind, socially committed, hard working and thoughtful. She moved to London to become a printer around 1980 and I lost direct touch but heard that she had died not long after.

Deborah Glass

Appendix

Contributors

Aileen Regan (née Kidd), 18, 45, 51, 84, 90, 130, 139, 179, 190, 196, 211, 215
Alison Litherland (née Hill), 8, 24, 36, 44, 68, 88, 95, 110, 129, 148, 153, 174, 194, 203, 209, 221
Alison Mawle, 114
Alison New, 21, 38, 232
Alison Wray (née O'Brien), 10, 67, 92, 103, 128, 137, 169, 210, 233
Angela Bailey (née Webster), 26, 85, 110, 140, 165
Anne Muir (née Borrett), 13, 23, 55, 91, 99, 109, 146, 171, 177, 183, 220
Charlotte Crawley (née Miller), 6, 38, 59, 98, 111, 119, 123, 143, 154, 170, 238
Deborah Glass, 5, 37, 41, 69, 77, 84, 99, 128, 146, 154, 156, 166, 189, 212, 236, 244
Denise Phillipson (née Milburn), 11, 40, 105, 139, 154, 176, 205, 212
Diana Kuh (née Lewin), 42, 100, 121, 134, 216
Diana Murray (née Collyer), 8, 39, 43, 62, 95, 105, 111, 117, 137, 144, 148, 164, 188, 207, 234
Dorothy Cade (née Clark), 10, 45, 69, 93, 140, 149, 160, 185, 237, 242
Emma Wheelock, 49, 84, 85, 118, 189, 216
Fiona Edwards-Stuart (née Weaver), 7, 30, 32, 37, 46, 57, 77, 80, 135, 136, 142, 146, 157, 191, 225
Gillian Blessley, 7, 27, 74, 76, 79, 96, 106, 145, 150, 161, 165, 173, 186, 213, 230
Helen Mayer, 11, 28, 47, 80, 96, 125, 132, 138, 162, 169, 181, 213, 218
Helen Morton, 21, 31, 38, 44, 71, 87, 94, 103, 116, 127, 133, 147, 156, 172, 179, 184, 190, 210, 232
Hilary Martin, 19, 34, 68, 100, 108, 156, 213, 224
Jan Sherman (née Phillips), 20, 27, 35, 66, 112, 139, 153, 157, 172, 174, 229, 244
Jane Dottridge (née Rooke), 20, 67, 136, 155, 231
Jane Mott (née Style), 1, 11, 40, 70, 107, 112, 129, 133, 138, 144, 147, 156, 169, 180, 186, 198, 237
Jo Edkins (née Dibblee), 13, 70, 78, 81, 86, 89, 97, 121, 128, 131, 133, 153, 167, 171, 172, 175, 182, 193, 197, 208, 217
Joanna Watts (née Sloper), 6, 64, 86, 91, 112, 132, 136, 155, 166
Karen Greenwood, 29, 36, 66, 102, 154, 188, 208

Liz Stafford, 31, 67, 102, 127, 230
Lorna Robertson, 46, 115, 132, 159, 168, 227
Lou Radford, 13, 30, 53, 85, 107, 114, 126, 142, 166, 175, 204, 216
Mary Anne Bonney, 51, 94, 104, 125, 137, 148, 159, 206, 239
Maryla Carter (née Ignatowicz), 79, 120
Maureen Bell, 14, 25, 42, 48, 55, 82, 92, 98, 101, 118, 124, 158, 174, 178, 208, 240
Nicola King (née Brown), 88, 167, 210
Pam Hilton, 10, 24, 33, 42, 52, 94, 115, 122, 131, 147, 157, 168, 173, 180, 184, 192, 203, 223, 240, 243
Pauline Whitney (née Micklam), 43, 111, 140
Penny Stirling, 50, 101, 107, 118, 126, 130, 133, 139, 164, 176, 187, 190, 202, 208, 224
Philippa Evans (née Taylor), 9, 24, 65, 84, 89, 173, 199, 212, 229
Ros Coward, 29, 37, 41, 76, 109, 125, 141, 147, 155, 203
Ros Morpeth, 31, 39, 63, 77
Rosemary Grande (née Temple), 5, 26, 33, 65, 81, 89, 105, 114, 138, 148, 159, 163, 176, 183, 195, 199, 211, 235
Rosie Boughton, 5, 52, 234
Sally Morgan, 22, 29, 68, 94, 108, 145, 151, 161, 169, 180, 209, 228
Sarah Watson (née Henley), 19, 28, 64, 78, 90, 108, 127, 135, 140, 154, 200, 207, 220
Sarah Wilson (née Stallard), 12, 36, 63, 80, 84, 91, 101, 141, 160, 163, 180, 202, 205, 222
Siân Crisp (née Jenkins), 14, 23, 62, 85, 135, 141, 146, 152, 171, 188, 198, 226
Sue Attridge (née Wood), 17, 27, 82, 99, 134, 155, 158, 163, 176, 182, 189, 215
Sue Whitham (née Addison), 15, 43, 73, 87, 90, 120, 139, 194, 206, 211, 221
Ursula Wide (née Buchan), 6, 28, 41, 56, 85, 120, 141, 174, 204, 219
Virginia Beardshaw, 25, 34, 47, 61, 92, 103, 113, 114, 123, 140, 143, 162, 163, 197, 208, 235
Wendy Joseph, 13, 23, 75, 132, 155, 227
Wendy Spray (née Coulson), 25, 32, 47, 71, 101, 128, 132, 142, 211, 217

Editors: Aileen Regan, Diana Murray, Jo Edkins, Mary Anne Bonney

New Hall entrance exam

In the 1970's, when you applied to Cambridge, you applied to a college rather than the university as a whole. There was an entrance exam which for most colleges was restricted to specialised knowledge. New Hall had its own entrance exam which encouraged a wider viewpoint.

NEW HALL
Entrance exam

TUESDAY 13 OCTOBER 1970

Time --- 3 hours

Candidates must answer **three** *questions.*

(a) *Candidates intending to read* NATURAL SCIENCES, MEDICAL SCIENCES, GEOGRAPHY or MATHEMATICS *must choose* **one** *question from Section A,* **one** *question from Section C, and a third from any section*

(b) *Candidates intending to read any other subject must choose at least* **one** *question from Section A and any* **two** *other questions.*

All candidates are advised not to neglect questions relevant to the subjects they intend to read or where they can use specific knowledge.

[TURN OVER

SECTION A

1 'Man is a slave to his own inventions'.

2 What kind of sources are the most useful for the reconstruction of an historical past?

3 'There is no reason whatever to suppose that the new possibilities of space travel will do anything to promote wisdom.' (BERTRAND RUSSELL).

4 Food.

5 Science and the Press.

6 How do you know you aren't now dreaming?

7 'Bigger means better'. Discuss with reference to modern means of transport.

8 Chance.

9 Define and discuss, with examples, one or two of the following: city-state, slavery, 'bastard feudalism' chivalry, baroque, anarchism, renascence, scientific revolution.

10 Is freedom of speech possible? Is it desirable?

11 There is no "useless knowledge".

12 Planning permission has been sought for a 2,000-berth caravan site on a stretch of unspoilt coastline; the local naturalist association considers the area should become a nature reserve. Discuss the factors that would need to be considered in weighing the strength of the two claims.

[TURN OVER

SECTION B

13 Attempt to analyse the way in which experience is presented in the following passage:

> He rose and placed his candle unsuspectingly on the floor near his loom, swept away the sand without noticing any change, and removed the bricks. The sight of the empty hole made his heart leap violently, but the belief that his gold was gone could not come at once – only terror, and the eager effort to put an end to the terror. He passed his trembling hand all about the hole, trying to think it possible that his eyes had deceived him; then he held the candle in the hole and examined it curiously, trembling more and more. At last he shook so violently that he let fall the candle, and lifted his hands to his head, trying to steady himself, that he might think. Had he put his gold somewhere else, by a sudden resolution last night, and then forgotten it? A man falling into dark water seeks a momentary footing even on sliding stones; and Silas, by acting as if he believed in false hopes, warded off the moment of despair. He searched in every corner, he turned his bed over, and shook it, and kneaded it; he looked in his brick oven where he laid his sticks. When there was no other place to be searched, he kneeled down again and felt once more all round the hole. There was no untried refuge left for a moment's shelter from the terrible truth.
>
> Yes, there was a sort of refuge, which always comes with the prostration of thought under an overpowering passion: it was that expectation of impossibilities, that belief in contradictory images, which is still distinct from madness, because it is capable of being dissipated by the external fact. Silas got up from his knees trembling, and looked round at the table: didn't the gold lie there after all? The table was bare. Then he turned and looked behind him – looked all round his dwelling, seeming to strain his brown eyes after the possible appearance of the bags, where he had already sought them in vain. He could see every object in his cottage – and his gold was not there.

14 Consider, with examples, some of the means by which a story-teller makes you want to know what happens next.

15 'To use a language poetically is above all to use it figuratively.' **Either** explain why this is so **or**, if you disagree with the assertion, give your criticism of it.

16 Could a fake be better than a genuine work of art?

17 What kinds of relevance to modern issues, personal or public, make a work of art worth study? (You may if you like confine your answer to a single art form.)

18 Discuss, with examples, what we mean by 'classical' in **either** painting and sculpture **or** music.

19 Define and, where possible, distinguish between: myth, legend, fable.

20. The role of music in worship.

[TURN OVER

SECTION C

Candidates intending to read MATHEMATICS *are strongly advised to attempt question 21.*

21 Either (*a*) A plane polygon is called a *face* and a straight line segment joining two adjacent *vertices* is called an *edge*. A geometric figure in real 3-dimensional space is built up from a finite number of polygonal faces 'glued' together in such a way as to satisfy the following properties:
  i. Two distinct edges are disjoint or meet in a vertex.
  ii. Two distinct faces are disjoint, meet in an edge or meet in a vertex.
  iii. At most two faces meet in any edge.
  iv. Given any two vertices it is possible to travel from one to the other along edges.

Such a figure is called *solid* if exactly two faces meet in any given edge. Let the number of faces, edges and vertices be F, E and V respectively. By induction on F for geometrical figures or otherwise, prove that
$$F - E + V = 2$$
for such a solid. A *regular* solid is one for which each face has n edges and r faces meet at each vertex. Prove $F = 4r / (2n + r(2 - n))$ for a regular solid.

What values of F are possible if r takes the values 3, 4, 5 and 6?

Or (*b*) Let $(a_1, a_2,..., a_n)$ be an ordered array of the integers from 1 to n. The integer a_1 is called the *first coordinate*. For $j=1,2,....,n$, let P be the permutation of the symbols $a_1, a_2,..., a_n$, which reverses the order of the first j symbols. Thus Pj permutes
$$(a_1,...., a_n) \text{ into } (a_j, ..., a_1,..., a_n)$$
The following operation is performed on the given array: if $a_1 = k$, apply the permutation P_k. This operation is repeated indefinitely, the first repetition being to apply P_{ak}. Each repetition is called a *step*.
  i. Suppose $a_1 = k \neq 1$ and after p steps the first coordinate is again k. prove that for some integer q, less than p, the first coordinate after q steps is greater than k.

ii. By considering the largest integer to appear arbitrarily often as a first co-ordinate, or otherwise, prove that after a sufficiently large number of steps the first coordinate is equal to one.

22 Discuss the variations in dominance of the special senses in different species. Explain why these variations have come about.

23 Discuss some of the ways in which the application of the science of genetics affects everyday life. What are the biological mechanisms involved?

24 Write on any aspect of cell biology which has specially interested you.

25 What do you understand by the term 'catalysis? Discuss, with examples, the importance of catalysts in the chemical industry and/or biological systems.

26 Describe, with appropriate examples, the methods available for purification of chemical compounds in the laboratory. Discuss briefly the physical principles involved in the procedures you give.

27 Either (*a*) Discuss any engineering failure: why it happened, how it was investigated, and the lessons learned from it.
Or (*b*) The fixed guides of an escalator may be thought of as having five sections: a short horizontal section, a curved transition from horizontal to inclined, a long straight incline, a second curved transition, and a final short horizontal section. The steps move at constant speed.
A man steps onto the bottom, stands still on a moving step till half way up the incline, then walks up the rest of the way and off the top. Describe in words, by diagrams, or both, how the horizontal and vertical components of the force from his shoes onto the step vary as he travels up the escalator.

28 Either (*a*) 'The more important laws and facts of physical science have all been discovered and these are so firmly established that the possibility of their ever being supplanted in consequence of new discoveries is exceedingly remote... Our future discoveries must be looked for in the sixth place of decimals.' (MICHELSON, 1899).
Or (*b*) Discuss, with appropriate experimental evidence, theories concerning the nature of light.

29 Estimate the magnitude of 3 (or more) of the following, making reasonable assumptions about any of the quantities involved, and stating these assumptions clearly:
- *(a)* The velocity of a torch battery if its electrical energy were converted to kinetic energy.
- *(b)* The potential difference in volts between the wing-tips of an aircraft flying over the North Pole.
- *(c)* The rise in temperature in the brake drums of a car when stopping from a speed of 60 m.p.h.
- *(d)* The orbital speed of a close satellite of the Moon.
- *(e)* The cost of heating (by gas or electricity) the water for a hot bath.

Questions 30 and 31 should not be attempted by candidates intending to read NATURAL SCIENCES, MEDICAL SCIENCES *or* MATHEMATICS.

30 Why may two streams with catchment areas of exactly the same size have very different annual discharge totals?

31 'The lower the annual precipitation total, the greater is its year-to-year variability.' Discuss the implications of this observation.

Timeline

1284	Peterhouse founded (oldest Cambridge college)
....	Sixteen more colleges founded
1869	Girton College founded (first college for women)
1871	Newham College founded (second college for women)
1954	New Hall founded (third college for women). At this time, Cambridge had the lowest proportion of women undergraduates of any university in the United Kingdom. The original location was in Silver Street. There were 16 students, and two tutors, Rosemary Murray and Robin Hammond, who were still there during our time. We always referred to them as Miss Murray and Miss Hammond. Rosemary Murray was the first president of New Hall 1954-1981.

Original site and blue plaque

1962	Members of the Darwin family gave their home, "The Orchard", to the College, on Huntingdon Road, about a mile from the centre of Cambridge. The building work began in 1964 and was completed in 1965. The new college could house up to 300 students.

1970 Age of majority in UK was lowered to 18, from 21. That meant that most undergraduates were now adults rather than minors.

1970 The Equal Pay Act prohibited any less favourable treatment between men and women in terms of pay and conditions of employment.

1970 December Power station engineers work to rule causes power cuts.

1971 The contributors of this book arrived in New Hall in October as freshers.

1972 UK miners' strike caused power cuts in January.

1972 Women were admitted to men's colleges (Churchill, Clare and King's) for the first time.

1972 New Hall received its Royal Charter and Arms.

1974 UK miners' strike caused power cuts and the three day week.

1975 Rosemary Murray became Cambridge University's first female vice-president.

Since 2006 Newnham College and Murray Edwards College (both in Cambridge) are the only colleges in UK with a woman-only student admissions policy.

2008 It was announced that New Hall would be renamed Murray Edwards College, in honour of the vision of its first President, Rosemary Murray, and the generosity of the Edwards family. A donation of £30 million by alumna Ros Edwards (née Smith) and her husband Steve Edwards secured the future of the college as a college at the University of Cambridge in perpetuity.

2021 Publication of memories by freshers of 1971.

The Arms of the college are *Sable a Dolphin palewise head downwards to the dexter in chief three Mullets fesswise a Bordure embattled Argent.*

The castellation round the outside shows the college's location on Castle Hill. The three stars are borrowed from the Murray coat of arms, while the heraldic dolphin symbolises a youthful spirit of exploration and discovery, and a kindly intelligence.

First published in 2021 by Jo Edkins

© Jo Edkins

The rights of Jo Edkins to be identified as the Authors of this work has been asserted in accordance with the Copyrights, Designs and Patents Act 1988.

All rights reserved. No part of this book may be reprinted or reproduced or utilised in any form or by any electronic, mechanical or other means, now known or hereafter invented, including photocopying and recording, or in any information storage or retrieval system, without the permission in writing from the Publishers.